CIVILIAN
AT WAR

by

Ken Parker

Ken Parker
4/10/09

To My Children
Marilyn, Nancy and Robert

Revised Edition
Copyright © 1984 and 2002 by Kenneth C. Parker

Published in the United States of America by

243 E. Front Street
Traverse City, Michigan

ISBN: 0-915937-14-X

On the Cover: Photograph from
Work Horse of the Western Front by Robert L. Hewitt
Washington Infantry Journal Press
Photo by U.S. Army Signal Corps

Book Design and Layout by Judy Albaugh

Preface

It is a great honor to write the preface to the revised edition of a *Civilian at War*. There are thousands of books on World War II that analyze every detail of this great conflict, but very few of these books reveal what it was like for the average soldier, the common infantryman of the U.S. Army. This narrative does just that. It dramatically unveils what it was like to be removed from civilian life and quickly transformed into a civilian in uniform.

The past comes alive as the reader moves through the hedgerows of France, down the lanes in Belgium, and across the fields of Germany with Ken Parker. He never lets you forget what these men did to liberate Europe and earn the title, "The Greatest Generation." These young men were truly civilians at war, not professional warriors, just average young men who got caught up in the century's most horrific war.

As you follow Ken across Europe, you will encounter his friends, the courageous captain whom they all admired and even Ken's cousin whom he met in France as the war raged around them. Ken survived a hundred days in combat, and his account of that deed is an outstanding tribute to all Americans who gave up part of their "civilian" lives in order to fight and die in World War II.

In addition, this narrative of World War II has enriched the lives of my students. As a community college instructor, I am constantly looking for historical accounts that will bring the past alive and inspire my students to continue their exploration of history. Mr. Parker's story fulfills both of these requirements.

His style is direct, honest and powerful. He takes my students to 1944 France where life and death were decided in an instant, and America's young men were changing the world. Thank you, Ken, for sharing with America your account of the Second World War and keeping alive the memory of the generation that did so much for, not only modern America, but the entire world.

James Press
Army Veteran and History Instructor
Northwestern Michigan College

Introduction

In writing this personal account of more than 100 days of combat with an infantry unit during World War II in France, Belgium, Holland, and Germany, I have endeavored to be as honest and accurate as possible. In so doing it is my hope that this book will give readers, and possibly historians, an intimate look at what World War II was like at the foot-slogging level.

In some cases, names have been changed to respect the privacy of the men and their families.

One element that cannot be strongly enough carried over in words is the constant fear that accompanies the front-line infantryman. It is a natural emotion that the soldier must constantly deal with and "put down" in order to function. So, if it appears that this underlying fear, and sometimes panic, is not adequately expressedl, it is because the combatants trained themselves to make light of these feelings in order to endure and perform their duties.

The first draft of "Civilian at War" was published in serial form in *The Antrim County News* in 1947-48 at Bellaire, Michigan. This book is a complete rewrite of the original with the addition of much material that was purposely left out as possibly offensive to readers of that time. The original version was written while the author's recollections were still fresh as to details, most of which were burned into his memory through the writing of awards and decorations for the combatants. *History of the 120th Infantry Regiment,* published in 1947 by the *Infantry Journal Press*, has also been a most helpful reference.

Some of the St. Lo experiences are related in fiction form in "West of St. Lo," a short story published by *Yankee Magazine* in June of 1979.

Materials regarding personal experiences at Mortain appear in *Stalingrad en Normandie* by Eddy Florentine (*Presses de la Cité,* Paris, 1965) and *Mortain dans la Bataille de Normandie* by Dr. Gilles Buisson (*Presses de la Cité,* Paris, 1971).

Originally published in May of 1984 this book now includes three additional sections titled "The Battalion Rear War," "The War Revisited," and "Post-War Talk." The first section deals with the Battle of the Bulge and final battles in Germany. The second deals with revisiting old battle sites, and the third reveals what was learned at Co. B reunions and other sources.

Ken Parker
Traverse City, Michigan
June, 2002

Table of Contents

Additions

St. Lo Breakthrough
July 16 through 25, 1944

The switch from a swivel chair in the office of a large utility company in Detroit to a hole in the ground in Normandy, France, took about eight months. It seemed unreal to say the least to be suddenly thrust into a war one had been content to read about a few short months before. Regardless of how intensely the Army had trained me in the art of warfare and soldierly conduct, the brown-clad, steel-helmeted figure who reported for assignment on a July afternoon in the hedgerow country of Normandy still housed the conservative and anxious mind and heart of a typically awestruck civilian who had been fascinated by historical accounts of past wars, but never dreamed he'd have a chance to "go abroad" with all expenses paid to take part in one himself.

Many of the men with whom I had trained at Camp Blanding in Florida had assumed that something would happen to save them from being sent overseas, but if they had the bad luck to be shipped out, that they would somehow draw an assignment behind the lines. I had shared this hope, but the Army's need for bodies at the front was constant. Furthermore, my record showed that I had qualified as an expert, the top rank, with the M-1 rifle. The record might also have shown a perfect score in the rapid-fire category.

About thirty of us, all recently landed replacements, crowded around the Captain of Company B, 120th Infantry, 30th Division, also known as Old Hickory. The Captain's name was Greer. He later became Lt. Col. Greer, returned to the United States on a furlough shortly before the war ended and was quoted in some newspapers as believing that boxer Max Schmeling was killed by members of his company in a battle on July 16, 1944.

On this afternoon of July 14, France's Bastille Day, the Captain was very tired. He was reclining on a bedding roll in a small rammed-earth structure, either a tool or animal shed. His head and torso were propped against the wall. He talked in a low North Carolina drawl and asked for our names and type of training. He had been on the line for thirty days since D plus 12, and his unit was back as far as the artillery emplacements for a bath and a change of underwear — the first cleanup since they had started fighting.

As the names were volunteered by the men, I tried to insert mine but someone always spoke up before I could. I decided to wait until all were done, then give my name last. This decision proved to be a factor in surviving the days ahead. I wonder now what guardian angel held my tongue, for a few hours later the Captain announced the assignments, and it looked to me as he read the names from the top of his list down that the first ten went to the first rifle platoon, the next segment to the second platoon, and the final group to the third platoon. My name had not been called. Almost as an after thought, the Captain told me to join a light machine gun squad as an ammunition bearer. The others were led like sheep to the rifle platoons, where they became captains of the Garand Automatic Rifle, M-1. For a great many it was the death sentence.

I was anxious to get some inkling of what the war was like, and I found the veterans talkative and friendly. Most of them were fatigued beyond words. Their sun-browned faces were bearded, and their clothing was impregnated with the brown French soil. Later, when I saw them in the hedge-row crouch, they looked more like gnomes than warriors. On this day they were relaxed and enjoying their brief respite.

I was impressed by their fervor and skill in digging holes as deep as four feet and placing massive covers over them. The tops were made of boards, doors, or tree limbs, packed over with dirt and sod. Hay was obtained from nearby barns and haycocks to spread on the floors of the holes and make them warm, comfortable and clean smelling. In basic training, nothing had been said about building covers. But the American GI learned fast. Many enemy shells were detonated by the trees and shrubs growing out of the hedgerows thus causing downward bursts of shell fragments. Most of the time the heavy covers stopped the shrapnel.

Since landing in France, these men had quickly advanced to the Vire-et-Taute canal and held at this line for several days while the Cherbourg peninsula was cleared in the north. When the time was right (July 17), they jumped off from the canal and captured St. Jean de Daye. Their division was now pushing yard-by-yard, hedgerow-by-hedgerow on the right flank of St. Lo.

Most of the men knew little of their military objectives. Their concerns were personal, "How good is the enemy observation in this position? Wouldn't it be nice to get a flesh wound and get the hell out of here? That 88 will be the death of me yet."

Connie Matausche (real first name Constantine) was my boss. He was a corporal in charge of our machine gun squad, which consisted of himself, the gunner and assistant gunner, two ammo bearers, and a runner. Connie was crowding the forties, but was still lithe and athletic. He had been a trapeze artist in a circus in Florida and came from a family of aerialists. I never inquired as to his ethnic background, but he spoke with a slight accent. Connie inspired my immediate confidence, because he was confident and told me a little of what to expect. I had replaced a man who had sprained his ankle in hopping down from a hedgerow. Otherwise, the machine gun section of twelve men had experienced no casualties in 30 days of fighting, which for the machine gunners consisted of giving supporting fire to the attacking riflemen and joining them as soon as the objective was taken to consolidate and defend the new position.

Connie was not highly religious, but he attended a religious service the next morning (July 15) and reported that it was very satisfying. The rest of us spent the morning giving obeisance to the machine guns and small arms, checking and cleaning them to make sure they were in proper condition. Jones, another ammo bearer and my squad mate, took me in tow and showed me some tricks about carrying the ammo. He took two boxes and tied them together with a wide strap so that they could be carried over the shoulder. The wider the strap the less pain, he pointed out. Jones was a freckle-faced lad who would have made a good model for Norman Rockwell, but all the same he struck me as unusually mature. War had apparently added a few years.

Word suddenly came down that we were moving out within an hour. We were to move back to the front to attack the following morning. The holiday, such as it was, was over.

Shortly before the column of heavily-laden infantry began to file out of the field in which we had been living to plod its way along the hedgerows and narrow lanes, a pistol shot was heard about fifty yards from where I was standing. Soon the call for medics came down the line, and a squad of litter bearers went to a prostrate form. As they carried a moaning towheaded boy past me a few minutes later. I saw that he was one of the replacements who had come up with me. He was shot in the right foot by his own .45 pistol, whether intentionally or accidentally I did not know. I thought I detected a faint smile of derision on the face of one of the medics, but the incident remained a mystery. In any event, we had our first casualty, and I learned that war has all sorts of ways to maim men.

As the column of infantry trudged through the "bocage" country, stopping and starting fitfully, each man maintaining an interval of five to ten yards to minimize casualties, I observed the countryside and the debris of war. Our route hugged the hedgerows which were earthworks thrown up by the peasant farmers to create a permanent fence for the fields. Out of these hedgerows, some of which may have been made centuries ago, grew dense foliage, bushes, long grasses, and even trees of good size. Sometimes a ditch ran along the hedgerow, where the dirt had been taken out to form the mound, but usually there was no ditch.

I was informed that German snipers hid on the tops of these hedgerows, concealed by the foliage and their camouflage suits.

I was impressed by the quiet of this sunny afternoon of July 15 — a stillness that heightened the unreality of my situation. The soil was underfoot, but it was French. The sun was shining peacefully in a clear sky, but one of our artillery observation planes droned above. I listened but there were no typical noises of the country in summer.

"Beautiful day," I said to Jones, "but I don't hear any birds."

Jones smiled. "No," he said, "they're too smart to hang around us."

So, the quiet was ominous, even to the birds.

Suddenly, I was aware of a language change since joining Co. B.

"How come you guys don't swear very much?" I asked.

Jones reflected a bit. "Guess you're right," he replied.

"Why?"

"Well, I dunno. Probably most of the guys figure that swearing won't change your luck any. Might even hurt it. But wait till we get in a real tight situation, when we're really desperate. Then you'll hear 'em let it rip. Can't seem to stop it then."

Occasionally we passed a knocked-out tank, either enemy or American. The tanks without exception were burned and blackened, with tracks or wheels usually destroyed. Trees were shattered everywhere and shell holes were equally ubiquitous. I was later to learn the sweetish smell of a freshly damaged tree and to fear what it meant: that the area had been recently shelled and might be again at any moment.

Even today the smell of newly cut or broken live wood, or the odor of damp earth and grass can transport me back to Normandy and other scents of battle and death, including my own fermenting sweat, the not unpleasant farm smells of cider and hay, and always the too sweet and sickening odor of the dead.

Presently, we emerged from the densely covered lanes and hedgerows into a larger field which was alarmingly open. As the column paused before making the next jerky movement forward, a rifleman with another company and another column of troops moved past us. He remarked to a companion:

"Geez, this is the place Birdie got shot. The Jerries had a machine gun over there," and he pointed to a spot on the opposite hedgerow.

The next move took us across a tarvia highway just south of a crossroads called Hts. Vents. This road extended south to St. Gilles, an objective west of St. Lo. The regiment was to bleed heavily before it achieved this goal. We then maneuvered through a maze of hedgerows and fence openings before halting and being ordered to dig in for the night. We were in an "assembly area," from which we would "jump off" the next day. It was not necessary to dig. The infantry which had occupied this section previously had already fashioned a defensive rabbit warren.

Jones and I teamed up in a double hole, one half of which was tunneled under the hedgerow. I wondered at the strength and tenacity of the men who had hacked out such a cave in the tough French clay.

Each of the two machine gun squads maintained its own guard throughout the night. To fill out the two-hour shifts one man had to stand twice. As the men discussed how it would be arranged this time, I thought I detected some glances at me, so I volunteered to stand two guard periods because "I've had more sleep than you guys lately." They didn't argue with me. I had done the right thing.

Before night fell we had a chance to look over the area. There was a farmhouse to our rear, and some of the men were finding "cidre," a fermented cider which tasted like vinegar, but only because we were drawing it from the bottom of the huge barrels in which it was contained either before it had properly aged, or after the good stuff had been tapped. Cidre was plentiful everywhere in Normandy, a fine apple-growing area. Sometimes we drank the vinegary liquid in an effort to quench our thirst, only to find that it left us thirstier than ever. I later found it better to shave in cidre and conserve drinking water.

As Connie, our trapeze-artist corporal, and I went to the farmhouse we ran across a pile of enemy machine gun belts. Connie opined that a machine gun nest had been here at one time and probably had been knocked out of action.

Barth, another member of our squad, was already at the farmhouse when we arrived. He was in a depressed state of mind. He drank heavily of the cidre and made solemn remarks about what would happen tomorrow. He held his head low, rolled his eyes upward, and smiled sardonically as he shook his camouflaged and helmeted head to indicate the hopelessness of the morrow's program.

As we walked back to our holes, Connie told me that he felt he had no business being in the war because of his age, but that he had faith that things would work out all right. He disliked Barth's attitude, though it might be shared by many. "It just makes things harder," he said.

I pondered Connie's remarks. The section had lost only one man in thirty days of combat and that because of a sprained ankle. It didn't seem to be a bad record — so far.

That night as I stood my second turn of guard around 2:00 a.m. the screams and curses of one of our riflemen on a hedgerow ahead of us suddenly split the air with paralyzing effect.

"Come out of there. I know you're there," he shouted into the darkness, punctuating his hysteria with curses and bursts from his BAR (Browning Automatic Rifle).

I alerted our squad and waited for developments. The aroused madman finally subsided, and quiet again prevailed. The next morning I learned that the BAR man was evacuated as a case of battle fatigue. The powerful effect of fear, even on veteran soldiers, was making itself evident. I wondered about myself.

We were to attack at 10:00 a.m. on July 16. It seemed oddly like a banker's hour. Perhaps there was some strategy behind the selection of such a time. More likely it was a careful estimate of the time it would take all units to get into position for the jump-off.

As we inched ever closer to the front, we passed a column of tanks parked under the concealment of leafy hedgerows. The men were standing about. Some were preparing food. One was playing with a kitten. I smiled at the incongruity of the sight, but I sobered at the thought that these tanks were waiting for us to probe ahead.

In England, while waiting for transportation to France, I had been impressed by the rapid progress of the fighting in the Cherbourg Peninsula. Past successes of our armies in Africa, Sicily and Italy, as well as the heavy concentrations of military hardware stockpiled all over England, had led me to believe that it would be a short pulverizing war in France and Germany. I estimated that I would be in combat for forty-five days before the war ended. I take no credit as an expert analyst, but the estimate would have been nearly accurate had our supply lines not proved a stumbling block, for on September 15 our unit sat on the Siegfried Line. The enemy had been routed, but we could not finish it off for lack of supplies and ammunition.

This July morning, the first of the forty-five days, was as full of sunshine as the previous day. We began to sweat under the heavy loads we carried and from the building tension. Suddenly we reached the front. No one told us. We knew from the crouching, mole-like brown figures in alert positions behind hedgerows, trying to get a glimpse of what was ahead of them. These watchful, alert, and silent men were elements of the 117th Infantry which had fought to this point the previous day and through which we were to advance.

Our column passed through a gateway in the hedgerow maze, and edged along the side of an orchard. Here I saw my first German soldier, a smartly uniformed member of the 14th Parachute Regiment, probably an officer. He had been hit in the foot and was lying sullenly against a hedgerow with his bandaged foot resting in the grass. I considered him a lucky fellow, but obviously he did not think so. Did his sullenness stem from fear, hatred, or simply pain?

Our column halted and the two light mortar squads set up their 61-millimeter tubes and began firing. The barrels were pointed almost straight up because of the extremely short range. They were aiming at a sunken road about 175 yards to the front.

The rest of us quickly assembled behind a hedgerow densely overgrown with brush and thorns. The riflemen spaced themselves at five-yard intervals behind the mound. Our machine gun squad was to attack with them. Connie told me that my job would be to go back after more ammunition if needed. He said that the machine gun boxes were stored at the road junction to our rear, and he described the best route to take.

As the men waited for the precise moment to hop the hedgerows, a laughing BAR man, kneeling with his heavy automatic weapon pointed past the tip of his helmet, said: "Lordy, thirteen hedgerows today! What a way to celebrate my birthday!" He made several other joking comments and ended by hoping that this wouldn't be his last birthday. Then came the "let's go" order, and the riflemen pushed through an opening hacked in the network of thorn bushes and slid over the hedgerow's top, showing as little silhouette as possible. I never saw the BAR man again.

Our mission was to cover the advance of the riflemen with the machine gun. If opposition were encountered and the men were pinned to the ground by enemy fire, we were to open up with our machine gun and cover their retirement or further attack, such as the case might be. In some instances when the next hedgerow was known to be defended, artillery and machine gun fire was first directed against the enemy line and the riflemen then moved ahead as soon as our fire was lifted.

We waited with our gun in position and ready to fire, but the next hedgerow was not defended. We then crawled through the holes in the wall of thorns and moved up to support the attack against the next hedgerow. This seemed quite simple. The riflemen were moving fast.

Our machine gun squad slid over another hedgerow and walked in a crouch across a field of tall grass to the next bastion, the sunken road which our mortars had fired on earlier. Here an enemy tank was still burning, and here, too, was our platoon of riflemen. I looked across the small tarvia road our attack was paralleling and saw another enemy tank which apparently had been destroyed the day before, for it was blackened and rust-colored from the heat.

Word was passed that there was an enemy tank dug in behind the next substantial hedgerow to our front. Enemy infantry was emplaced about this fort, and they made themselves known with machine gun and rifle fire, for the bullets began clipping the grass above our heads.

This hostility seemed to enrage the sergeant in charge of the riflemen.

"Get up on the line and fire, you guys," he bellowed. "Give 'em that fire power. Whatdya think you're here for!"

Like sheep everyone hugged the hedgerow and peered over the top to fire their weapons. I realized for the first time that I was not sufficiently armed for this kind of combat. I had only a .45 pistol, the sidearm issued our replacement package when it was thought we would be fed into heavy weapons companies. My pistol was of little use at this range. Jones, however, dropped his boxes of ammunition and fired the carbine he carried.

"I see where that machine gun is," Jones exclaimed. "Gimme that thing," he demanded of a rifleman who had a rifle grenade mounted on the end of his weapon.

Jones fired and slid down the embankment from the recoil. He got another grenade and climbed back up. This time he kneeled on top of the hedgerow, heroically exposing himself, I thought, to get a better bead as he fired a second time.

At that moment, an order came to get down, since our artillery was going to blast the enemy position. I plopped on the ground. Soon the reports of our guns could be heard. The shells hissed in and shook the ground a bare 100 yards ahead of us. Several concentrations whined and hissed with what we hoped was devastating effect.

"O.K., guys, we're goin' to get 'em," the sergeant said, as though that's all it amounted to. The men apparently were too slow in moving, for the sergeant began to act as though besotted. He cursed and berated them, even shaking his fist, to get them into action.

This was the first time I saw men moving to keep an obvious buzz-saw appointment. I doubt that they would have moved at all without the sergeant's violent prodding. There was no elan. They were simply obeying, doing what was expected of them by the Army, their country, and perhaps the memory of those back home who honored them. The crouching, sodden column rounded the end of the hedgerow at the highway and, armed with rifles, grenades, and a bazooka, began the challenge of the entrenched enemy infantry and tank.

War is mostly costly mistakes and deadly confusion, with victory usually going to the side which makes the fewest damaging errors, although not always. The next few hours were my introduction to this assessment of war.

Our machine gun remained set up on the hedgerow the riflemen had just left. Connie remained alert but calm. We were alone. The decision to follow the riflemen rested with him.

After a few minutes of relative quiet, he ordered our weapon dis-mounted and we, too, rounded the hedgerow. We stepped briefly on the tarvia highway and dropped back into a thorn-infested ditch to the left of the road and began crawling forward. It was like crawling through a tunnel of barbed wire. The thorns scratched, pricked, tore clothing and even pulled helmets off. After about fifteen yards of this, we paused for a minute, and I was glad for a chance to catch my breath.

Barth turned on his knees and asked: "How do you like it?"

"If It doesn't get any worse than this, it'll be all right," I said.

He nodded mournfully. "Wait'll they start throwin' 88s, then tell me," he said.

Connie gave the order to turn back. Apparently he was bewildered

UPPER LEFT — An American tank fired over this hedgerow to knock out a dug-in enemy weapon on July 16, 1944. Photo shows dense foliage which was not present during the battle, nor was the paved road.

UPPER RIGHT — The author occupied a slit trench at the base of this hedgerow when U.S. planes bombed American as well as German lines on July 24 and 25, 1944.

BELOW — This barn at which the author fired some shots during the German counterattack July 16, 1944, was never rebuilt. Photos taken in 1967.

as to what he should do with his squad. It was too quiet ahead of us, and we plainly could do nothing bottled up in a briar patch.

It didn't take long to return to the hedgerow again. Our gun was mounted once more. At this juncture, the roaring and creaking of American tanks could be heard. Soon three of them lurched into our sector, apparently to engage the enemy tank.

The two lead tanks burst daringly into the field ahead of us and began firing their cannons in great earth-shaking explosions. A third tank lumbered down our sunken road with its gun just high enough to fire over the hedgerow in support of the tanks in the open.

The enemy reaction was quick and devastating. The 88mm gun on the dug-in tank fired at our lead tank and knocked it out of action. Enemy fire was then directed at the second tank and scored another hit. The driver of the second wounded tank desperately tried to back over our hedgerow and into our defilade position. Its rear was high on the top of the hedgerow when a second enemy round set it afire. It remained with its snout in the ground as though praying.

Meanwhile out third tank, but five yards from our squad, continued to blast away. All of us were stretched on the ground, holding our helmets on and expecting the next moment to be our last. The concussion from the friendly weapon combined with the return fire made the ground shake and raised such a cloud of dust and dirt as might have been beaten from a gigantic mop. The noise was terrifying, but comforting, too, because we knew it meant an end to the enemy tank, which it was.

After our gun stopped blasting, enemy 88s, probably from self-propelled guns further to the enemy rear, began whistling shells with terrific speed over our heads and to our rear. This was the weapon Barth was warning me about. Its rifle-bullet speed took one's breath with it. As I was to observe later, its shell, upon ground impact, made a shallow hole about the size of a hat, which meant that its fragments got maximum ground-level killing dispersion. Our shells, on the other hand, seemed lazy and indolent as they whined their approach. Furthermore, they dug large craters and sent shrapnel flying at a higher, less effective angle.

Connie now thought we should try to rejoin our rifle platoon. Again we began crawling ahead through the thorny bramble patch until we met a wounded man crawling toward us. He dragged himself painfully by the head of our small column, but when he came to me, he stopped and asked me to cut off some of his equipment, including his gas mask and pack. I obliged and tried to be cheerful about his wound. He said he had a piece of metal in his back. He seemed dazed, but clear on one point: He wanted to get out of here and back to the rear for medical attention. Most ambulatory wounded felt the same, their greatest fear being that they might be abandoned to the enemy.

Again we retreated from the ditch and back to the sunken road. Connie had learned something that he didn't tell us. This time our squad got out of the road and behind the second hedgerow to avoid flying metal from the still burning American tank, which was now also exploding as its stores of gasoline and ammunition reacted to the heat.

At this point, Captain Greer appeared and gave us information and new orders. The enemy position had been taken by another platoon on our left. We would be attached to this new unit. What had happened to our men? I got the horrible answer when a helmetless rifleman named Silver approached from the front to talk to the Captain. I remembered Silver as a replacement who suffered intensely from sinus trouble in England. His expression indicated he was still suffering, but not from the same affliction.

"There isn't anybody left," he said, trying to control his voice. "Our tanks blew us apart — arms, legs, guts all over the place."

None of us, including the Captain, said a word. Now I knew why Connie had been silent. An enormously stupid mistake had been made. Two tanks were gone. An entire rifle unit was wiped out. But this was no time to moan and cry about it. We had to go on. The battle must continue.

Silver slipped off to the rear, and it was the last I saw of him. I heard much later that he was killed by an 88 shell a few minutes after this interview.

At this juncture a tank officer approached the Captain and asked for help in removing a wounded tanker. The Captain told Connie to give him one of his men. Connie said, "O.K., Parker, you go."

I noticed that part of the tank officer's helmet was sheared off and that his left ear was cut and bleeding. He guided me, a medic, and another to the same corner we had rounded before in attempting to advance in the thorn-infested ditch. In the open field near the burning tanks, we found two wounded men. One was smoking and seemed comfortable as he lay on his side on a stretcher. A piece of flesh had been gouged from his thigh. The second man was burned all over, although in my judgment not severely. He had shell fragments in his arms, but his worst wounds were in his legs. The medic cut his pants off and his limbs were revealed as swollen masses of darkened flesh which appeared to have been sliced by a knife in several channels along his legs.

The man was still conscious. He said he did not know why we bothered with him, because he was loaded with metal. "I'm a mess," he said.

"Aw, come on, Charley, you don't look so bad," the tank officer said optimistically.

The medic considered putting tourniquets on the legs, but we all virtually spoke in unison in advising against it. We said it was more important to get him out of this exposed position immediately. Furthermore, we reminded the medic that tourniquets might do his legs more harm than good if not properly watched.

As we carried the man out, enemy shells continued to startle me with their terrific speed as they seemed to pass within inches over our heads. On one occasion, I involuntarily fell to one knee. The others remained standing and my end of the litter dipped. I felt ashamed and quickly resumed my share of the load.

When the job was done, I returned to the machine gun emplacement, only to find that the squad was gone.

I guessed that my squad had moved forward, but which route to take to find them I didn't know.

"Your squad is ahead two hedgerows," an authoritative voice informed me. "You can reach them by going through that gate on the left." Captain Greer was speaking to me. I noticed that he held a photographic map in his hand, with hedgerows clearly outlined and numbered. These maps, probably obtained through aerial photography, were one reason our artillery was able to fire so quickly and accurately on objectives.

Unencumbered by machine gun ammo boxes which another member of the squad had carried for me, I followed the Captain's directions and found myself in more open ground. I passed through a gateway into the second field and saw my squad stretched on the ground behind a skimpy hedgerow. I approached in a crouch, but even so, when I rejoined the group, Jones spoke with a fear-motivated sharpness: "Get down! They're shelling us!"

"Keep well apart," Connie said. "Don't keep so close together."

I fell to the earth and crawled to Connie's left and past Barth. I nestled against the protecting mound which was only about two feet high, although it was grown over with bushes. The Normandy farmer who tended this field, however, had strung a line of barbed wire through the brush as an added means of containing livestock.

Enemy mortar shells began dropping in the field to our rear. We could tell they were mortar rounds because they announced themselves only at the last moment with a menacing hiss.

The ladder technique of firing was a favorite with the Jerries, especially when they were pulling out. This meant firing at a greater range than the target and stepping down the increments with the next four or five shells to cut a swath across the objective. One or two of the group of shells would thus land close enough to be effective.

I thought of what I had learned in basic training as each succeeding shell landed closer to our hedgerow. Finally, one struck in our midst with a deafening crash. Dirt pelted my back and a cloud of dust obscured my vision.

"My back, Connie! I think I'm hit in the back." It was Barth's excited voice. "Connie," he called, but there was no response.

Barth crawled over to me. "Look at my back," he said. Barth had had back trouble the last few days. This morning someone pulled him out of his hole because he was temporarily paralyzed by his cramped position during the night. He really wasn't sure if he had been hit or his back was bothering him again.

I saw a fluffy-looking rip in his field jacket.

"Yeah, you've been hit," I told him.

Ignoring caution, Barth jumped to his feet and ran to the rear. I was not to see him again until the latter part of September.

I thought I had better tell Connie that Barth was gone. I crawled over to Connie who was on his knees with his head resting on the ground as though listening for earth tremors, His face was already black from a head wound. Herr, our gunner, who was a few yards to his right, looked glum and said simply: "He's dead."

A still-smoking, 12-inch shell crater was about a foot from our squad leader's head.

For the first time during the battle, I was shaken and stupidly afraid. Our little trapeze-artist corporal, who had attended Catholic church services the day before and had expressed such faith and confidence in our future, who had been so alert and poised, and apparently in command of the situation, was gone with the snap of your fingers. I felt sick and weak. I supposed that was the moment I ceased being a raw recruit and became a combat "veteran," a soldier who has learned to fear everything, even the quiet times, and who becomes wily, suspicious and unashamed of being selfish and afraid if that is what it takes to stay alive.

The order came to move ahead. Herr was now in charge of our depleted squad. He carried the gun, Jones the tripod, and I the ammunition. We crouched our way quickly through two fields and came to a lush, five-foot high hedgerow behind which some riflemen were standing guard. Jones set the gun on the bank after hacking a hole in the dense brush. We were to hold here temporarily.

The men began to talk loudly about the advance — too loudly, I thought. Why broadcast our position to the enemy? Some queried anxiously about what was on our left, so men were posted to watch the flank. Skeeter, our little Mexican-American runner, guarded an open gateway on our left, and I stood to his right. Our gun was set up about ten yards further to my right with Jones and Herr manning it.

Suddenly word was passed that an enemy tank was approaching on our right along the tarvia road. The men were electrified. They executed an orderly abandonment of the hedgerow and swung as though on a hinge, based on the gateway, and set up a new line perpendicular to our former defense line.

We waited fearfully for the tank to appear, but nothing happened. Slowly the men began to reassemble on the former line. Sgt. Barbuzzi, whom I came to know much better later, came along the line cursing and fuming.

"You can't see nothing standing there like that," he said to me. He used his bayonet and bare hands to tear a hole in the brush and thorns. "Now get your head up there and keep your eyes open. We're stickin' out here like a sore thumb."

I obediently leaned against the slope of the hedgerow and burrowed my head into the opening to see what was ahead. I saw another field identical to ours, except that the hedgerow on the left angled into our gateway. It was part of a sunken road leading to a farm to our front about 150 yards. A substantial wall was around the house and barn.

At this point I was joined by Walt Paige, a well-educated Andover graduate who had actually volunteered for service and whose luck at rising in the ranks had been slightly better than mine. He was a Pfc. We had had long talks about the war and its probable course while waiting in the kitchen area to join Company B. His home was in New Bedford, Massachusetts. He had been in France before the war studying textile manufacturing, a business he expected to enter in the States after the war. Now he was a mere rifleman getting his first taste of battle.

We chatted a bit. Another sergeant with a noisy walkie-talkie radio passed us and the gateway, and climbed on top the hedgerow where he sat in the brush with the radio still in his hand. I thought he was foolhardy. I later came to know emotions of despair and hopelessness which engender such behavior, sometimes known as battle fatigue. I was never able to precisely define battle fatigue since it seemed to affect men differently. Some wanted to get it over with and would get reckless as though dying would be a welcome release. Some wanted to hide in a hole. And some just wanted to get out. They might run away, or they might calmly walk off as one would from a bad movie.

A burst of enemy small arms fire which originated from the other side of our hedgerow and clipped the leaves around our machine gun caused us all to drop instinctively behind the cover of the embankment.

Jones, who was much quicker than the rest of us in sensing enemy tactics, jumped up, seized the machine gun from the embankment, and fell to the ground again with the weapon pointed at the gateway.

A loud explosion came from the gateway and a metal object slithered in the grass and stopped at the gun. It was an anti-tank round, but it didn't go off. We discovered later that the pin had not been pulled.

At the same time enfilading automatic fire streamed down the length of our hedgerow sending white tracers zipping past our bodies as we hugged the bank.

Despite our efforts to be vigilant we had been flanked through the gateway.

As the tracers and bullets cracked around my body, I stood against the hedgerow in stupefied wonder that none were hitting me or the others near me. In contrast to my bewilderment, Jones frantically worked at the bolt of our machine gun to get it into action, but the gun would not fire.

A bullet had penetrated the exterior of the weapon and frozen the block in place.

But we had a supporting tank almost next to our hedgerow. It was probably the intended target of the anti-tank round. Guided by one of our infantrymen who hid behind its protecting armor, the tank backed up a few yards to bring the gateway in line with its angle of fire and then poured .50 caliber machine gun slugs into and around the opening.

Meanwhile, at the highway-end of our hedgerow, an enemy tank began to creep around our line, apparently with the hope of catching our armor napping as it fired at the gateway. Sgt. O'Brien, a gunner in our other machine gun squad, was waiting for it with a rifle grenade. As soon as its front sprockets were in view, he fired from extremely short range and succeeded in halting its progress. A bazooka-man in another platoon on our right knocked it out.

Sgt. O'Brien fired from such short range, however, that a fragment from the grenade struck him in the chest. He later walked past our position on his way to the rear, blood streaming from his exposed torso. He had a grin on his face, so he drew nothing but kidding and envious remarks.

As we reconstructed this part of the counterattack later, we deduced that the enemy had crept up on the other side of the hedgerow, spotted the nose of our machine gun and fired the bullets to put it out of action. Meanwhile, other elements in the attack fired from the gateway at our tank and defense line. The strategy was brilliant, but the execution, save for knocking out our gun, was faulty.

As soon as our tank had silenced the enemy automatic fire, Sgt. Barbuzzi came along again and shouted for "firepower."

"Get up there and shoot, for God's sake," he shouted.

I had had the typical civilian's attitude about shooting only when a target is visible. But in this kind of warfare, when little is visible (I hadn't

18

ABOVE — Occasionally a rifleman got a good shot at a German.
Photo: *History of the 120th Infantry Regiment*, Infantry Journal Press, 1947
BELOW — "...a terrific rush of air and the receding whistle of a shell passed over my head followed by a hair-raising explosion to my immediate rear. The shell took part of my breath with it, and I fell into a sweaty, vitiated heap...I felt as though the enemy could count the hairs on my neck, as I waited helplessly for them to improve their aim." Photo: U.S. Army Signal Corps

seen an enemy soldier in action yet), a stream of fire to the front whether anything can be seen or not, had the effect of putting the enemy undercover and forcing him to take the defensive.

I fired my .45 pistol just over the hedgerow and directed downward. I didn't reach over too far, because I had heard the story about the GI who had pushed his hand through the brush to drop a hand grenade on the other side, only to have his hand caught by one of the enemy. The grenade went off, killing the German and removing the American's hand.

My pistol was a most unsatisfactory weapon for my purpose. Seeing an abandoned M-1 rifle on the ground, I used it to punch another hole in the shrubbery and began firing at the top of the wall at the farm complex. The gun was jammed with sand and would not fire automatically. I had to cock it each time. After seven or eight rounds, I threw it on the ground again.

The entire action took about ten minutes, but it seemed much longer. The main thrust, we learned later, was made on our right to the south of the highway. Here, one platoon of our company and elements of Company C engaged a strong infantry attack, supported by tank and half-tracks. The attackers were members of the 1st and 3rd Battalions of the German 14th Parachute Regiment. They boldly leaped from personnel carriers and charged our lines while carrying their arms at high port and yelling at the tops of their voices. Our BAR men, riflemen, and machine gunners opened up on this easy target, and they fell in closely concentrated numbers on this killing ground. These bodies were inspected in silent awe later by our GIs. One corpse looked like Max Schmeling who was known to be a parachuter. In any event, the enemy charge was a terrible mistake which more than offset our day's errors.

We remained on the alert behind the hedgerow long after the firing had died down. I noticed with relief that twilight was beginning to descend. Where the time had gone, I didn't know.

Skeeter was concerned about the sergeant who had been sitting on top the hedgerow at the gateway. He got up enough nerve to walk past the opening to the intersecting hedgerow. He found that the sergeant was dead with a bullet hole in his head and still holding his radio.

The enemy had ruined our squad's table of organization. Our leader had been killed, Barth had been wounded, and Herr also had been hit by a

20

shell fragment in his leg during the last action. Only Jones and I were left and our gun was useless. We joined forces with the other machine gun squad, which still had its gun, and had lost only one man, Sgt. O'Brien.

Taking a lesson from the tank which had poured bullets into the gateway to save our lives, we moved back a hedgerow and set up our remaining gun with its line of fire directed at the opening. Our riflemen continued to hold the hedgerow to our front.

Jones and I teamed up and began to hack a two-man hole in the ground between two dead cows and next to a tree which had been toppled and shattered by shell fire.

Dead cows were scattered about, for they had been exposed, placid spectators and victims. I had watched some of them die. They first went down on their knees, mooed once or twice and then were gone. Most of them were brown and white beauties, meek and peaceful, but their cud-chewing days were over. In time, they ripened and rolled on their backs with their legs stiffly pointing upward.

The day's action now came across my mind as a nightmare. The objective had been 13 hedgerows, if the birthday boy was right. I mentally counted seven. We hadn't done it then? What would the dispatches back home say? "Elements of the 1st Army hammered out another 1,000 yards in the stubbornly defended hedgerow country west of St. Lo today." That would probably be all.

After two or three hours work, Jones and I had a hole about three feet deep. "Good enough," Jones said. I was exhausted and more than willing to quit.

C rations were brought up when darkness fell and we had hot food out of cans. I couldn't believe it when I was also issued a carton of cigarettes as though it were a kind of bonus for the day's work. Not being a smoker, I had no use for the cigarettes. When this was learned, I was besieged with offers to trade for chocolate bars and other goodies, which I readily accepted. After I had forced down as much food as I could — my fear-racked body did not crave sustenance — I fell to the bottom of the hole. I was ready for sleep.

Jones nudged me. "Your guard will be at 2:00 tonight. You wake up Halbrook after two hours for your relief."

"O.K.," I said, as I stretched on my side in the hole, my helmet on my head as a pillow, and the raincoat over my body as a blanket. Two a.m. seemed like a long way off. Let me sleep. Let me get away from this damned war for a while. Let me sleep.

Someone was pulling my leg and whispering, "Parker! Parker!" I smelled the rich French soil, and the realization of where I was came back in a sickening wave.

"Your turn for guard," Jones said, as he handed me a wristwatch with a luminous face. I stiffly crawled out of the hole shivering with the night's cold. My long winter underwear, which I was wearing on the advice of the veterans who knew how chilly the nights could get, was still damp with sweat from the day's exertions. I thought I smelled somewhat like fermenting hay.

"Don't stand here," Jones said, meaning next to our hole. "Get back in the open where you can see anything that moves," he directed, pointing to a spot about three or four yards behind our hedgerow. "The Jerries like to sneak snipers in during the night, so stop anything that moves." Nothing was said about a password. That was for the movies. Just shoot anything that moves.

Jones crawled in our hole and I stepped back to the place indicated. The watch read 2:00 a.m. I stuffed it in my pocket and began the boredom of standing guard. I was impressed with the quiet peace of the dark. I could distinguish nothing in the blackness.

My quiet was broken by the hiss of shells passing overhead. I recognized them as friendly artillery rounds. They landed well to the front. My combat ear was sharpening.

The remainder of my guard period was uneventful, save for periodic concentrations of friendly artillery which gave a reassuring feeling of security as they crashed in the distance. No enemy fire was returned.

It was only the night before that I had been on guard duty at 2:00 a.m., but that seemed eons ago. So many men gone, killed or wounded. But what had I expected? I had anticipated nothing. I had refused to think about it. Now after my first day of combat, I admitted that I had never been so frightened and tired in all my life, that I couldn't point to any personal glory or achievements in the battle, only that I had stuck it out. What were my future chances of survival? Better with the machine gun squad than with the riflemen. I had learned we had a slight edge.

At the end of my two hours, I woke Halbrook and went back to sleep, to a welcome respite from the war.

The next three days at this position were quiet, except for occasional 88 rounds and enemy sniping. We feared the 88's which came with lightning speed. One landed on our hedgerow, but did no damage since everyone was under cover. The sniper fire was merely a nuisance and lasted only through the first day.

"They can't hit anything," Jones said, with a grin on his freckled face. I noticed that every time I exposed my head at a certain place on our hedgerow, bullets would clip the branches above. The sound of the German "burp" gun became familiar. The crack of the bullets would be first heard overhead, and then the pattern of sound would be repeated in a lower tone as the report of the weapon reached our ears. Thus a staccato: "Teet-te-te-tee" was followed by "tah-ta-ta-tah."

Jones and I built a rickety kind of top for our sanctuary. Boards from C ration boxes and branches from trees formed a framework upon which we loaded as much sod and dirt as it would take. GIs were constantly occupied with the digging and improving of holes in the ground. I have said before that they looked like moles. They spent most of their time living like them. The entrenching tool was the most important defensive weapon.

The two dead cows lying on either side of us in the hot July sun reached a stage of decomposition which made Jones and me social outcasts. Our olfactory senses had become fatigued, and the odor, although still offensive, didn't stop us from eating. We began to realize how bad our situation was when some of the light mortarmen, located down the hedgerow a bit, began running past our position and holding their noses as they did so. Largely immune to the smell, we were at first puzzled as we saw them flit back and forth.

The cows finally got so swollen that they rolled on their backs. Then, one day one of them, unable to contain her gaseous ballooning any longer, burst an opening in her side with a hideous bubbling and whistling sound. One humorous GI shouted: "Dinner."

Skeeter stopped the music by shoveling dirt on the bovine whistle.

Toward dusk on the afternoon of July 20 our unit was ordered to move forward. During our days of relative idleness, the 2nd Battalion had pinched us off and pushed ahead about 1,000 yards, and the 3rd Battalion had gained another 200 yards. We had gradually pushed the Germans off most of the ridge west of St. Lo. At the time, I had no idea we were on a ridge. From prone positions I had examined the excellent pasture at very close range. My world was microscopically limited, rich in minute detail but barren as to the big picture.

"We're going up to the front and we'll be on outpost duty tonight," Jones said. My stomach tightened at the thought.

"It might not be so bad," Jones added.

I hooked up my equipment, got my boxes of ammunition together and was ready to move out. We waited, however, while a column of Company B riflemen filed past us. Some still had the red faces that were wind burned from training days in England. But about half did not. All were heavily loaded with rifles, grenades, and bandoliers of ammunition, and some carried rifle grenades, bazookas, and bazooka ammo. They made a rustling, clanking sound as they waddled by. There was no wisecracking. They were the veterans, the lucky ones who had survived the last battle, now leaving their dugouts to expose themselves to the "beaten" zone of the real front and roll the dice again. Would they, and I, continue to be lucky?

We moved at the usual slow pace, stopping and starting, and maintaining about five yard intervals between men. We passed through the gateway from which the enemy had attacked on July 16. The gateway opened into the angled hedgerow I had noted before, but now I saw that it was part of a sunken road leading to the farm buildings. (We called all French lanes or trails with high banks on each side "sunken roads," probably because they gave the illusion of being below ground level.) I saw bodies of three Americans lying face down, suggesting they were in a collecting point for battle casualties. The real front could not be too far ahead.

The column advanced in a seeming tunnel, since the dark and somber lane was covered with a canopy of trees and brush. We reached the farm structures which I had shot at during the counterattack, then crossed the highway and continued on another sunken road for a few more yards before a round of enemy artillery crashed into the head of our troops and wounded two men. Word as to their identities quickly passed down the line. One was a man whom everyone in the replacement package had known as "Tennessee." He claimed he was 38 and said he had a family at home, to whom he wrote frequently. We knew this because he made us all partners in his letter writing by constantly asking how to spell certain words. He also quietly let it be known that he had made "expert" rifleman, the highest Army award for marksmanship, but he must have been bewildered by the lack of opportunity to use his skill in this war. Now he was wounded in the leg. "Hurt bad," someone said. I didn't see him, but I was glad he was out of the war.

Our column inched further south, until we came to fairly open ground. We all felt naked and alarmed at being exposed to enemy view. Here we moved as rapidly as we could, crouched behind the low hedgerows for what little concealment they afforded. Nonetheless, the enemy probably saw us, for shells again hammered into our line.

I fell into a ditch beside a dead American to wait for the barrage to cease. I noticed a green mold around the blackened ears and neck of the dead soldier, indicating he had been there some time.

We jumped up and moved again. Gross, one of the members of our combined machine gun squad whom I have not mentioned before, passed me in a crouch, heading for the rear, with blood flowing from a small cut on his cheek. His eyes protruded in seeming amazement that this could have happened to him. I mirrored his expression.

We passed through another gateway, where an American soldier was lying comfortably on his back in the death rest. The riflemen began to assume defensive positions, for we had arrived at our new sector, all, that is, except our machine gun squad and a squad of riflemen who were to proceed to a listening post about 150 yards ahead of our lines.

Crossing another field to the south as darkness began to settle, we found elements of Company A entrenched in another typical sunken road, which, however, did not have trees or shrubs on it. The road ended abruptly at the edge of a small woods. A trail, densely covered with brush and small trees, descended along the side of the woods, and gradually widened and deepened at the bottom into a sharply cut ravine. This was my first indication that we had been on high ground, for we were now at the base of the ridge on its south side. A hedgerow protected us on the left, facing open ground. I noticed several neatly cut firing steps in the bank as well as a broken German rifle and an empty box of enemy machine gun ammunition. The enemy had fought from here once.

It was completely dark by the time we had set up our gun at the extreme corner of the woods and at the bottom of the ditch-like ravine. A sound power phone had been brought with us. Someone tested it and got a response from the rear. Everyone talked in whispers.

"We're out here all alone," Jones hissed. "Don't make any noise, and don't go to sleep tonight. If the Jerries try to attack, they'll probably try to use this approach. That's what we're here for — to slow them up and give the word when and if they come."

"You'll guard the rear tonight," he added. 'We're setting up a perimeter defense to guard from all directions."

Maybe I'm lucky I thought to myself. If anything does happen, I'll be the get-away man, the guy who gets the word back; unless they come at us from the rear and cut us off, then I'll be the first one to get it, I reflected soberly.

I didn't like this, but I was very willing to cooperate as far as keeping quiet was concerned. It proved to be an agonizing night, both physically and mentally. Every snapped twig could signal something fearful in the dark, or any similar noise on our part could alert the probing enemy. But it was impossible to remain motionless for long; the strain of standing or kneeling in one position was too much. Each body change, had to be made in stealthy quiet. Despite my extreme fatigue, fear kept me bright-eyed and alert until dawn's relieving light.

With the coming of daylight, it no longer seemed necessary to be as quiet and motionless. I climbed the hedgerow and peered through the brush, but could see nothing but a field and more trees to the north. I expected that we would retire from this impossible position, but we stayed on. I looked at the dense overhanging tree branches. No shell could ever penetrate that mass without being detonated, I thought. Therefore, an overhead burst would be the result—the most deadly kind of shell-fire. I spotted a shallow tunnel in the side of the hedgerow. It was as yet too small to hold me. If enlarged, the tunnel would give overhead protection, but little at the exposed side. I went to work with my shovel and started to hack out a larger opening. Presently, I had a space large enough to hold me if I assumed a cramped sitting-down position.

Jones and another GI were also getting overhead cover. They had a door or several boards — where they came from I didn't know — which they threw over a depression in the ground. They were exposed at the head and foot, but they improved their overhead protection by piling dirt and sod on the cover.

At about 10:00 a.m. enemy shells began to fall in the vicinity. Most of them went over our heads, but now and then one would land close to us. The enemy must have sensed that this corner of the woods might harbor observers.

Walt Paige, who had been one of the riflemen lying on the open ground all night to our front, came back to visit with me.

We were glad to see each other again. Walt had a stubby black beard which made him look like one of Mauldin's characters. His glasses spoiled the effect somewhat, and when he talked you knew that here was no typical GI.

Our conversation was interrupted by a cluster of enemy shells slamming into the woods all about us.

"Stick your head in here quick," I shouted. Walt obeyed but not with alacrity. He did it as though annoyed.

When the barrage was over he pulled his head out.

"Parker," he cried, "isn't this whole thing ridiculous! All this senseless killing, and for what! Why couldn't this be settled some other way. It's absolutely ridiculous!"

I couldn't help recalling our talks in the kitchen area where he had said that Hitler and the Nazi machine had to be stopped. Now he saw the war as farcical tragedy. All the same, I marveled at his disdain for danger and his continued objectivity, although it was leading him to different conclusions about warfare, if not the war. I was later to wish that Walt could have been more subjective, more interested in his own safety. It might have helped him survive.

(Walt's reaction was not unlike that of many Americans who witnessed the Vietnam War in their living rooms via TV coverage. Could it be that there never again will be broad-based support in this country for the sort of fighting we did abroad, no matter how worthy the cause may seem to be?)

I learned the meaning of "combat fatigue" from a personal stand-point during the next several hours. Our position in the wooded draw was becoming more and more untenable as enemy shells devil-hammered the vicinity. Another man and I were sent to the rear at noon to get rations and water. We walked across the open ground just north of our ravine to an orchard where we picked up C rations and a can of water. We returned across the same open stretch, apparently in full view of the enemy, and descended into the draw. Not long after, shelling of our woods became more persistent and closer to our outpost.

The exploratory tenacity of the enemy artillery finally brought hor-rifying results when a shell stopped the world right over our position. It was like having one's wind kicked out in a football game. There was a moment of stunned silence as the shattered leaves floated down and the dust began to settle. Then came the cries of the wounded as though babies were being slapped into life. Two men who had been lying on top the hedgerow over my tunnel were hit, and little freckle-faced Jones caught a piece of metal in his ankle. The shell had burst in the trees as I had expected, and my tunnel had saved me from injury.

One of the wounded was a rifleman named Holland. He had a one-inch gap in his neck which gave his breathing a rasping sound. I examined the wound, but there was no noticeable bleeding. The jugular vein had been missed. Holland later told me in September when he returned to our unit that the doctors had gathered around him to marvel at his wound, since the shell splinter had passed so close to the vital jugular without cutting it.

"Another fraction of an inch in the wrong direction and you would have been a goner," he was told. The miracle of escape was later nullified by the laws of chance in November when Holland was struck by a shell and killed while in a supposedly secure hole on the outskirts of Altdorf, Germany.

On this July afternoon in Normandy, Holland still lived. I was ordered to help him to the rear for medical attention. I grabbed my carbine (I had added this weapon to my collection two days ago), and left my pistol, ammo belt, machine gun ammunition, gas mask, and raincoat, thinking that

I would be back later to get them. Holland staggered along the pathway for about 25 yards, before we both stopped as more shells whistled in.

"Is it bleeding?" Holland gasped.

"No, you're all right, you lucky stiff," I said. "But you better take your sulpha pills." I undid his first aid packet, attached to his belt, and got the pills out. He had difficulty swallowing water to wash them down.

We reached the top of the slope and the end of the woods, where we found a medic who put a bandage on his neck and tied a tag on his field jacket.

I turned to go back, but at that moment more enemy shells began falling. I saw a roomy hole with a door over it. Two men from Company A were in it. One held a communication phone to his ear.

"Can I get in until his shelling stops?" I pleaded.

"Sure. We got plenty of room," the GI with the phone said, giving me a wry grin. I squeezed in beside them with a feeling of relief and gratitude.

The shelling increased in intensity, but I began to relax in the relative security of the hole. The GI with the phone tried to keep the tension out of his voice as he talked into the mouthpiece: "We're getting quite a bit of mortar and artillery," he reported with understated authority.

Then he spoke to me: "Did you see our friend Joe out there?"

"You mean the guy draped over the tree stump?" I said. I had noticed a dead GI lying on his back against the stump of a fallen tree. The body had a ghostly grey appearance caused by an overlay of dust thrown up by the shell which had killed him. One foot was laid open, reminding me of the sectional shoes on display in store windows.

"Yeh," replied my host. "Joe had to have a hot cup of coffee, so the fool built a fire. The Jerries probably saw the smoke."

During the subsequent conversational quiet, I found that the sleepless night and the strain of the day's action were piling up on me. My lights went out, and I fell asleep or simply passed out.

I don't believe I slept more than ten minutes. When I awoke and realized what had happened, I was anxious to rejoin my squad. I reluctantly left the hole and expressed heartfelt thanks for the temporary haven.

At the entrance to the woods, I met Jones being supported by Paige and another GI. I greeted them and was about to continue into the draw when they detained me and informed me that we were pulling out.

"All my equipment's down there," I said.

"Leave it there," Walt advised. "It's as much as your life is worth to go down there now."

Jones, who had a bloody bandage about his ankle, said, "Let's keep moving."

"There's a medic back there about 25 yards," I said, pointing up the sunken road toward Company A's position.

More shells said, "Excuse me a moment while I try to kill you." Walt and I and the other GI scrambled into a nearby hole. We couldn't get Jones to dive in also, and he didn't want to.

"You guys can stay here," he said. "I'll crawl on back."

The last I saw of the very courageous Jones, our most intelligent and effective fighter, he was crawling to the rear with his wounded ankle cocked in the air to keep it out of the dirt.

We huddled in the hole, wondering what to do and where to go, when another GI crawled in with us. He was a kid, just old enough to be in the war.

"Geez," he said in large-eyed fear, "they just dropped a mortar right in my hole. I didn't get hurt, but my buddy was killed. The blood spurted out of him like a fountain. I had to get out of there."

He would have gone on, but he was interrupted by Paige who told him to shut up.

"It's bad enough now without rubbing more blood in our faces," he said sharply. The youngster became silent and his body began to shake.

Halbrook, who was now in charge of our squad, had been seen going to the rear. We decided it was safe enough now to try to find him. Paige and I gingerly walked down the sunken road about 100 yards before turning into a field formerly occupied by a heavy mortar section. They had suffered, too, before moving out. We came upon a helmet about a quarter full of blood. Bandages and equipment were strewn about.

Despairing of finding our unit right away, we crawled into a spacious and well-built hole which the Jerries had dug. Since it was getting late and rain was beginning to fall, I suggested that we stay put until morning and start looking again.

Walt thought that he should continue looking while I remained in the hole to keep it for us in the event he was unsuccessful. I assented. Walt disappeared over another hedgerow. I stretched out on the bottom of his spacious dugout, thinking that jerry-built and Jerry-built certainly had opposite meanings. I fell asleep to the pitter-patter of raindrops falling outside.

I had not long to sleep. Walt returned with Lt. Pulver (later Captain Pulver), who was in charge of the 1st Platoon of Company B. Lt. Pulver was a poker-faced, brief-spoken officer of great courage. His erect six-foot or more carriage, which remained erect whether in battle or not, was to become his trademark and an inspiration to his men. He also became known for the many rifle grenades he clustered on his body before going into battle. He found them superior to hand grenades in knocking out machine guns and even tanks.

"I don't know where the weapons platoon is," Lt. Pulver told me. "You might as well come with us until we can find them."

I hated the idea of becoming a rifleman, even on a temporary basis, but I submissively followed the lieutenant as he led the way back to the front. Rain was continuing to fall lightly.

At the front, Paige and I were assigned to a two-man hole which we occupied for a short while before Lt. Pulver ordered us to take a position on the right in the open ground leading south to the wooded draw which our outpost had recently left.

I considered the order a death sentence. The hedgerow in this open ground was low and without the concealment of shrubs and trees. There were no adequate pre-dug holes with substantial covers, and the area had been subjected to heavy shelling. It was the same ground I had crossed when bringing up rations, and it was the same place an enemy shell had dropped squarely into one of the holes, the news of which had been graphically given us earlier by the surviving occupant. We did not reckon on a lucky downpour of rain which came at the moment to cover us as we ran in a crouch to the exposed ground.

Paige and I found a shallow hole with a flimsy top of wooden strips and boughs which had not yet been filled in with dirt and sod. The hole was partially full of water, but we accepted it as the only thing available. We took turns standing guard, while one of us worked digging chunks of sod to add to the feeble cover.

Meanwhile the rain came down in such torrents that we were soaked to the skin. The temperature cooled considerably to add to our discomfort.

Another rifleman joined us to stand guard, so Walt and I loaded as much more earth on the top as we thought it would hold and crawled in. I should say that we slid in on the mud bottom. Neither of us cared that our trench was slimy and wet so long as it afforded a bit of protection. We soon found that our roof was far from rain-proof, for the water dripped through in several places and chicken plops of mud hit our faces.

I was standing guard an hour or so later, while the rain continued to pour down, when a runner from the first platoon appeared in a half crouch barely visible through the haze caused by the sheets of rain.

By this time I had acquired a strange attitude toward danger. I simply didn't care. I believe at that moment I would have welcomed a piece of metal in the right place to put me out of my misery. It was a perilous attitude for an infantryman, one which could lead to quick extinction from bold, careless action that, however, might be viewed by others as extremely heroic.

I laughed at the crouching anxious figure of the runner and kidded him about being still alive.

"How did you manage to survive this long?" I had never seen the runner before and had no business being so personal. He seemed puzzled by my hysterical laughter and chose to ignore my behavior.

"Lt. Pulver says for you guys to come back to our lines again," he said.

It was joyous news. It was also my first exposure to Lt. Pulver's battle wisdom. He had an instinct for enemy tactics and how to counter them, thus often saving his men unnecessary casualties while still getting the job done. We wasted no time getting out of that exposed location before the rain could perversely stop and reveal us to the enemy.

Lt. Pulver met us and led us north into an apple orchard. I noticed a dead GI in a grotesque posture. He was on his knees with his head on the ground in an ostrich pose. In a final touch of disrespect, the rain had washed the shirt off his back so that it was bunched at his neck.

We were assigned some well-constructed Jerry holes and our new sergeant gave us orders for guard duty. My turn was two hours away so I prepared to surrender myself to Morpheus, since I had had only a few catnaps in the last 36 hours. I had barely stretched out when the sergeant told me to go back to the supply sergeant and bring up some cigarettes.

This made me angry. Strange how GI anger was usually directed at each other instead of the enemy. I didn't smoke, and to give up my sleep to further expose myself to enemy fire to get some useless bits of tobacco seemed like the last straw. However, I went.

As I moved past some rain-soaked riflemen on guard duty, I saw that, for waterproofing, the ends of their weapons were covered with unrolled prophylactics. GI manhood was no longer at stake. The only potent thing they had left was the rifle.

I found the supply sergeant in another orchard after inquiring at several damp and dark-looking holes. He had a raincoat fitted across the opening to his sanctuary. I moved the raincoat aside and spoke into the darkness.

"I came to get some cigarette rations.'

"Who are you?" the hole queried.

It was the question I had been waiting for. I blurted out that I was with a bunch of riflemen up front, but that I was a weapons man and couldn't find my unit. It wasn't exactly what the supply sergeant wanted to know, but he took it in good spirit and responded with some vital information.

"The light machine gun section, what's left of it, is with the mortars right behind this hedgerow," he said.

I didn't bother to verify his story. I grabbed the smokes and flew back to the rifle squad sergeant.

"Here's your cigs," I said. "I'm taking off. I found my machine gun squad."

The sergeant wasn't too pleased, but he didn't try to stop me, so off I went.

The supply sergeant was right. I found my friends of the mortar and machine gun squads where he said they would be. They looked at me in astonishment, not only because of my mud-caked appearance, but because they thought I was dead.

"Where the hell have you been?" Halbrook asked with a grin emerging through his red-whiskered face.

"Yeah, and where the hell did you slip off to?" I replied with disgust as I threw my carbine to the ground. And that was all I had to throw. All the rest of my gear was at the bottom of the ravine. But my gesture of disgust could not conceal my pleasure at being back home and I began to tell Halbrook, with animation, the tale of my adventures. The horrors of war were already beginning to fade as I relaxed in the aura of friendship and security I felt about me. Such temporary feelings of well-being were to occur again during the war. They were always delicious moments, but they did not happen often enough.

Again I was concerned about getting myself into a hole in the ground. In the five days I had been with Company B, I had occupied nine burrows, most of them dug by others. I had no shovel now, my equipment having been left in the ravine. Halbrook steered me to a substantial open trench near him. It was invitingly deep and wide, but its clay bottom was holding about two inches of water.

"Whitey," a daredevil member of the light mortar section, saw my predicament. Now that it had stopped raining he was cavorting in the grass, even doing backflips for a bit of exercise. He had been more adventurous than others, wandering about the neighborhood while most were under cover. Thus, he knew about the little French house on the highway to our left.

"Let's go to that house," Whitey said. "There's a bed there we can tear apart for a top, and I even seen some hayshocks in the rafters that we can take to put on the bottom of that hole."

We found a fine old French bed that antique lovers would have cherished. We ruthlessly pulled it apart, and together we carried the headboard to my new quarters. It was just the right width. The cocks of hay, when thrown on top the water, absorbed most of it and elevated the level of the bottom so that the hole was warm and dry. I found an extra gas cape — a plastic transparent shield intended for our bodies in the event of a gas attack — and fitted that over the bottom. The final touch was more hay over the cape, and I had a deluxe haven.

"Whatcha got here?" a soldier I hadn't seen before asked. "Mind if I share it with ya?"

"Who are you?" I asked.

34

"Sgt. Horne," he replied. "I'm the section sergeant for the light machine guns."

The sergeant told me that he had taken a wounded man back to the rear during the July 16 battle and that he was just now returning. He didn't explain the lapse of time. I later learned that he had been delayed by battle fatigue. In time, it was revealed to me that many good men suffered from this ailment and that some of them kept trying anyway. I came to realize that they were exhibiting a kind of courage that the rest of us had no right to judge, especially since we might become "fatigued" ourselves. I felt I almost had reached that stage the day before.

Our machine gun section (normal strength twelve) was now down to four men. Sgt. Horne, Halbrook, myself, and Skeeter, the runner. The others had been killed, wounded, or evacuated for combat fatigue.

Sgt. Horne said that replacements were coming up and that he could make me a squad leader. Advancement in rank could be speedy for combat survivors, but I turned the offer down.

"Why not?" he asked. "You've had the experience, and these fellows will be new."

"Everyone of those new guys will know more than I do about the machine gun," I explained. "I'm not mechanically inclined. I'll stick to being a pack horse. I'll carry the ammunition."

I had spoken truly. Halbrook had torn our gun apart to clean it and I was unable to help him put it back together again.

The sergeant didn't give me an argument.

Meanwhile, word had been passed that we were going to attack again tomorrow (July 22) if the weather was right. Good weather was needed to allow an air armada of 1,000 bombers to soften up the enemy before we jumped off. This sounded like the beginning of the pulverization of the Germans that I had been counting on.

My immediate concern was to replenish my equipment. I remembered the dead GI with green mold growing around his neck and ears. I found the spot where he had been, but he had been picked up. Luckily, the body-removing detail had cut away his equipment. Thus, I acquired a pistol belt, gas mask, canteen, canteen cup and cover. The latter was infested with ugly, white. crawly maggots. I was about to throw it away, but Halbrook intervened. He brushed them off and showed me how to dig them out of the folds of the cover, which I did. My need was greater than my squeamishness.

I still had to get a raincoat and an entrenching tool. Skeeter gave me his raincoat. He said it was too big for him, and he knew where he could get another. A battlefield is a treasure trove. I still lacked a shovel, the infantryman's most important defensive weapon.

On July 22 it rained again, and there was no attack, so I got a reprieve. The replacements came up and began to dig in. One of the group was a veteran of our section who had been sent to the rear for battle fatigue. He took the squad leader job I had refused. Halbrook was the leader of my squad. We were at full strength again — for a while.

That afternoon we watched a body-removing detail pass. The officer in charge wore a trench coat; his helmet strap was under his chin; and he sported combat boots. He was definitely rear echelon. (None of us wore the chin straps. They were looped over the edge of the helmet. The fear was that concussion might blow your helmet off and damage your throat and chin in the process.)

The combat boots were a dead giveaway, too. The frontline infantry men who were doing the "combating" were still wearing leggings. The combat boots didn't filter down to us until just before the Rhine River crossing.

The littermen were carrying a corpse which I believe was the GI in the orchard who was on his knees with his head on the ground. In any event, the body was twisted in strange ways to resemble a Rube Goldberg lamp base. We all looked and started laughing. Whereupon the officer ordered his men to stop.

"What's the matter with you men!" he barked. "You laugh at a man who has died for his country. Haven't you got any God-damned respect!"

We were shocked into silence. The officer ordered the litter bearers to pick up their heroic load and they trudged off.

Years later in a short story, "West of St. Lo," in the June 1979 issue of Yankee magazine, I had my protagonist respond to the officer as follows: "Sir, you might be right, but when they carry me away I would be pleased if I could give these men the small amount of relief you have just heard."

July 25, 1944, is a bigger day in my life than the traditional July 4 Independence Day, for the former date marked the liberation of our

36

Company, Battalion, Regiment, and Division from the murderous ridge upon which we had been fighting. Our deliverance was not without tremendous cost, but as prelude to the great St. Lo breakthrough the price was tolerable.

Rain cancelled attack plans on July 23, and set them ahead to 1:00p.m. July 24. Friendly planes came over at about 12:30 and planted their deadly loads on our lines as well as the enemy's. We lost 14 killed and 65 wounded, mostly in Companies G and H, which were near us. This caused another postponement. I was personally relieved since I still had not found a shovel.

The mighty drone of U.S. bombers, about 1,000 strong, was heard at 10:00 a.m. the next day. Sgt. Horne and I were standing outside our hole to watch. It was the last time I ever dared watch airplanes, friendly or enemy. The sergeant was the first to see the black specks dropping from the bellies of the planes.

"My God, they're dropping them on us," the sergeant cried.

We scrambled under cover, even though it was no protection against one of those huge bombs, two of which could demolish a small Normandy field.

Outside it was one big rushing noise, as though a tornado were churning our way.

The sergeant must have had a good Baptist upbringing for he shouted repeatedly: "Oh, Lordy save us! Oh, Lordy save us!"

I'm ashamed to admit that my refrain was some typical GI profanity.

It seemed as though we were under a waterfall of sound as the bombs cascaded upon us, and the earth quaked and shook and bounced us about. We sensed the center of the storm rushing toward our hedgerow and we braced for its earth-shattering impact.

But it never came. The Ninth Air Force ran out of bombs about 100 yards short of overrunning us.

Neither Sgt. Horne nor I congratulated each other on surviving. I think we were ashamed of the fear we had so volubly expressed. Still, I thought the sergeant's words were more appropriate than mine and that perhaps I should have thanked him.

To our astonishment the order came to attack. We wondered what with. Later tabulations showed that the Division's loss in this brief bombing was 662 casualties- 64 killed, 374 wounded, 60 missing, and 164 cases of combat fatigue. The enemy had never been able to do that well.

Ironically, the 2nd Battalion, which had suffered the most (175 casualties), began the attack. They soon bogged down against stiff enemy machine gun and tank fire. (Hadn't they heard about the bombing?) The 1st Battalion, including Company B, was then ordered into action.

When I heard that we were moving out, I felt naked for lack of an entrenching tool.

Skeeter came to my aid. "There's a kid in a hole down there about 25 yards who's too scared to come out of his hole. Maybe you can get his shovel."

I went to the designated hole and crawled in. I found a runt-sized GI, quivering and sobbing. I asked permission to take his shovel. He nodded and I looted him of his precious entrenching tool.

I felt no contempt for the man, nor did I feel sorry for him. I had experienced the same emotions that he couldn't let pass. On the other hand he was staying behind and I was going ahead, and he was simply a convenient source of something I needed. My capacity for sentiment was nil. I was happy about the shovel, but nothing else, as we began the crouching stop-and-start movement toward the beaten zone of action.

Later we learned that Ernie Pyle, the famous war correspondent, was two or three hedgerows to the north of our position during the aerial bombardment. He described the experience in graphic style for the newspapers back home. He reported that General Lesley J. McNair, commander of the Army ground forces, who was visiting our lines, was killed instantly in the bombing.

Meanwhile, despite our losses, it was imperative to attack while the enemy was in greater disarray than we, or so we believed. We had been told, as well, that Patton's 3rd Army lay behind us, and that the tanks and trucks were stretched out for miles, waiting for us to pick up a few hundred more yards before they came bursting through with all their power and speed to sweep across France. We believed that this would happen, without question, and it did. We were wrong in supposing, however, that this would mean the end of the war. It was merely the end of the desperate beachhead phase of the war, and certainly the beginning of the end for the Germans.

Our column crossed the tarvia road at the farm house. I noticed that a group of dead cows had been ruthlessly plowed to the side of the road by a scraper, evidence that preparations were being made for the motorized column behind us.

We advanced alongside the St. Gilles road for two or three hedgerows and then stopped. We waited so long that I and Gibson, a new member of our squad, began to dig in. It was always prudent to get cover if one remained long in one spot, especially in an attack that has apparently bogged down.

Finally, a tank colonel came along.

"What's holding things up?" he demanded. "Why, there isn't anything left up there. Their defense is as thin as a paper bag." Nevertheless, enemy machine guns and tanks were proving troublesome, enough so that when we started to move again it was getting dusk. About two hedgerows further on I saw the crew of a German tank. They were dressed in green camouflage suits and stood helmetless, their hands clasped behind their heads. Col. Birks, our regimental commander, was interviewing them.

At one point in the advance two or three rounds of direct tank fire screeched at us. One round struck as I was climbing out of a huge crater made by one of our aerial bombs. The shell hit the rim of the excavation, but since I was still below ground level I was unharmed, only momentarily stunned by the bright flash and concussion. The Ninth Air Force which had nearly killed me a few hours earlier could now take credit for saving my life.

It was nearly dark when we came out of the series of hedgerows into a small settlement. I got separated from my unit and found myself with riflemen from the 2nd Battalion, who said they were shorthanded and invited me to join them. I declined the honor. At this point, Lt. Ziegler of Royal Oak, Michigan, who had taken over command of our weapons platoon and who was in his first fight, appeared out of the gloom. I learned that my unit had circled a barn and was lying in an orchard behind. I was glad to return to familiar faces again.

While stretched in the orchard, an enemy burp gunner occasionally sent streaks of red tracers our way. We did not worry. It was too dark for him to fire accurately.

Within a few hours, we left our comfortable orchard to inch forward again. This no longer seemed like an attack. It was simply a problem of assuming a new position in the dark, for what was left of the Germans was pulling away and letting us take what we wanted with little or no resistance. We now encountered many huge craters, indicating that the bombardment had done some good after all. At the crest of slightly higher ground, we came upon a burning tank which ominously illuminated the area and made targets of us all.

"For God's sake don't bunch up. The Germans still got a few shells left." It was Captain Greer talking. It was true that the men were getting too close to each other, but maintaining close interval was the only way each man could see the one ahead of him in the darkness.

We passed a lone German prisoner being questioned by some enthusiastic GIs.

"Ask him if he knows that the Russians are headed for Berlin," someone said. The Russians had made tremendous advances lately, and we all believed they would be in the German capital within a short time.

We milled about in a field south of the burning tank, and learned that this was the end of the line. We started to dig in, riflemen in the lead hedgerow and mortarmen in the next hedgerow to the rear. The machine gunners were left to shift for themselves. Gibson and I were forced to dig a hole near a gateway on the enemy side of the hedgerow the mortarmen were using. Two riflemen with us refused to dig. They flopped on the ground and went to sleep. Gibson and I worked through the night and took our turns at guard as well. I was so tired at times that I lost my balance frequently and fell against the side of the trench I was digging. At about 2:00 a.m. we stopped, satisfied that we had excavated enough.

I rested against the side of the hedgerow and gazed at the starlit sky which cast its peaceful spell. I reflected on my ten-day introduction to war and how fortunate I had been. I offered a grateful prayer. It seemed to me now that the war must end shortly, and that I had a good chance of surviving. Patton's column would come through us at daybreak and we would virtually be through fighting — so we thought.

The Sweep To Tessy-sur-Vire

July 26 through August 5, 1944

As July 26 began to show a bit of daylight I was able to spot a German ammunition truck hidden under the foliage of the hedgerow on our left. Next to it was a huge crater created by one of our aerial blasts. I marveled that the truck had not been blown to bits. Several large craters were in the field to our front. So much topsoil had been blown away that I doubted that the area could be productive again.

Behind our hedgerow I now could see a hated enemy artillery piece that had been abandoned. What a joy that one of their 88s could no longer be used against us!

I found some boards by the ammunition truck and placed them over our gateway entrenchment, after which Gibson and I shoveled some soil on top to add to our security.

Suddenly we were electrified by the sound of approaching tanks—ours.

"Here they come," someone shouted. An American tank with several GIs crouched around it, with rifles ready, advanced slowly in the field on our left. They saw the gateway and directed the tank through it. The Goliath swung perilously close to our hole, and, as it turned, pushed a huge quantity of dirt on top of it. The boards held, and we felt fortunate in having been saved the labor of moving that much soil.

One of the advancing riflemen asked me: "Where's the front?"

"See that next hedgerow with our riflemen behind it?" I must have sounded unduly cheerful, but to us it was a tremendous relief to have another unit take over the war.

None of us missed the historical importance of the first tank and infantrymen which slowly moved past us and pressed the attack. We knew this was the beginning of the breakthrough, and we were childishly happy about it.

Other tanks churned past our hole and more dirt was thrown upon the top. I began to worry about a cave-in, but not too seriously. It was fun having a front seat at one of the great moments in history. Soon the sound of tank and small arms fire came to our ears, after which two or three rounds of German artillery whistled over our heads. One landed directly behind our hedgerow, but, fortunately, no one was hurt.

A column of German infantry, with hands over their heads, came marching back to our hedgerow with some GIs guarding them. The last thin crust had been broken. The race would now be on.

Throughout the day, the tanks, throwing up huge clouds of dust, continued to stream by. They no longer bothered with the fields on their flanks, but moved along the main highway south. In the afternoon, the armored vehicles were followed by truckload after truckload of infantry and supplies. The procession continued throughout the night. The breakthrough had indeed been made.

By this time, we were completely relaxed and freely wandered about the area. An enemy tank on the road was found to be booby-trapped. Knowing this, we didn't toy with the enemy artillery piece or the ammo truck. Even Jerry cans of water were left strictly alone.

On the afternoon of the next day, we got our orders to "move out." There had been talk of going back to a rest area, but we were to learn that there would be little rest for any of the units landed thus far in France.

We were to follow the route of the 2nd Armored Division for a distance and then strike our in an arc to the south of St. Lo until we reached the Vire River. This area was to be cleared out to protect the flank of the armored thrust.

Our route seemed an endless maze of hedgerows and circuitous pathways. We seldom traveled a roadway, but stuck close to hedgerows and areas of dense foliage. Ours was an intimate tour of France: through a farmer's front yard, his back yard, down the lane and through a valley, then up to high ground and across a road, a creek, and into another farmer's domain. I saw many buildings of rammed earth construction with red tile roofs and barns housing great hogsheads of "cidre," which our boys tried to drink, but as usual, found too vinegary.

I noticed, too, the neat German entrenchments and the occasional empty bottles of wine and champagne left on the ground, The Jerries weren't leaving anything for us but the undrinkable cidre.

The dead cows and men we ran across seemed freshly killed. It was a sign that the advance was moving fast and through virgin territory.

We struck a snag at a bit of high ground called Le Pont Hain where some Germans put up stiff resistance. We rounded a horseshoe bend on the main highway and crossed a bridge, at which point the familiar, fearful high velocity 88 artillery opened up.

I flopped into a shallow ditch beside one of our tanks. The shells were hitting to our rear about 300 yards, and, I later learned, caused some casualties. When the order came to move, I jumped up and began climbing, with the others, up the roadway leading to the hill held by the Germans.

Col. Cantey, who was commanding our battalion now, shouted into his radio to an infantry unit farther up the hill: "Blast 'em out of there, blast 'em out."

Presently one of our riflemen, whom I recognized as a non-digger at the end of our night attack on July 25, came by clutching his left shoulder.

"What happened?" someone asked.

"Aw, they got me with a rifle grenade," the soldier replied, not unhappily. He had got his ticket out of the war.

A firefight rattled at the top of the hill, and soon a procession of about thirty Germans and officers came down the road past us. One had been shot in the hip and groaned as two of his comrades helped him stagger by.

At the hill's crest, we found a farm house with some damage from bazooka fire. We passed through a farm yard and cautiously walked along a sunken lane with fields on either side of it.

I next saw a German in a camouflage suit lying dead in the lane. He had been preparing something to eat, when one of our lead scouts surprised him. We then encountered five Germans who quickly surrendered. Col. Cantry was questioning them joyfully and reporting back to rear commanders of his catch.

This was easy going. We all felt jubilant, and yet fearful that the easy successes would come to an abrupt halt.

The lane led to the highway to Conde-sur-Vire. We passed a farmhouse, which to our amazement was occupied by French civilians, who to our further amazement greeted us with flowers and drinks of water. We felt like heroes and conquerors for the first time. I still remember the thrill and the difficulty in holding back the tears of welling emotion. It was a moment of happiness that is now difficult to impart. The war had been dirty, fearsome, and unglamorous to this point, and now, in an instant, it was like a football game with crowds cheering us on to another touchdown.

A flower-decked tank sputtered and roared in our mock parade. Cries of "watch the flanks" kept us from being too ebullient. After all, we were an exploratory finger in unknown territory.

Rounding a bend, we saw the symbol of our victory, a dead German in a ditch. Passing us toward the rear was a live one, hands behind head, ashen. At another point, the road was littered with letters and papers. Sgt. Horne picked up a German rifle and smashed it against a tree to break the stock and render it useless. This was common practice which backfired once for a GI of our unit in Germany. The impact exploded the rifle and sent a bullet into his chest.

Then came a weird order in this increasingly weird war: "Double time with arms at port."

Loaded down as we were with ammunition and the various parts of our machine gun, we thought the order was slightly balmy. But its very absurdity seemed to fit this new kind of war, so we obeyed with abnormal cheerfulness.

The column jogged off the highway and into hedgerow terrain

again, where we came to an abrupt halt and none too soon for the pace was exhausting.

"This is as far as we're going," someone said. Smiles and laughs. A tanker, looking like a flower child, passed a bottle of Calvados around. I thought it was wine and drank it as though it were water, only to find that I had ingested firewater instead. I immediately resorted to my water canteen to dilute the terrible burning in my throat and stomach, but I had only a few drops in the container and no one else had water either. I undid a D Bar, an emergency chunk of chocolate we all carried, and ate it, hoping to absorb the acid-like liquid, but even this was not enough. Was I to become a Calvados casualty? I was later to learn that Calvados, a cognac made from apples in the Department of Calvados, was so powerful that GIs used it successfully in their cigarette lighters.

We set up a defense line and my agony continued. We had moved so fast and so far during the day (12 miles in all) that our supplies hadn't caught up with us. So we didn't get any water that evening and I got no relief.

That night a patrol of riflemen went before our lines to check out the ground ahead of us. They ran into enemy fire at a farmhouse held by the enemy some 250 yards to the southeast. I was standing guard at the time and saw the tracers from our weapons. The skirmish was followed by piercing screams of agony which came from a horse. Later, one of our GIs who had been hit in the leg crawled into our sector.

"Don't shoot," he called out. He was recognized and helped over the hedgerow. He lay on the ground near our hole and stayed there throughout the night.

"I'll be O.K.," he said, as he curled up under his raincoat. It must have been a long night for him, even more so than for me.

At about midnight planes droned over and bombed the area ahead of us. One of our riflemen chortled. He thought it was Jerry dropping bombs on his own troops, which it could have been since their planes ventured out only at night.

Toward morning, while again on guard, my thirst and stomach burning was so unbearable that I licked the dew off the leaves of the bushes. There was some moisture, but only enough to further whet my thirst.

Finally, with the full arrival of morning, water, precious water, as well as food arrived, and I enjoyed the ecstasy and balm of lengthy gulps of water. I drank my fill and replenished my canteen. (Throughout the remainder of the fighting in July and August water was a primary need. I learned not to depend upon our supply and supplemented my water ration from whatever source I could find — a pump or a cool fresh-running stream. In such cases, I added Army-issue halizone tablets to cancel out any possible impurities.)

At 10:00 a.m. we moved out. The riflemen filed past us first with that peculiar glazed look of fatigue and fear. Once when the column paused a moment, one of the riflemen who had evidently been with Company B from the outset, flopped on the ground by our hole and talked in a morosely confidential tone.

"Here we go again," he moaned. "More blood, more guys to get killed. How long do they think we can keep this up? I'm so damned fed up with killing and spilling blood every damned day." His words trailed off. His despair was controlled. He was not hysterical. He was just tired and sick of the whole business.

We soon shouldered our equipment and arms and followed the riflemen to the farmhouse where last night's patrol had been in action. We saw the results: a dead horse lying next to a German soldier, probably an officer, naked save for a towel wrapped around his middle. He may have had his bath interrupted by the skirmish.

The farmhouse was in a rare and beautiful setting. A small brook ran through a lush green valley about 200 yards wide, with sheer elevations on each side. At the northwest end of one of the elevations, the ground sloped off and the brook, the farm buildings, and the hill merged into an inviting tree-shaded haven for broken down infantrymen looking for a rest.

But there was no rest. We worked hard for a bit to dig some holes and then left them to retrace the ground we had covered. We went all the way back to an assembly area in an orchard near the highway we had used yesterday. While stretched on the ground here, the electrifying whistle of an enemy shell sent us scurrying for cover. More shells quickly hammered the ground around us, telling us that Jerry had regrouped and was going to stand his ground vigorously again.

We accepted the challenge, and began the maneuvers of combat — falling face forward into ditches, jumping up again, and scurrying short distances ahead. To our relief we left the targeted highway and began to wade a small creek, walled in with hedgerows on each side. This was security again.

But the column soon emerged from the creek and advanced across open ground and uphill toward Le Mesnil Raoult. It was to be one of the bloodiest and costliest fights the Battalion experienced, to be referred to later as one of the several Purple Heart Lanes in our combat history.

Climbing the hill to Le Mesnil Raoult would not have been difficult if we had not received the order: "Light machine guns up front —- on the double!"

Our two squads began to dog trot up the hill past slower moving units of riflemen, or some who stood or leaned against hedgerows to let us by. We traveled about 1,000 yards through fields and lanes, always uphill, and as fast as our unwieldly and burdensome equipment of machine guns and ammunition would permit. The ascent was physically the hardest thing I ever did in combat. My breath came in terrible gasps, which seemed about to tear my lungs out if pushed much further. My face became livid and the expression of torture on it must have been ludicrous. Still, I was recognizable, for a soldier I had known in one of the replacement depots and who was now a member of Company C said "hello" to me as he walked to the rear supporting a vacant-eyed officer who had been shot in the neck.

Others along the route, seeing the gun we were carrying, said from time to time, "give 'em hell." I didn't know whether they were being funny, or whether it was a corny effort to buck us up. I didn't feel capable of giving anything or anybody hell. I was too far gone with exhaustion.

My agony was relieved when we reached the crest of the hill where our riflemen were lined up in defensive positions along the sides of another Normandy sunken road at a point where it intersected the main highway at the outskirts of Le Mesnil Raoult. I flopped on the ground and waited for my breathing to get back to normal and for my heart to stop pounding. Enemy bullets were zipping over the tops of the hedgerows, but we were perfectly safe behind them. All might have been well if an enemy half-track which we had cut off to the north on the highway had not decided to bull its way back to the German lines.

Anticipating the return of the half-track, we had set up a roadblock

ABOVE — This wall encloses the shrine at Le Mesnil Raoult. The author ducked behind it on July 28, 1944, while an enemy half-track fired down the lane at fleeing troops behind him. Photo taken in 1962. BELOW — It doesn't look it now, but Tessy sur Vire was a tough nut to crack.

at the intersection, but the crew in this enemy vehicle proved to be exceptionally alert and skillful. I saw one of our bazooka men standing at the road juncture ready to fire when suddenly the lane erupted in a mass of flying metal, dirt, and tree branches. Concussion from the shell blast knocked all men in the vicinity to the ground. I was felled with the others, and the calf of my left leg went numb as though it had gone to sleep.

Before the dust and bits of leaves floating in the air had settled, all but three of the men who had been knocked down got up and ran past me down the curving sunken road. I looked where the bazooka man had been. He was now lying motionless on the ground. Behind him a high bulk of black metal, partly hidden by the foliage of trees in a small garden or park in the center of the trail, explained to me the sudden exodus of the other GIs.

I frantically crawled behind a retaining wall surrounding the little park (which I later learned contained a shrine), and while waiting out what I thought surely would be my last moments, I watched our men climbing over hedgerows on both sides or running around the bend in the sunken road, while the half-track created a deafening and terrifying noise with its heavy caliber machine gun.

I had company behind the wall. Col. Cantey and his radioman shared it with me. We were the only ones left in the trail. The Colonel shouted at me to fire at the half-track. He was using his .45 pistol by putting his hand over the wall and shooting blindly at the half-track. He then wanted to borrow my carbine, but I paid no heed to his request. My strategy differed from his. Perhaps we were both right, for within another ten seconds the half-track roared back into the village and our men slowly began to reassemble in the lane.

Col. Cantey was slightly wounded in the chin. I examined my leg, but could find nothing wrong with it. Apparently a muscle spasm had given me a cramp, or the leg had been hit by a stone or stick.

Our machine gun section came back to the congested road intersection, and we were ordered to cross the highway, which was under intermittent enemy machine gun fire, and set up our weapons on the other side.

We successfully crossed the highway by sending each man individually in a quick dash. To my amazement, our weapons were set up five yards apart on a hedgerow at the intersection. It was to my mind a foolish and tragic decision. Halbrook, our squad leader, was wise enough to have Gibson and me fall back of the gun emplacements at five to ten-yard intervals. I was flat on the ground when the enemy half-track opened up with direct fire at our guns as well as at a heavy machine gun on the other side of the road.

Again — the experience of concussion, flying dirt, and clouds of dust. Some of the dirt fell on me. I began to wish that lots of it would fall on me and cover me up, take me out of this terror. Halbrook appeared out of the heavy dust to order us to evacuate. He had one of our guns. The other was destroyed. As I crouched past our former gun position, I saw the vanquished parts of our machine gun section lying in brown heaps. One of them was still coughing as though the dust were too thick for him. The others were motionless. The tally was two killed, including the squad leader of the other gun — a job that I had been offered and turned down. One man was knocked unconscious by a rabbit-punching piece of metal in the back of his neck, and another was wounded in the leg. A fifth was evacuated for shock and battle fatigue, and a sixth ran from the scene and was lost for a time. There were four left of the original ten.

A few yards away, I noticed a rifleman sitting with his back against the hedgerow. His eyes were open but unseeing. His face was pale green. It was the veteran who had complained that morning about going into another day of bloodshed. The war was ending for him.

Following Halbrook, our depleted squad hugged the side of the hedgerow, past a rifleman who was bandaging his leg, and quickly moved over open ground to the hedgerow behind us as sniper bullets kicked up the ground near our feet.

Behind our new natural fort, we discovered that there were still some live GIs left. These were huddled and holed up.

"Watch out for that sniper! Get down!" one of the riflemen commanded. I flopped on the ground with the rest.

"Why don't they have us drop back and let the artillery pound the damned place?" a bearded rifleman asked. It was an obvious tactic, one which our command put into execution eventually, although it wasn't necessary to move back. Our infantry had suffered a temporary defeat, but the artillery cancelled it out, as it often did under similar circumstances. The infantry had a great love for our artillery and for the cub plane which hovered overhead to spot artillery targets.

As I lay in the grass and let a delicious wave of relaxation roll over me, I reflected on the sudden loss of six men from our section, as well as the other numerous casualties I had seen. The experience had a numbing effect emotionally. And yet, despite the fear-laden, fatiguing treadmill of war, there was a dimly felt boredom. A pattern of conflict had been established and it was repeating itself: hedgerows, holes, guns, red-faced fighting men, bullets cracking, shells exploding, trees and men shattered, sweat, fatigue, and death in various postures of relief, pain, and absurdity.

I had now witnessed the second big loss in personnel in our section. Was I becoming what the newspapers called a "veteran," a soldier of weary but hard cunning, relentlessly stalking the enemy? I laughed to myself. I was merely a packhorse, an observer, a soldier without verve or transcending beliefs. The war was my cruel master which would take all my strength and demand a certain debasing selfishness to survive. And it would take luck, too, and where could I find an endless supply of that?

As I lay in the lush pasture, I thought of the lines: "He maketh me to lie down in green pastures." I thought, too, of my intense thirst for water and of the lines: "My cup runneth over." The poetry of the 23rd Psalm and its peculiar appropriateness to my situation gave me a deep satisfaction. I knew now how the ancients must have felt in those days of barbarism and how they groped for a greater power to help to relieve the pressures of constant insecurity.

Our artillery concentrations discouraged the enemy and the sniping stopped. Since it was getting dark, however, we did not move forward. Our machine gun squad of four men was tied in with riflemen of Company C to set up a defense on the hedgerow behind which we had cowered for the last few hours. Our gun, curiously enough, was faced not toward the town, but to our rear. It was the first indication I had that we were sitting exposed on nearly all fronts on the little hill.

As darkness fell, we were annoyed by several explosions of hand grenades about 25 yards away. They made little red flashes like glow worms and caused no trouble. They were an annoyance which served to keep us tense and alert.

Gibson and I found an entrenchment which had already been dug. We were told to maintain a continuous guard from this position, taking turns of course at watch during the night. I was desperately tired, but the extreme danger of our position was a good no-nod stimulant.

When it was completely dark, I was assigned with several other men to go to the rear for rations. I groaned inwardly, for the job meant more backbreaking labor.

Our column of five men returned to the road intersection where we had been decimated by the enemy half-track. We crossed the highway and went down the sunken lane. After about forty yards, word was whispered back: "Watch out for the bodies. Don't step on them." Enemy mortars had zeroed in on this part of Purple Heart Lane.

After picking up the rations near the base of the hill, we began the arduous climb with our loads, but by a different route to avoid stumbling over the dead.

Back in our lines, I learned to my astonishment that the officer in command of Company C had decided that he couldn't feed our machine gun squad —- this after I had helped carry the rations to his unit.

"Why not?" I asked the officer.

"Haven't got enough for my own men." he said.

"Did you have four casualties today?" I asked.

"Sure, more than that!"

"Well, there's only four of us and you've been issued rations for the strength of your platoon before it went into action today," I pointed out.

We got our food and water. I remember that there was white bread in the ration, the first baked goods we had had since landing in France.

The enemy, during guard duty that night, was sleep. Several times I sagged, but caught myself before I fell to the ground. Toward morning, I attempted to awaken Gibson to take another turn, but exhaustion had overtaken him too. He couldn't get up. Finally, after I had punched him for several minutes, he rose from the hole, swung at me with his fist, missed, and slumped back into the hole and went to sleep again. And so did I.

The morning of July 29 introduced us to a clear, sunshiny day complete with a panoramic view from our hilltop position of the beautiful Vire River valley to the north and east. With such a commanding view it was now clear to us why the Germans had fought so hard to hang on to Le Mesnil

Raoult.

I saw occasional white clouds of smoke rising from the miniature-looking hedgerows on the east side of the Vire River. Out artillery was using smoke or phosphorus shells to zero in on targets as the infantry attacked to bring their line up to ours on the other side of the river. Under the peaceful greenery below, I realized, men were still fighting and dying.

Anticipating a union with these GIs who were fighting their way up on the left, our command deployed us off the hill, to the east of Le Mesnil Raoult, and nearer the Vire River. We moved about 500 yards south and east in accordance with this deployment to help close the gap. The hedgerows were very thick and observation was extremely limited on the lower ground. However, at one farmhouse near the river, I borrowed some field glasses from one of our mortar observers and spotted smoke coming from another farmhouse 800 yards further east and apparently on the river's bank. French civilians were busy around the house packing a cart with their valuables. One of the women left the group, got behind a bush, pulled up her skirt, and relieved herself. I felt like a voyeur. After this, she was ready to help the others push their cart away to the south.

Our machine gun squad was assigned a position near our Company headquarters. We set up our remaining gun to the north again, indicating that the unit on our left hadn't come abreast yet. I dug a snug hole in the rich clay soil, lined it well with sweet-smelling hay, and caught up on my sleep that night. I felt unusually secure for the first time in several days.

To add to this feeling of well being, our kitchen served pancakes for breakfast the next morning. Then came the ultimate luxury — mail — the first since landing in France. I avidly read the letters and prized some photographs of my infant daughter taking her first steps for the camera. My wife was shown in a backyard picnic scene with a glass in her hand. I was emotionally overwhelmed. I immediately wrote a letter, my first since going into action. I can't remember what I said that would be intelligible to the family back home. In any event, the letter never reached its destination.

July 30 was relatively calm, save for some shooting on the left as our mortars fired to help a patrol of GIs from the 35th Division cross the river and make contact with us. There must have been some Jerries about, for Whitey, the blond youngster in our mortar section who was fond of doing back flips, was shot in the left thigh. I happened to be peeking over our hedgerow down into the sunken road via which he was being taken to the rear. He was on a litter and his leg had been given first aid. I wished him well as he passed. He grinned up at me, but he was in great pain, and fear was in his eyes.

The next morning we resumed the push south and through part of Le Mesnil Raoult. Apparently the units on our right and left had caught up, and the attack, or sweep, was being resumed. The village was a shambles. I saw one German with his head blown off and another dead German in a wheelbarrow with his head tilted back almost to the wheel.

After a short advance, we left the road and set up a defense for the evening in an apple orchard. Rish, who had been lost from our squad, had found us again, so together we dug a fine two-man slit trench, complete with substantial top and camouflaging.

I struck up a conversation with an officer in the heavy machine guns company. He was "fed up," he said, "I'm never going to feel sorry for anyone again the rest of my life," he declared bitterly. As an afterthought he added: "Wonder how long that will be?"

While in a nearby barn getting some hay, I overheard an exchange of experiences between a medic and a rifleman. The latter was being treated for a shoulder bruise caused by an enemy rifle grenade. He had unexpectedly come face to face with a Jerry, which was easy to do in the Normandy bocage country, and the enemy soldier had been so startled that he fired the grenade without pulling the pin.

This story reminded me of a similar incident related by a rifleman I met when I first joined Company B. He had come upon a German suddenly, a sniper who was hiding in a ditch. This GI, however, had remembered to pull the pin, so his grenade split the enemy soldier's body in two. Our riflemen had many such harrowing stories to tell, for they were indeed at the razor edge of combat at all times.

I slept soundly again that night, although an enemy plane came over and dropped a heavy bomb near us. I never heard the plane, nor the bomb, I was so far gone, but I did see the crater about two fields ahead of us when we began our march toward Tessy-sur-Vire, a little French village which cost our company heavy casualties again before we finally captured it.

Much is made of the terrifying noises of battle in fictionalized accounts of war, but the veteran fears as much the quiet and silent things that precede the outbreak of conflict.

In the march toward Tessy-sur-Vire, the sun was bright and the air was calm and still. Our unit was feeling its way toward the enemy, cautiously and alertly, and fearing the sudden outburst which we were consciously trying to create. Would the next hedgerow be our fort for the day? Or would that hill ahead prove to be the enemy stronghold?

We passed many dugouts and foxholes in the rather hilly terrain. Some of their locations puzzled me. Which side had fashioned them? We came across a freshly killed German youth with blond hair. He was apparently climbing the hedgerow in retreat when hit, for his feet were elevated against the mound and his head, a beautiful wax-like model, was on the floor of the trail, his long flaxen hair feathered in the dirt. All of us took a good look as we walked around him. It might be one of us some day.

Soon we crunched through the broken slate and glass of another still-smoking hamlet. All was quiet, save for the small noises of our movements and the occasional words of command.

We reached the Vire River and proceeded parallel to it via a sand road up the crest of another hill. At the top I looked over the edge of a hedgerow to see the beautiful Vire River valley on our left and the high ground on the opposite side. The river was about twenty yards wide. Another Division was supposed to be on the other bank pushing the enemy south.

Intersecting another main highway, we used it awhile before turning off to the side roads again. We met a French peasant, an old woman. Someone asked her for "cidre," for we were getting thirsty. The GIs who made the request had to move on, so by the time she got some cidre with a pitcher and glass to serve it in, others moved up and got the benefit of the request. This cidre was sweet and bubbly, not the vinegary dregs we had previously tasted. The old woman appeared to be sorry for us, for it sounded as though she repeated in French: "My poor children."

Presently the column reached a field just north of the village of Tessy, which was impossible to see since it was located on the reverse slope of the hill ahead of us. We knew it was there for our advance patrols had run into resistance.

Our machine gun squad was assigned a position behind a hedgerow facing the village. We started digging in when suddenly the quiet we had been dreading to lose was broken by the nerve-shattering whistle and crash of enemy shells hammering the road about 100 yards to our right.

We were ordered to fall back one hedgerow. Fine! It might be a safer place. In assembling behind this new fort I kneeled in some human excrement, the stench from which nearly gagged me. It was on the wrong side of the hedgerow for a German to have done it. Could it, however, be a new sort of booby trap? I barely had time to clean myself up when the order came to attack. I could feel my queasy stomach giving way as we stumbled toward the road which was being shelled. We avoided the highway proper, crouching in a two-foot-deep ditch and disregarding the possibility of mines. A shell fragment whacked the hard surface near me. I reflected that my helmet would have turned it since the fragment's full force had been expended.

After about 25 yards, we turned left into a small lane, bushy and high-walled. Here were cover and concealment, the best friends of the infantry. As we walked through, I noticed Sgt. Munn, our platoon sergeant, sitting against the bank, a pained and tired look on his face. He was suffering an attack of appendicitis, for which he was later evacuated. We didn't see him again until January 24, after the Bulge fighting was over.

We kept moving south into a valley at the base of the hill of the town. In the floor of the valley, the wall of hedgerows disappeared mercilously and we were forced to run across an open spot of about fifty yards.

I was in the middle of this dash when a terrific rush of air and the receding whistle of a shell passed over my head followed by a hair-raising explosion to my immediate rear. The shell took part of my breath with it, and I fell in a sweaty, vitiated heap. Another shell made me squirm into a small wagon rut, desperate for protection. I felt as though the enemy could count the hairs on my neck, as I waited helplessly for them to improve their aim. I was only too glad when the column moved again to rush toward the hill ahead. I ran with a noisy brushing of leather and clothing as well as the clanking of machine gun boxes. I felt like a red-faced clod entirely incapable of dealing with a clever and relentless enemy.

My breath was coming in gasps by the time we reached a heavily covered ravine which led sharply up the side of the hill. Men were all around us — riflemen of squads which hadn't yet been committed, heavy machine gun squads, mortar squads, and sergeants bawling orders such as, "Sgt. Nowicki's squad, number three, 1st platoon, up front, on the double." It was a fine and sad thing to watch nine red-faced men, solemn and sweating, as they rustled past and climbed the small trail. No one shouted words of encouragement. Cheap heroics was inappropriate, for these men were offering the dearest possession, their lives.

At this point, a new horror began. We heard the popping of enemy mortar shells, no doubt intended for us in the draw, which seemed like a gigantic funnel as the mortars began crashing about us. One hit the bank above, and another went over. It was like playing bean bag. The next one might be in the hole, on target, good for no one knew how many casualties in the game of war.

The shell for which we were tensely waiting — one which crashed in the center of the trail — impacted mainly on the body of one man, a member of a heavy machine gun squad a few yards ahead. Nonetheless, flying fragments wounded three more in our machine gun squad: the squad leader, Halbrook, was slightly wounded in the hand; Gregory, our gunner, was hit in the leg; and Skeeter caught some metal in the hand and side.

The firing stopped, allowing Halbrook and Skeeter, both grinning, to take off for the rear. They were soon followed by an unescorted German prisoner whose hands were shaking as he held them over his helmeted head.

I carried the machine gun now, replacing Halbrook. Gibson took the tripod, and Rish followed with the ammunition. It seemed as though in every action we were being reduced to one gun and three or four men. Sgt. Horne was still with us, and he walked in the lead.

At the top of the hill we came onto the main highway again as it bent south leading directly down the slope into the village. At the turn in the road, a heavy machine gunner, his weapon across his body, was lying still in death. His face and hair were sprinkled with the fine dust of the roadway.

Suddenly direct 88 fire bolted the length of the highway directly overhead. I fell to the ground and squeezed my helmet tighter on my head as each shell shrieked past and slammed behind us. Just as suddenly it was

Dr. Jean-Claude Lemoine of Tessy-sur-Vire, shown here in a 1962 photo, was a small boy when his village was liberated August 1, 1944. The author is showing the doctor the ravine behind them via which 1st Battalion troops advanced to capture the town.

quiet again. Sgt. Horne returned along the line and bawled me out for being too close to another GI, part of a group we were passing.

"Keep your distance," he warned. "Keep your distance."

It seemed an inappropriate admonition since there were too many men on the road to permit following the rules of basic training to the letter. However, the sergeant was doing his job.

Further down the slope we came upon the enemy artillery piece. Its long barrel was pointed at me as it hugged the same side of the road I was on. There was a small round hole in the gun's shield. Behind it were two dead Germans, one sprawled over the other. Sgt. Groves of Company B had crawled ahead under the fire of this weapon to knock the crew out of action with an anti-tank grenade fired from his rifle. He received a well-earned Silver Star for this action, but it was a long time coming. I wrote it up for him about a year later while on occupation duty in Germany.

The Germans had employed devilishly clever defense tactics on this hill. When our riflemen had burst out of the ravine shortly after the mortar fire was laid down, they were met by the direct fire of the artillery. When they leaped the hedgerows on each side of the road, they encountered fire from two "burp" gunners, one on each side of the road. These gunners were intending to keep our men in the road for further slaughter by the 88. Our GIs preferred small arms fire to artillery, however, so they overran the burp gunners, one of whom was captured. Groves had then crawled ahead to dispose of the 88.

"Watch the flanks. Don't shoot our men on the right." These commands were passed along, as we moved slowly forward down the hill and into the outskirts of Tessy-sur-Vire, another typical brick and stone village with red-tiled roofs. Some of the buildings were burning from an air strike delivered only moments before. (On a peace-time visit to Tessy in 1962 I observed that the name of this street had been changed to Rue de Aout 2, 1944, and that the square to which it led was called Place de la Liberation. Actually, it was August 1 when we first entered Tessy, not August 2 as the sign said.) At the central courtyard I noticed a high church steeple, which seemed to me would be a good vantage point for a sniper. I worried about it as we turned left on another street leading toward the river.

Enemy shells, fired from the opposite bank of the Vire on high ground, began to strike the town. One of the artillery victims was lying face down over the curb as I passed. It was Walt Paige, but I didn't recognize him since I could see only the back of his head. He had been struck in the head by a shell fragment and died instantly. When I eventually learned that it was Walt, I was badly shaken, since his passing meant more to me personally than the many others who had died. We had a community of interest that had developed surprisingly fast despite our brief encounters and conversations. He was a highly educated young man, who, although he could have qualified for far less dangerous military duty, chose instead to carry a rifle. In my mind, he was one of the many true heroes of the war.

Our column stopped in the street after a few more yards advance, while more shells crashed but a short distance in our rear. The buildings about us made us feel somewhat safer. All the same, the man who was lying near me on his back had been hit by a shell. The wounded man jerked convulsively at the hips. He was lying in an awkward position, but the medics did not dare move him. The man seemed too seriously hurt to be conscious, so he startled me by speaking. Was he talking to me?

"For God's sake, I'm bleeding to death. Help me." And with that the blood gushed from his mouth, as his heart pumped his life away. The medic returned but there was nothing to be done. His internal injuries had made it impossible to stop the bleeding. Where a few minutes before there had been a life pleading for help, there was now a sunburned heap of brown, with staring blue eyes, still pleading. The medic said: "He's dead."

The riflemen who were slugging it out with the Germans at a bridge at the southern outskirts of town were engaging elements of the 2nd Panzer Division, which had been rushed to this part of France to stem the breakthrough.

Our squad ducked into a store building, apparently an electrical or auto supply shop. Bits of junk were scattered all over. Some of our GIs were examining the parts and gadgets and tossing them about. No matter how miserable their lot, American soldiers never seemed to lose their sense of playfulness.

After Sgt. Horne learned we were not going to be used in the action at the bridge, we moved back a building or two to a cement block garage. There were two other men in the building, including a squad leader from the heavy machine gun company. He was a light, delicate appearing youth with glasses. He talked in a treble of approaching hysteria. "I've had enough," he said. "How can they expect a man to keep going day after day at this business. Freddy killed today, and so was Harsha. Day before yesterday it was..." We left before we could hear more.

About an hour later, we were told that the Germans had retaken the bridge and that we must fall back to the northern end of town. We found another cement block structure in which to await further orders. We shared this new post with a black, horse-drawn hearse, which the boys joked about grimly.

I crawled under the hearse and into a corner under a small window. After sitting there for some time, I became concerned about the unusual quiet. I remembered similar periods which had been broken by a stealthy enemy attack. I pulled myself up to the window, a small opening near the ceiling by, in effect, chinning myself with my arms and hands. I looked into an adjacent garden but could see nothing of interest.

I heard a rustling noise, and looked harder, but still saw nothing. Again a rustling noise and this time I saw the source, a bird sitting on its nest not four inches from my face. The bird did not move. We stared at each other a few seconds. Then my arms grew tired and I slowly slid down to the paved flooring.

Our momentary peace was destroyed by our air corps which scared the living daylights out of us by strafing and bombing the town without much concern as to what they hit, it seemed.

When this excitement had passed, I heard someone say that water was available at a house about 25 yards up the street. I stepped out into the open again and quickly dashed to the designated dwelling. I was afraid of snipers and enemy artillery and did not want to remain exposed longer than necessary.

At the house I learned that the water was at a well in the garden and that someone was out there filling his canteen now. I waited until he returned and entered the garden with two canteens, mine and another man's. My containers clanked as I set them down. I was also noisy in lowering the pail into the well. The pail had hit the water level, when I heard the pop of mortars being fired. Experience had taught me that mortars are unpredictable and give no warning as to where they will drop. I imagined that the

61

Wine cellar in Tessy-sur-Vire in which troops stayed during a lull in the fighting. Author got permission from occupants in 1962 to inspect this former haven for troops.

rounds would be directed at me because of my clumsy, noisy efforts. So my vivid imagination caused me to run toward the house. No sooner had I passed through the kitchen door than two or three shells exploded behind me and a piece of metal broke the door's glass as a kind of spiteful warning.

I decided to skip the water since the Germans were zeroed in on the well, but the moment I stepped out the front door to return to my unit a close shot by a sniper convinced me that I had better stay put.

A few minutes later, some of our tanks roared into the main street and began strafing every building in sight. Lt. Ziegler was walking beside them — a madman.

"Let's go," he shouted. "We'll go down and blast those blankety blank blanks." And he and a group of riflemen, with some light mortars as well as the tanks in support, went down to the bridge and drove the Germans out. The battle ended, except for sniping and occasional shelling and mortar fire.

Nightfall, as usual, was a relief. Sgt. Horne found a basement in a large apartment building and obtained permission for our machine gun squad to stay in it. The mortar section joined us. It was the first basement we had found to occupy in France to date, since we had been living in the countryside without benefit of more urban amenities. I slept on the basement floor under an archway to get all the protection I could. I was covered with a down-filled quilt which was light and warm. It was a happy and comfortable night.

Some of the most enjoyable days of the war, August 2-6, 1944, were spent by our unit in Tessy. Overnight, everything became peaceful. The first day a shell dropped in the garden behind us, but otherwise we experienced no enemy fire.

Our rolls, poor bedraggled affairs, were dumped in a hotel courtyard. After some searching I found mine. The clue was a blue and white case for my shaving stick which had slipped out on the ground near it.

We went through the strange formality of being paid, as though some unfamiliar French francs could recompense us for what we had gone through. I arranged to send all my riches home as I plainly had no use for money. I wrote some pious letters home, and composed a piece about what combat had been like and sent it to Stars and Stripes, but nothing came of it. The Army paper confined itself to glorious or humorous accounts of war. I remember a few items about GIs being caught with their pants down while relieving themselves, and yet succeeding in killing or capturing the enemy.

We had the luxury of a bath. The facility was several miles to the rear and it was operated by black servicemen, the first I had seen in France. No new clothing was issued.

A Red Cross mobile unit was set up in a field about 200 yards behind us and served coffee and doughnuts several times. There was no charge, I can assure you. Col. Mainord, commander of the 1st Battalion, stood in line with the rest for his coffee and doughnuts. I heard him tell one of the RC girls that he was a "two-timer."

"Oh," she said coyly, "what does that mean?"

"I was in World War I, too," he replied.

Military intelligence units arrived and questioned returning French civilians, who reported the location of huge underground garages where the enemy kept tanks. The civilians shared our K rations and were grateful. They were usually headed northward, hoping that their homes had not been destroyed.

A placid French farm youth showed up and wanted to join us. We couldn't accept him, but he stayed with us in our makeshift basement quarters for two nights until French authorities could take him for military service. He was so quiet that we could not credit him with intense patriotism. We kept an eye on him for fear that he might be a spy. The language barrier made it impossible for us to get better acquainted.

I perused many French pictorial magazines in the apartment overhead. I found a pewter spoon on the floor in the hallway and kept it throughout the remainder of the war as my dining utensil. It survived in my pocket along with two .45 bullets and two German rifle bullets, one red wooden round and the other a steel-jacketed bullet. The latter items I picked up on the battlefield July 16. The Germans used the wooden bullet as a blank round, a fact I learned many years later.

The apartments were a shambles from frequent lootings, but one could see that they had once been comfortably furnished and neatly maintained. The Germans had looted first and our boys shamelessly picked over what was left. A large steel safe stumped some of our aggressive foragers. But with chisel and hammer they finally forced it open, only to find that it con-tained — to them — worthless items. Others, I was told, found jewelry and silverware in a smashed store and promptly mailed the finds home. I abhorred such behavior and was unable to understand eagerness for materi-al things in the face of our constant exposure to the loss of our lives, a far more valuable possession.

Finally the owner and some of the occupants of the apartment house came back. The owner was a dowager-like French woman, whose broad face and dour expression reflected the sadness she felt at seeing the ruins. She insisted, however, that we stay where we were. She would occupy other quarters. I took her upstairs to show her a "chien noir," which had lived in one of the bedrooms, completely cowed and unable to leave the spot or eat any proffered food. The dog immediately showed its joy upon seeing her, but the woman could not respond. She saw only a bedroom with mat-tresses and bedding on the floor, drawer contents spilled and scattered every-where, and an open window out which the curtain was floating. We both turned around without a word and went downstairs. The dog remained for-lornly in the bedroom.

We were surprised the next day by the return of Halbrook and Gregory, both of whom had been wounded in the taking of Tessy. They had bandages on their wounds, which were apparently considered minor enough to warrant their return to duty. Manpower was still a short item.

During this period we had what the Army calls "hot meals:" that is, the kitchen moved up with us and we ate cooked foods out of our mess kits. We usually had guests every day, a few French civilians who drifted in and out.

More interesting new arrivals were some replacements who seemed cocky to me, especially one lad whom we later concluded was insane. He was sent back finally as an incorrigible, but not until after he had performed sev-eral zany and foolhardy exploits which probably should have earned him medals. While at Tessy I became aware for the first time that Co. B had a set of twins, Harold and Harry Chocklett. The latter was captured at Mortain. Harold survived it all. Decades later I met both at a Co. B reunion.

At the time feeling was running high that the war would soon end; perhaps we had seen our last fighting. This feeling was augmented when word came on August 5 that we would move out that night at 2:00 a.m. in, of all things, trucks. It was a novel way for us to travel. We concluded that we must be far, far behind the front. What were we going to do? It was said that we were to hold a defensive line and relieve another outfit. It seemed like easy and safe duty, but it turned out to be one of the most terrifying experiences of my life — the German counterattack at Mortain.

German Counterattack at Mortain

August 6 through 13, 1944

The battle at Mortain was one of the great victories of the war in Europe. The Germans twice attempted major counterattacks: once, in the Ardennes, known as the Battle of the Bulge, and the first time at Mortain, where they committed four armored divisions in a desperate effort to cut off Patton's thrust and slice into the twenty-mile corridor established along the sea coast. The 30th Division, however, happened to be in the way.

For most units, Mortain was an intensive bloody, nerve-wracking, and exhausting fight. Our company was stationed on Hill 285 west of Mortain and Abbaye-Blanche. It was a new and sometimes panicky experience to be on the defensive, not knowing when or where the next blow would come. Miraculously we escaped the heavy losses that other companies suffered.

We arrived in the countryside near Mortain on August 6 to assume defensive positions already dug by troops who had previously held this ground. From our hilltop vantage point we looked over a wooded valley to some of the taller buildings of Mortain. A large piece of statuary was visible as well as the rocky crest of the hill on the side of which the town was situated. This rocky promontory was where our 2nd Battalion was later cut off. Their stand against steady German pressure for six days was later heralded in the press, and the outfit was labeled the "lost battalion" of World War II.

Since our machine gun squad did not select a position where others had dug before, I was forced to fashion a new hole. While doing so, I heard the town, or church, clock in the village tolling off the quarter hours. All was quiet until a small group of enemy planes suddenly appeared and strafed us a bit. I dropped in my hole, which was almost complete, and sweated out the attack. I did not attach much significance to the aerial attack, since it seemed so small in scale. I should have noticed, however, that it was done in daylight, a tactic the German air force had not dared use before because of our dominance of the skies.

That night at about 4:00 a.m. my leg was shaken as I lay sleeping. Halbrook hissed out the information that an enemy tank was approaching. "Get ready to move," he said. I put on my belt with the raincoat looped over it, hitched my carbine over my shoulder, and grabbed the two boxes of ammo. I was ready.

Visibility was virtually nil because of a dense fog as well as the early morning darkness. The sound of the tank seemed only 25 to 30 yards away. Perhaps it's our own, I thought hopefully. But this hope was quickly blasted when a stream of red tracers flew down the length of our position, followed immediately by the awful and shocking roar of the tank's gun. We were enfiladed and cut off from Company B headquarters.

Our first thought was to get a hedgerow between us and the tank, and to do this as quietly as possible, for the only way the enemy could sense a target was by sound.

The voice of the officer in charge of the enemy group rang out giving further chilling evidence of a powerful presence out to destroy us.

"He's telling his men to move forward again," Gross frantically whispered. German-born, he understood every word of the command. Gross had been wounded under the eye in the St. Lo action and only recently had returned to us. He had told us that he came to the United States at the age of ten and learned English by going to movies. He was an alien when drafted, but hoped to get his citizenship by serving in the Army.

The tank rumbled closer, and red tracers, mingled with white, streaked over our heads. We retreated further down a slight embankment, at which point I fell into a big hole, perhaps a crater, and my ammo went flying noisily. I fully expected enemy bullets to be sent my way, but nothing happened. I couldn't find the boxes and didn't have time to search, so I left them and joined the others in a wide wagon trail which was full of infantrymen scurrying for cover. We may have been badly disorganized, but at least we were being quiet and fairly calm.

The rifle platoon in this sector was commanded by Lt. Jack Grimshaw, a somewhat chubby young man who had an air of disgust with the bother of war — an annoyance with the alarms and excursions which were constantly arising. He was known affectionately as Jack. Some of the older fighters may have thought he did not give enough weight to their experience, or correctly size up new situations, but I suppose that is the cross all replacement officers have to bear in taking command of a bunch of veterans.

In any event, Jack loomed out of the fog and darkness to see what was up.

"Where the hell do you guys think you're going?" he demanded of the men milling about him. It seemed to us that he was talking in booming tones that would give us away to the Germans.

"Get back on those hedgerows and set up a defense," he ordered as he sauntered toward the enemy.

The men mysteriously and quietly disappeared in the darkness. I presumed they followed his orders, but I couldn't see that they did. Our machine gun squad obediently took a position facing east toward Mortain, although our immediate trouble was to the north, on our flank.

Gregory, a member of the other machine gun squad, ran across the wagon trail with a white band of machine gun ammunition draped around his neck. I believe an enemy gunner saw him, for we were enveloped in red tracers. One bullet hit the machine gun Gregory was carrying and knocked it out of action.

Apparently Jack was now convinced that we were hopelessly flanked and cut off from Company B headquarters for he had us fall back about 200 yards to set up a new line hinged on the old and facing north. It was the only time Company B gave ground to the Germans.

In the meantime, the Jerries were free to move toward the area occupied by the headquarters platoon and our mortar section, behind our former line. These troops put up a spirited defense and slowed the enemy advance, a factor which I believe was extremely important to us when the fog lifted.

Our new line was along the northern edge of a triangular field sloping to the wagon trail. The hedgerow provided a heavy canopy of trees and shrubs drooping so low as to touch the ground in some places. This leafy archway was to be a lifesaver.

Our remaining gun was established over a two-man hole which had been hacked in the side and partially under the hedgerow. I regretfully took over a small hole at the base of the hedgerow in one of the few open spots. I didn't like the lack of concealment.

For the moment we were happy about escaping with our lives, even though this had been at the expense of lost ground as well as lost equipment and weapons abandoned in our haste to retire. As day started to break, though, we became alarmed by the fog which limited vision to about 25 yards. The enemy tanks, which were still moving about, were more than ever a menace, for we realized that the moment the fog lifted the battle would be on in earnest.

At about 10:00 a.m. vision improved greatly and we thought we were in for it. We didn't know that we had an anti-tank gun in place on our left next to a small road at the top of our hill and that it was waiting for the right moment to take advantage of the situation, for the German tanks were now clearly in view and had not yet had an opportunity to conceal themselves or become aware of our exact location.

Our anti-tank gun crew, enjoying its concealment as though in a duck blind, blasted the two visible tanks, knocking them out with two rounds in each. We laughed and joked as we listened to the armored Goliaths popping and crackling while they burned. Then word came down the line that the enemy tank crews were trying to get away. I stood up on the hedgerow with the rest and tried to see something to shoot at. I thought I saw a green-uniformed German crouched against the hedgerow to my front, the one we had recently hid behind. I slowly squeezed the trigger, but it wouldn't move. The safety was still on. I tried again and got off a few rounds, but later, when the fog was completely gone, I saw that I had been shooting at a bush. It is an odd fact that this was the only occasion I fired the carbine during three and a half months of action.

After the enemy thrust at our sector had been blunted by knocking out two of their tanks, our troops began working intensely on improving their holes and camouflage. The Germans were but a scant 200 yards to our front, and we believed that their headquarters were set up in the farm houses and barns another 50 to 100 yards behind their front line. No doubt they were digging, too.

The hole which I had inherited must have been dug by a midget. I tried to enlarge it, but found the digging very difficult in the dry clay. I had a chance to test the hole when a barrage or mortar shells began to fall. I jumped for cover head first, and found that my head and torso were accommodated, but that a portion of my hindquarters was exposed. After the barrage was over I crawled out and noted a smoking crater about five yards behind my hole.

I was congratulating myself on taking cover with such alacrity, when Piatrowski, a blond, likable Polish rifleman on my right said, "What you afraid of, Parker? Those things won't hurt you."

I looked at him in disbelief. "Are you crazy?" I inquired.

He was crouched beside the hedgerow with his rifle leaning against his body. "I sat right here watching you," he said. "I didn't get hurt. Those Jerry mortar shells ain't no good."

"They can only kill you, that's all," I responded in disgust. He laughed.

We soon learned where the enemy had set up its machine guns. One fired from the corner that our own machine gun squad had occupied the day before, and the other fired on the left from near the road.

My part of the hedgerow with its lack of dense foliage provided excellent observation of enemy positions. I spotted one of the destroyed tanks, which seemed to me to be parked over the slit trench I had labored so hard to construct.

An observer for 81mm mortars came to our sector to deliver the first important counter fire on the enemy troops. He selected my position as the best from which to observe. We enjoyed pointing out targets for him, for we had seen much troop activity. Some Germans even rested brazenly on the

The author finds the hole which he occupied during much of the battle of Mortain. Except for caved-in tops, the complete line of defense was intact when revisited in 1962.

ground in the orchard just out of effective small arms range. The resultant havoc that this observer and his radio caused was very satisfying to all of us. Just when we were warming to the target practice, however, he left, saying that he now had his weapons properly zeroed in.

(In 1962 I revisited the Mortain battlefield. A farmer took me to the orchard our mortars had pounded and showed me a human jaw bone hooked over a tree branch and partially covered with moss. He said that one of his pigs had rooted out a German helmet next to a fence. Upon examining it, he found the fragmented jaw and placed it on the tree. I probably was seeing some of the results of the shelling 18 years earlier.)

Our men began to talk about how the Germans had been able to slip in on us with tanks. Blame was passed on to Company A, which had been on our left and still was. Some said that there were supposed to be friendly tanks in front of us that night, and that sentries had thought the approaching tanks were ours until too late. I never knew, but obviously the proper weapons could not be brought to bear in time to stop them.

At about noon, British Spitfires flew over our sector and terrified us by firing rockets rather indiscriminately. Throughout the day both enemy and friendly planes bombed us.

No other action of importance occurred until about midnight when the quiet was broken by a grenade exploding to our left near the point where our hedgerow and the road intersected.

An enemy patrol of four or five men, one of whom carried a portable flame-thrower, had crept up the ditches beside the road within a few yards of our lines. One of our sentries heard a noise and threw the grenade. The flame-thrower was brought into play, but since it malfunctioned it succeeded only in spraying oil on one of our men.

More grenades were tossed. Gross crawled up to the trouble spot and threw a couple. I pulled the pin on one with the intention of throwing it to my front to discourage any Jerries there, but it suddenly grew quiet again. I held the grenade, knowing that it would have to be used since I couldn't find the pin in the darkness. Gross came crawling along the ground from the road. I told him I had another grenade if he wanted it. He accepted with pleasure, for he enjoyed giving his former countrymen as much discomfort as possible. I gingerly passed the grenade to him and he quickly crawled toward the road. Soon there was another explosion.

A section of an old bazooka is inspected by the author in a 1962 visit to Hill 285. Farmer Marcel Genevée was using the tube to convey water from a pump.

Shortly before daylight, one of our riflemen snaked out ahead of our lines to investigate. He found a wounded Kraut and the abandoned flamethrower. He brought the enemy weapon back and left the German, who refused any assistance. The flame-thrower was passed along our line for inspection. It eventually ended behind my hole where it stayed throughout the remainder of the fighting. It looked like gear for portable spraying of a garden, and not a deadly weapon.

We had welcome visitors when an artillery observer and a radioman arrived. The observer selected my point on the hedgerow as his Observation Post and had begun to set up his equipment when word came that three enemy tanks were moving slowly down the road toward us. The Germans were attacking again.

We joked nervously about having the artillery observer on the spot at the right moment.

"Give it to 'em," we urged, wishing all along that the anti-tank gun was still around to meet the onslaught.

The radioman worked feverishly at his set's telescoped antenna. But it was stuck. He tugged harder, yet the willowy length of metal would not come. In the meantime, we could hear the tanks creaking and roaring as they slowly moved closer.

"For God's sake fire on those tanks!" This frantic plea came from the road intersection.

The radioman fumbled harder, and his face grew red and his hands more clumsy.

"Has anyone got a knife," he asked shakily.

"A knife? Get the man a knife!"

When he had the knife in his hands, he was visibly trembling as were the rest of us who did not have the terrible responsibility that was his. We all knew we would die if he did not get the radio operating soon enough. We believed that our lives and the outcome of the battle hung upon this man's struggle with a jammed antenna. Our hearts, our stomachs, our hopes sank.

None of us in our sector knew that the plan of defense against tanks had been carefully laid, and that the road had been mined the previous night. Our anti-tank gun was still in position at the side of the road, well hidden, but it was playing a dangerous waiting game in the hope that more than one tank could be destroyed.

The plan was to wait for the lead tank to reach our mine field and become disabled. Our anti-tank weapon would then open up on the third tank in the rear, knocking it out and trapping the second tank between the two immobilized ones.

However, as the lead tank crept closer to our lines, our gun crew apparently gave up the war of nerves and knocked it out with two quick rounds when it was but a scant twenty yards from out hedgerow. The explosions were so violent that a huge cloud of dust enveloped the area for several minutes, during which time the other two enemy tanks hastily withdrew. Soon we heard the satisfying snapping and crackling of a burning tank, followed shortly after by the larger explosions of ammunition and gas tanks. Again we enjoyed the relief and elation of stopping and destroying enemy armor.

Gross, who was proving himself to be an exceptionally aggressive soldier, detected one of the enemy tanks behind some foliage, and he said he could see the tank commander in the turret. He hurriedly borrowed an M-1 rifle, took long and careful aim, and squeezed off a shot which brought forth a heart-rending screaming which lasted so long we cynically thought it might be faked.

By this time the artillery observer and the radio were working, and his battery was firing salvo after salvo. Clouds of dust and flame spurted but a short distance ahead of us. Since some of the flying metal clipped the brush overhead, I decided it was a good time to retire to my asylum in the ground, inadequate though it might be. One short round could mean curtains, but as I crawled into my tiny hole, Jack, the platoon leader, who was walking along the hedgerow from the scene of the recent tank action, bawled at me derisively: "Don't you know that's your own artillery firing?"

So I crawled out in obedience to an implied order, reflecting, as I did so, that I could feel insulted and angry at his jibe at a time when such emotions should have been directed against the Germans. But this perversion of being angry with each other rather than with the enemy was often the case, I discovered.

After our artillery firing had ceased, one of the oddest incidents of my combat experience occurred. A GI stationed at the road intersection ran past, crying "German tank, German tank." In the terror of the moment, some of the men crawled on top the hedgerow and slid down on the enemy side, for to our amazement an American tank with a swastika painted on it had bolted down the road and ripped through our lines without opposition and without detonating any mines.

I jumped into my hole and peered above the ground level to see what was going to happen. I trusted that my camouflaged helmet would blend into my background to avoid detection. The tank stopped behind some sapling trees in the road about fifty yards behind us. The tank commander looked all around, but there was no sign of life at our hedgerow, which as I have previously described, was heavily overgrown with a leafy bower. Everything was deathly quiet. I fully expected the tank to begin spraying the length of our hedgerow with machine gun bullets. After what seemed an interminable length of time, however, the tank lurched further into our rear positions and disappeared.

The men began to reassemble and laughed excitedly about the incident. Then Jack appeared with two GIs, one of whom carried a bazooka.

"Where you goin', Jack?" someone called out.

"Oh, goin' to see if I can get me a tank," was the reply as they moved off in the direction the tank had taken.

Jack had no success, for within a few minutes the maverick armored vehicle rumbled back through our lines again as calmly as though it had been on a practice maneuver.

The incident belongs with many that I'll never fully understand. What had happened to the anti-tank gun and its crew which had accounted so valiantly for three tanks up to this point? Why hadn't the invader shot us up a bit? I really believe that we were so well concealed by the foliage that the tank commander could not see us. Perhaps he reported that only a few snipers could be on this hedgerow, plus an artillery observer or two, for there was no evidence of a line. Perhaps the enemy felt he was on his objective, and, pending further orders, his only job was to hold and reconnoiter. But how to reconcile that with the previous aggressive action? Information is everything in war.

Our sector was quiet during the remainder of the day, but that evening we were disturbed to learn from the runner, when food and water was brought up, that we were moving out in the morning. That could only mean an attack. Some said we were going to make contact with the Lost Battalion on Hill 314 on the east side of Mortain.

The next morning, August 9, we did indeed pull out, headed toward Mortain. Company B was apparently scheduled to help someone else out of a hole, after having stalemated the enemy in its own sector.

By simply walking away from the area we had been defending, it appeared that we were abandoning it. Actually, another unit moved in to hold the line, but we did not see them when we left. All of our movements this day were puzzling, for there seemed no purpose to them, nor was there any clear idea of a front, either ours or that of the Germans.

As usual we marched single file at suitable intervals. Shortly we reached the small road leading east and downhill to Le Neufbourg, a sort of suburb near Mortain. We followed this road at our customary stop-and-go pace. At one point, I stretched on the ground by a huge hardwood log, felled as part of a roadblock, and went to sleep. My nap was quickly interrupted when the column moved again. I learned to take cat naps at every opportunity to make up for the lack of sleep at night.

Reaching an assembly area near a farmhouse, we were assigned defensive positions. We spent considerable time digging in and constructing tops for our holes before being told to leave them and cross a small sunken trail into an apple orchard behind the farmhouse. In the orchard we saw a jeep perched crazily on the side of a hedgerow. The Germans had raided the area about an hour ago, we were told. The enemy captured some of our medics, and one of the Germans tried to drive the jeep over the hedgerow, apparently believing glowing reports about the vehicle's capabilities. He was caught in this bizarre position by our troops and shot dead at the wheel. His body had just been removed.

We amused ourselves by reading the identification cards strewn on the ground, where they had been tossed by the Germans as they searched their medic captives. One card had a photo of a Medical Corps 2nd Lieutenant mounted on it. Included among this officer's papers was a picture of his pretty girl friend, or wife, with a suitable word of endearment written on it.

It was now about noon, and Gibson and I were told to dig in again. We didn't know how long we would be here and, having already expended much energy in constructing underground quarters which we had been ordered to leave a few minutes before, we were half-hearted in our efforts to build anew. However, I learned that the enemy was throwing 88 shells at intervals and I could see the evidence — several small craters dispersed in the orchard. Accordingly, I was anxious to get some sort of cover.

After digging a shallow depression in the ground, we were told not to bother too much since we were to move again in a few minutes. I stopped digging, but I was still concerned about protection. I asked Sgt. Landis who had charge of a mortar squad near us if I could share his covered slit trench.

"I suppose so," he said without too much enthusiasm since it meant crowding.

I had hardly crawled into the hole when a shell shrieked in, exploded, and shook the top of the hole so that dirt sprayed over our bodies. The confusion and terror of the moment was heightened by smoke and flame at the mouth of our trench, the smell of exploding ammunition, and the screams of a man who had been hit by a shell fragment.

I got out to look around and saw the wounded man, still crying out, as he was being carried away by a medical jeep. One of the medics was holding a blood-soaked bandage at the wound in the man's back.

Both of my boxes of machine gun ammunition had been hit. The first box had been blasted about ten yards to the entrance of our dugout. The ammunition had been set on fire, and this is what caused the smoke and flame. The other box had a few pieces of metal in it. The container rattled when I shook it. Some of the .30 caliber rounds were damaged. My carbine, which had been leaning against an apple tree about two feet from the crater, was undamaged. As for me, I had survived again by refusing to be careless about cover.

Shortly after this incident, our column left the orchard and began descending the hillside via the road. I remember a roly-poly Mexican-American sweating profusely as he waddled uphill past us. The rest who passed are a blur now, except for the French civilians who were being evacuated from the village. One woman wheeled her baby in a buggy, the wheels of which were bent and warped, making it even more difficult to push uphill on a gravel road. I was grateful that my own family was home, even if I was

This boulder in a field on the crest of Hill 285 at Mortain represents the furthest point of advance by the enemy armored thrust in August of 1944. The German dugout under the huge rock had been filled in when visited in 1962.

not. I must confess that my thoughts of home during these days of combat were rare. The popular notion that a married man with a family thinks of his wife and children as he goes into a fight is rather silly. A soldier who is any good is a realist. He thinks of his job and of survival, and he also is concerned about his fellow soldiers. Probably the main worry is keeping one's courage screwed up sufficiently to behave calmly and with dignity in the face of danger. After that come the physical needs: enough water, food, and sleep in that order.

As the road flattened out, we came upon a long chain of American tanks, decorated with red panels to identify them to our air arm. Figuratively, a sword of steel was being driven into Le Neufbourg, Abbaye-Blanche, and Mortain. We passed under a railroad bridge, turned left, then right, past a cemetery from which chunks of granite had been blown into the road. Some of the caskets had been unearthed by the huge craters.

Now we were in a village (Le Neufbourg), walking cautiously behind a high retaining wall for defilade. We came to a public well, or fountain, and some of the men fell to with great zest, drinking and filling their canteens.

We progressed another 100 yards toward a road block at Abbaye-Blanche when the quiet was broken by dreaded enemy mortars slamming the earth about 25 yards to our front. The column quickly ducked off the street and into a group of wooden buildings. We continued to advance, despite the increased intensity of the shelling. During a pause, I found myself lying on a flat stretch of ground as bits of metal slapped the earth about me.

One shell fragment rolled in front of my face. I reached out for it, but it was too hot to pick up.

"Come on ahead. We've found a swell dugout." It was Rish talking. He had crawled back to inform me.

I followed him in a low crouch for about fifteen yards to the entrance to a cave-like dugout that one of the French villagers had made. There was a narrow slit-trench entrance with steps leading into the dugout proper. The top was constructed of heavy timbers covered with two or three feet of earth — in all, a most happy and badly needed find.

I snuggled up to a five or six-week old calf which was bedded down on the hay-covered floor. Since there were four of us to share the crowded quarters — Halbrook, Rish, Gibson, and myself (Gross was not with us now, inasmuch as he had been selected the day before as battalion interpreter) — we decided to release the calf. Halbrook and Rish untied the rope which held the animal in the shelter and together they pushed it unmercifully into the open where it wandered about grazing, unmindful of the continued shelling.

We remained in the blissful security of this shelter for about an hour and enjoyed every minute of it. But our euphoria was disrupted when we were ordered to withdraw, not only out of the town, but back to our positions on Hill 285. Whether we had been a success or a failure in our day's movements, we didn't know.

It was well after midnight when we arrived in our old area. I flopped into a ditch with some other men and slept the sleep of exhaustion once again. At daylight, those who had relieved us at this position left, and we began to set up a defense line behind the old familiar hedgerow, but this time further down the slope in a bushier section. I pulled rocks out of the hedgerow and piled them over the top of the hole I inherited. I filled in around the rocks with sod and dirt. The green branches I used for support were pliable and bent precariously under the load, but managed to hold.

The GI grapevine, which seemed always to be operating, had it that after we had left the hill the day before the relieving unit became involved in a sharp enemy attack and suffered heavy losses. How true this was, I never knew, since I had no opportunity to talk with the departing troops.

Halbrook, our Pfc. who was still serving as squad leader, tinkered with the new type machine gun we had received recently. The gun was somewhat lighter and had been re-designed for hedgerow use. The principle change was a small, approximately six-inch tripod, mounted at the muzzle end of the gun, thus making it possible to rest the weapon on top of the hedgerow and fire immediately. The old, clumsy tripod, which supported the gun at its center, was eliminated. To try the new gun out, Halbrook prudently went up the hedgerow a short distance, poked through the foliage, and squirted two or three bursts into the thatched roof of a horse barn to our front. The tracers set the barn on fire, much to the delight of a mortar observer, who claimed he had been trying to hit the building all morning. However, we paid for this audacity when the enemy reacted immediately with several rounds of mortar fire which sent us scurrying into our holes. I ducked into mine to find a hot piece of metal already there waiting for me. Somehow it had gotten through my elaborate maze of rocks, wood, and sod.

The afternoon of the next day, August 11, we went on an attack maneuver into the wooded valley below us. After cautiously wandering through dense growths of shrubs and small trees and finding nothing, we began to realize that the enemy had withdrawn and that the battle for Mortain had been won.

We returned from the wooded valley and boldly walked along the road that the enemy tanks had used in their attempts to break through. It was a deliciously satisfying experience to enter the area held by the enemy during the previous five days. We had had our ideas as to where the German defenses had been situated, but now we were able to determine the precise locations of their machine guns, as evidenced by discarded ammo boxes and hand grenades. We also found the American swastika-marked tank, abandoned in the road, with a dead German in camouflage suit lying beside it. Also in the road were three dead GIs and the body of a gray-haired French peasant woman in a long black dress and black stockings. The story was that the Germans had tried to attack two days earlier with the GIs and the woman in the lead, and that our soldiers had mowed them down indiscriminately. We were also told later that some Germans had been dressed in GI uniforms. I still don't know what to believe.

Our defense line was now about 150 yards higher on the hill from where we had been when the Germans first attacked on the fog-covered early morning of August 7.

Halbrook, Gibson, and I occupied a magnificent German dugout. The entrance was in the center, with two covered rooms on each side. On one side the dugout was tunneled under a huge rock. We had heard the sounds of digging at night, and now we knew what they had been up to and how well they had done it. (When I returned to this site in 1962 I made a special point of locating the huge rock. The hole, of course, had been filled, but I discovered depressions in the ground near it. These were the slit trenches that other GIs had dug while there.)

Not having shaved for some time and finding things very quiet indeed, I ventured to the farm buildings and discovered the usual hogshead of cidre from which I drew enough to give myself a shave. Water was still too

Marcel Genevée's souvenir hangs on a tree at his farm at Hill 285, Mortain. The jawbone was found in a German helmet near a fence line many years after the battle.

precious to waste on one's toilet.

On guard that night, I had a beautiful view of the valley to the east, as well as a sky full of stars and streaks of enemy fire. The night was also occasionally illuminated by flares and exploding shells. I saw some "screaming meemies," as they arched a red trail in the darkness, and I heard the terrifying sound of their discharge without experiencing the reflex of fear, because I could see where these rockets were directed.

Quiet prevailed the next day, August 12. We sensed the end of the battle without being officially informed. We even felt secure enough to take the machine gun apart and clean it. In the afternoon, we received word that we were going to move forward, not into an attack, but to a rest area. It sounded crazy, and it turned out to be crazy.

The route of march to our "rest area" took us along the same leaf-covered secondary road down the hill and into Le Neufbourg. Our part of the column was at the public drinking fountain when enemy shells began to fall some distance away, indicating that things weren't altogether quiet yet.

While the shells were falling and the men were listening, trying to judge their meaning, Parks, one of the sergeants in the mortar section, asked me: "Parker, do you think we'll live through this?"

"I don't see how we possibly can," I promptly replied, and we both laughed. No one dared assume a personal happy ending, although we were confident that the Germans were being licked.

Parks was a tall handsome boy, who managed his mortar squad with a quiet reasonableness. I think his question was an effort to be friendly and somewhat humorous. Nonetheless, it cut to the heart of the matter.

The column moved past the point where we had been shelled off the road a few days earlier. We rounded a curve and began ascending a steep slope lined with knocked-out enemy vehicles and half-tracks.

Then came a strange sight — a German medic carrying a large Red Cross banner as though it were a sail propelling him through our lines. Some of our medics stopped him, offered cigarettes, and talked to him in German. I could only wonder at their cordiality as we continued to move up the hill.

Soon we had enough elevation to see other parts of the town and a beautiful park with a waterfall. Some French civilians were sitting along the roadside amid the destruction, but they smiled and gave the V-sign as we passed.

We eventually ascended out of Mortain and into the northeastern outskirts of the town. We were assigned a field and told that this was our area for the night.

"Dig in fast," Lt. Ziegler told us. "This is the lousiest rest area I ever saw. They've been shelling it regularly ever since I've been here." He had been part of an advance party.

Rish and I selected a two-man hole which had already been dug, but which was too shallow and in need of a more substantial top. I tore the old cover off and widened the hole, while Rish went for some heavy boards.

While hacking away with my entrenching tool and at the moment that Lt. Ziegler passed my position with his arms loaded with boards for his dugout, an enemy barrage came pounding in. The lieutenant threw his boards aside and fell to the ground behind the hedgerow, and I hit the bottom of my hole. Shortly after this bit of shelling, Rish returned with the boards and we hastily completed a much more solid refuge than the one we had inherited.

In a few moments another barrage hammered the ground around us. Rish and I were huddled in our shelter waiting for the fury to die when one of the mortarmen came to the entrance and asked permission to get in.

After crawling in beside us, he explained that the first shells had caught his mortar squad before they had had a chance to dig. We saw one of his companions wandering around in the dust-filled air, and although we called to him to join us, he did not respond. He seemed dazed and uncomprehending.

When the barrage lifted, we learned that no one had been hit, but that two mortarmen were suffering from profound shell shock — the man already described and Parks, the sergeant who only a few hours before had asked if I thought we would live through the war.

Parks was a pathetic case. He was both deaf and mentally stunned. We later received reports about him from a hospital in England, but none of them were encouraging. I have always hoped that he recovered his senses and returned to a useful civilian life.

Captain Pulver, bless him, decided that as a "rest area" this location would best be abandoned. Night was falling, but we packed up and moved further east to higher ground and dug in again.

Rish complained of a sore heel and asked permission to see a medic. It was the last we saw of him until he returned the middle of September when we were in Holland facing the Siegfried Line.

Gibson and I dug a two-man hole on the edge of a potato field and a few feet from an embankment which dropped sharply to the highway about 25 feet below. I scrambled down this embankment, holding onto brush and trees, and found my way through the darkness to a farmhouse. Here I located a chicken house door, removed it, and brought it back by a longer and less difficult route. Still working in the dark — we were as fervent as ants — we completed our new quarters in the loamy soil and got a little sleep between turns at guard.

The next morning (August 14), we received mail. Included in my batch was a photo of my wife, done by a professional studio. To preserve it, I covered it with a K-ration cellophane bag and stuffed it in the breast pocket of my shirt, which was now bulging with snapshots and other items. We all carried similar photographs. A favorite form of entertainment was to show each other pictures of our wives, girl friends, and relatives — our connections with a past that seemed more and more remote.

After a K-ration breakfast, we hiked back to Mortain and assembled at a large hospital building, or perhaps it was a monastery being used as a hospital, where we were met by trucks. We were happy to pile in and become motorized again. We did not know that we were being carted off to another hard battle before the day was over.

Closing the Falaise Gap
August 14 through 18, 1944

After a short truck ride, full of joking and laughing about past war experiences and highly optimistic predictions about an early end to the war, the column pulled off the main highway and we were deposited in some nearby fields. We all headed for the nearest hedgerow, or point of concealment, and stretched out on the ground for a nap, another GI friend. I hoped that it would be a long time before any orders were received.

After a bit, Lt. Hunn, leader of the third platoon and an exceptionally courageous and vigorous soldier, returned from a briefing session and waved a map at some of his men.

"If you think the last one was tough, wait till you see this one," Lt. Hunn shouted almost gleefully. With this knowledge that we were going into another attack, our former light-heartedness disappeared.

The assault on Domfront began with an approach march of about five miles along an asphalt highway. Our machine gun section, badly depleted again, was composed of Halbrook, Gibson, and myself. Since carrying the gun and ammo with only three men left was exceptionally burdensome, we

Rocky promintory at Domfront over which troops clambered to outflank the town.

dumped the works on a jeep which was traveling down the center of the road at the same pace we were. It was a Company D jeep and already was loaded with ammunition for the heavy mortars and machine guns.

"Just as soon as something happens jump for the weapons," Halbrook warned.

We passed some French civilians who stood by their houses watching us silently. They knew that we were headed for a hornet's nest and they had the good grace to be solemn about it.

At one point behind a heavy mass of trees, I saw a large French manor house which the medics had taken over. One of the medics leaned lazily against a pillar at the lane entrance and watched us slowly trudge by. He and his fellow medics were waiting for us to give them some business.

Presently we sighted a curve in the road, but before we got to it several shells screamed and shattered the hot afternoon quiet. We hurriedly got our gun and ammo from the jeep and dove for the ditches. We determined that the artillery was hitting the road about 300 yards ahead of us, so it was safe to advance to the curve where there were a few buildings to give protection. Some of the men broke down the door of a structure about the size and shape of a country schoolhouse. Property destruction for the sake of safety did not bother me as much as the inevitable looting. I went to the front of the building and discovered a well with a pail for dipping. I lowered the pail and brought up some welcome cold fresh water to fill my canteen. I also dropped in a halazone tablet and waited for it to take effect before tasting any of it.

With the return of quiet, we pushed ahead around the curve and into the western outskirts of Domfront. The shelling broke out again, however, and we were forced to duck behind some buildings on the right side of the road.

We waited for about an hour behind a typical French stone house and barn. Lt. Ziegler got out a box of K rations and ate some cheese and crackers. I had no appetite at the moment. Meanwhile, I became concerned that the buildings were too flimsy to afford good protection, especially the roofs. But these worries were supplanted by new ones when we were ordered to advance toward the shelled area.

I should have known that Capt. Pulver wouldn't lead us into such obvious danger, however, for we turned to the left off the highway and met a group of about forty Germans with hands upraised. They were command-ed by an Esquire-looking pink and white officer who carried a cane. An interpreter questioned him as we, the still active ones in this war, quietly filed past.

Our route now was cross-country, via a small cut in the ground. After crossing another highway, we began to climb — through an orchard, over a high hedgerow, and down into a deep ravine which had been freshly hit several times by artillery. Bullets began to snap in the air, but well over our heads.

The ravine led uphill and into a wooded area. On the left now was a huge pit with the peak of a rocky hill rising precipitously beyond about 300 yards. The column wended its way down into the moss and leaf-covered chasm and began the perilous ascent of the sheer side of the rocky hill. Strangely enough, squared off boulders were conveniently spaced to serve as giant steps for the climb.

Near the top, where a glance down made one dizzy, I could not make the next broad step upwards because of the weight of the ammo boxes. I took them off my shoulder and threw them ahead to Halbrook who deft-ly snagged them. I then easily scrambled the remaining distance. I still think of this incident as a fun experience, slightly equivalent to visiting a tree house.

The top of the hill was spongy from years of accumulated and rot-ted vegetation. The trees, mostly evergreens, towered above us, and at their base the roots had cupped the ground. We fitted ourselves into the depres-sions, taking advantage of these natural earthworks.

But the terrifying shriek of shells, just missing the tops of the trees, alerted us to a new danger — tree bursts from which there was no protec-tion. We sweated out more screeching artillery rounds before starting to advance down the reverse slope. We were eager to move this time, for once off the hill we were inside the arc of enemy shelling, or so we thought.

After passing a stone quarry, we stopped on exposed ground in front of the highway leading north of Domfront. This highway curled into the hilly countryside beyond. On the right we could see the village of Domfront for the first time.

Our sight-seeing mood was short-lived, however, for a barrage of hissing mortar shells suddenly caught us, falling on men at the head of the column. A rifleman and a mortarman were wounded, but worse was the death of Lt. Ziegler, who had been with us since the St. Lo breakthrough.

Crow, the mortarman, limped by and we kidded him about being hit, but it was plain that he didn't relish going back through the beaten zone of the shelling, even if he was going to the rear and out of the war.

Moving into the area where mortar shells had just fallen, I watched two of our medics working on one of the wounded men. His shirt had been cut away to reveal the grayish shell fragments imbedded in his back and shoulders.

Jack, the plump lieutenant, returned from his forward position to see what could be done for Lt. Ziegler, our Royal Oak, Michigan, weapons platoon leader. Jack silently examined the officer's head wounds and shook his head. I could see tears in Jack's eyes. It was a rare thing to see men weep at the loss of a friend in battle. Opportunity for strong friendships to develop was limited by the rapid rate of personnel changes.

We heard the pop of enemy mortar shells again, and naturally we expected them to fall in the same exposed ground we were now occupying. Jake Haglebarger, a gunner in the mortar section whom I later got to know very well, hovered in a ball at the top of the slope by the wagon trail, which was bordered by three or four trees. I asked Jake why he huddled near the top of the bank, instead of the base.

"I figure I got a better chance if there's a tree burst," he said. I respected his longer experience in the war by crawling up near him. The drama failed to come off, for this time the shells fell elsewhere.

Looking at the town south of us, I spotted a flashing light, repeated regularly, from a balcony on one of the larger apartment buildings. I pointed it out to Barnett, the mortar section sergeant who, because of Lt. Ziegler's death, had now been elevated to weapons platoon leader. He reported this information to Capt. Pulver. I never learned the outcome, but an enemy observer could have used the flashing signals to inform the Germans which routes we were taking north of Domfront.

Toward dusk, which came at about 10:30 p.m., we were joined by two tanks, which had rumbled through Domfront on one of the main shelled roads. We began to attack again, moving uphill on the main asphalt highway. The tank was on the road and the infantry walked in a ditch which was about two feet deep and provided good cover.

At the crest of the hill, we ran into an enemy roadblock consisting of a tank and enemy infantry in support. An amusing sidelight to this engagement was provided by a French civilian who had stumbled into the battle by accident. He was walking down the middle of the highway toward us, and our men motioned for him to move out fast. Suddenly the firing began at the roadblock, and the Frenchman threw himself into the ditch with vigor and ran past us as fast as he could.

Close to the point where the civilian had leaped into the ditch, I found a bottle of red wine with a cork stopper. Had the Germans left this for us to poison ourselves, or had the Frenchman dropped it? I showed the bottle to a platoon leader behind me. He willingly offered to be the taster. Since he pronounced the wine "very good" and suffered no ill effects, we passed the bottle among us and finished it off quickly.

Fortified by the wine, we took a more disinterested view of the minor skirmish ahead. One of our infantry squads tried to outflank the roadblock by advancing to the high ground about 25 yards to the left of the highway. As the lead man climbed over a hedgerow, he was shot in the shoulder and fell to the ground with an agonized howl.

Darkness overtook us, but one of our tanks fired on a hill to our right some 800 yards distant and succeeded in starting a grass fire which spread and illuminated the sky for most of the short night.

Our machine gun squad of three men and Sgt. Horne joined the riflemen on the high ground and set up the weapon on the densely covered hedgerow where the man had been shot. Standing guard that night, I was so fatigued that several times I almost fell to the ground asleep, but fortunately I caught myself just as my knees began to buckle. Between stretches of guard duty, I tried to dig a hole, but I ran into a large boulder and made little headway. Disgusted, I gave up and slept for a time in my shallow hole with my raincoat over me.

No rations reached us that night because of the intense shelling of the road and village behind us. I heard heavy explosions to the front during my turn on guard. The Germans were busy blowing trees across the highway and planting mines.

At daybreak, the men, not on guard, creaked out of their holes.

Some commented that this sort of life was developing arthritis that would bother them later in life, provided they survived "this damned war." We hurriedly ate C rations and stuffed two boxes of K's into our shirt fronts before moving ahead again. The trees across the road slowed us up, and we had to be careful about the mines. I saw a Teller mine for the first time. Fortunately, these personnel killers were detected and marked so that we could gingerly step around them.

At midday our attack bogged down on the outskirts of St. Bomerles-Forges, a tiny hamlet which was the last obstacle between us and the British who were driving down from the north in the Falaise Gap action. An enemy tank hugged the edge of the highway at a curve and would not move. German infantry protected it, and our tanks refused to barge into what they considered an ambush.

Sgt. Bahylle, a giant of a man who came from an Indian reservation in Oklahoma, succeeded in routing out a young German machine gunner who had been posted in a ditch in front of the curve. To encourage the German youngster to move to the rear faster, Sgt. Bahylle fired several rounds from his rifle at the feet of the prisoner, who responded frantically with a quickened pace.

An artillery observer tried to get his guns to fire on the enemy tank. After much cursing and shouting over his radio, he learned to our disgust and shock that our artillery support was out of range and could not fire. The observer's loud sputterings may have been heard by the Jerries and helped them determine just where we were, for shortly after the radioman's outburst mortar shells began searching for us.

Capt. Pulver had us move from the ditches to positions on the hedgerows in the fields to our right. He told us we could cover the road just as well from there and avoid the shelling on the highway.

I spotted a well in the middle of the field, and, since a lull had set in, I took Halbrook's, Gibson's, and my canteens and filled them at the pump. Another GI thought it was a good idea and followed my example. To my amazement, he was shot by a Jerry sniper.

Another barrage of mortar shells fell among us, wounding a rifleman about ten yards to our left, near the highway.

Capt. Pulver's erect form appeared again and directed us to retire to the rear about 100 yards.

"We can hold this road junction back there just as well if not better than we can here," he said. Our captain's flexibility and sound assessment of battle situations accounted for his effectiveness and longevity in combat. Naturally we were delighted to leave. We dashed singly across the open area in the field which was in line with the water pump. Behind the next hedgerow we found GIs from another unit, so we continued further to the rear into a wheat field which had recently been harvested. The sheaves were neatly stacked against each other.

Behind the next hedgerow were riflemen of the third platoon under Lt. Hunn. Equipment was scattered about and most of the men were taking their leisure, although some were busy digging in.

We tried to find a place to tie in with the riflemen, but the hedgerow was crowded, so we flopped on the ground and waited for Halbrook to scout out a better site.

Sgt. Bahylle, the Indian platoon sergeant, was using field glasses to observe the high ground about 800 yards to our rear. He had a pair of powerful German glasses taken from a prisoner earlier in the war.

"There's someone up there looking at us through a pair of glasses," Bahylle said. "It's a German. I can tell by the long boots."

Hardly had the words been spoken when the ground in front of us began to erupt in little spurts of earth, after which we heard the faint ripping sound of a German machine gun. Those who had holes jumped into them and the others scrambled to the other side of the hedgerow or lay flat on the ground.

I had only about ten yards to go to gain protection through a gateway to the other side of the hedgerow, and I wasted no time in doing so.

The machine gun bursts were immediately followed by mortar fire, this, too, from our rear. Apparently a sizable group of the enemy had been bypassed in our attack and was now daring to make things rough for us.

Halbrook appeared and said he had a spot for our gun. He led us through the gateway and back into the open field where we had been machine-gunned. We walked in a low crouch for about twenty yards when machine gun bullets erupted once more forcing us to hit the ground. The three of us turned around on our stomachs and snake crawled back to the gateway and safety.

In my haste, I had abandoned the two boxes of ammo, which were impossible to carry on one's shoulder while crawling. Halbrook set our gun on the hedgerow facing the enemy machine gun fire. Halbrook and Gibson looked at me accusingly when they saw that we now had only one box of ammunition.

"I'll go back and get those boxes," I said ashamedly, for I had put personal safety above duty. When I approached the gateway and began stripping myself of extraneous gear to make crawling easier, some riflemen standing nearby asked me where I was going.

"I've got to go back and get the machine gun ammo," I replied.

"Say, while you're out there, get my rifle," one of the GIs said. "It's opposite where I'm standing now," he explained, "and it's leaning against the hedgerow."

"Yeah, and bring in that bazooka that's out there, too, if you possibly can," another rifleman pleaded. "They's enemy tanks rumbling off to our left now," he groaned. I listened and could hear the roar of several armored vehicles in movement. It sounded like a battalion of them driving bogie-wheel to bogie-wheel.

I snaked through the gate and hugged the base of the hedgerow. I was flat on my stomach and chest and moved with a kind of swimming motion. To my right a two or three-inch stand of clover or alfalfa was my only concealment from enemy view.

I inched my way past several pieces of army equipment and noted a pair of field glasses as well as a bazooka and several rounds of bazooka ammunition. The rifle was there as described, leaning against the hedgerow. When I reached my boxes of ammo, I slowly and cautiously turned my body around, hoping that I would continue to be lucky in avoiding enemy detection.

Now my problem was to push the boxes back to my starting point and collect the other items requested. I shoved the ammo ahead of me and when I reached the bazooka and ammo I added them to the collection I laboriously and slowly propelled, while continuing to remain as flat to the ground as I could.

As for the rifle, I hesitated, but decided against moving it, since any enemy observer would surely notice if the weapon were disturbed.

I picked up the field glasses, however, and was successful in pushing the entire load around the end of the hedgerow and back to our lines.

"Did you get my rifle?" the GI asked me anxiously, and his face fell when he saw I hadn't. I explained why, and he didn't complain.

I gave the glasses to Lt. Hunn. He had been knicked by a shell fragment on the chin, but was still full of fight. He observed with the glasses, then hopped the hedgerow on our right where one of our tanks was located and directed its fire on the enemy position.

I found Halbrook and Gibson digging fervently.

"A couple of rounds of artillery just came in from the other side now," Gibson said. "So dig in as fast as you can."

I unhooked my shovel and began hacking. I had barely got the depth to a foot, when the whistle of enemy shells sent me plunging into the hole. What kind of a spot are we in, I asked myself, as the shells crashed all around us. Now we're being fired on from both sides. Who's supposed to be winning this war and which way is the front?

When the barrage had spent itself, I crawled out and went to see Halbrook, but the plucky little Pfc. who had been our squad leader for so long was lying helplessly in his hole and snoring loudly. I examined him more closely by tilting his helmet back. A lengthy shell fragment had pierced his helmet and penetrated the side of his head. It wasn't a large wound, but it was enough to end the life of one of the most courageous men in our unit.

My hole was only a few yards from his. Why had he been hit and not I? I think the difference was that I had dug at the base of the hedgerow, whereas Halbrook, as was his custom, had started his trench about a foot higher into the side of the hedgerow, thus making him more vulnerable to the upward spray of metal. If he had had a few more minutes to excavate, however, the extra depth would have saved him.

Gibson and I went in search of medics for Halbrook. Beyond the next hedgerow on our right we found a sunken road full of soldiers, some of whom had been hit and were lying on the ground. Here, too, were medics. Gibson led them to Halbrook, who was removed to the rear. We heard later that he died in a field hospital.

The enemy was now firing rockets known as "screaming meemies."

The concussion from these shells was terrific and the smoke was black and heavy, but the shrapnel was not exceptionally dangerous.

We began to sense that the Germans were pulling out again, since it was their practice to throw the book at us to slow down our pursuit. The tanks we had heard rumbling earlier were apparently retiring toward the Seine River and weren't coming after us, or they would have hit us by now. Because it seemed that the Krauts were withdrawing and because we felt that any place was better than our current shelled area, the order to attack again was, for once, sweet music to our ears.

Lt. Hunn's 3rd platoon was again in the lead, and the route was along the ditch by the side of the highway. The GI who had left his rifle leaning against the hedgerow under enemy machine gun fire complained to his sergeant that he didn't have a weapon.

"It's too late now," his sergeant replied. "If you don't know enough to hang onto your rifle that's your tough luck," he said.

"Well, if this isn't crazy," the rifleman cried, turning to his companions. "Goin' into an attack without a rifle."

We all laughed despite the seriousness of the man's situation.

It was now growing dusk, and we welcomed the concealment it gave as we hugged the green banks. At the curve in the road, where the German tank had previously held us up, we encountered no opposition. A street on the outskirts of St. Bomer-les-Forges met the curve to form a road fork. When we advanced along this new route, red tracers from a German machine gun whipped along the road and ditches. Fortunately, we were on the protected side of the hedgerow, parallel to the road, and were unharmed.

We paused in a small field in front of an orchard, and our light mortars were ordered into action. Three tubes were set up quickly and Sgt. Barnett barked out fire orders. Soon a widely dispersed barrage of mortar shells was pounding the area a few hundred yards ahead of us. It was the finest display of the use of mortars I ever witnessed during the war. When the last round had exploded, the infantrymen quickly followed up.

We entered the orchard and hugged the buildings on the left. At this point a shell fell some fifty yards away and a flying piece of metal clanged against the helmet worn by one of the riflemen.

"Well, I'll be..." he said, taking off the helmet and noting the dent in it. "These cans are some good after all." For the second time during the attack, we all had a good laugh.

The man without a rifle added to the growing comedy by constantly complaining. I was beginning to feel that this was a lark, and that nothing was going to harm any of us. This feeling was further supported when a hand grenade, either thrown at us or set off by a booby trap, exploded in our ears. Gibson said he was deaf for a while, and it affected my hearing also, but neither of us was hurt. German hand grenades did not have as much shrapnel as ours; they were largely concussion.

I saw some apples on the ground, picked one up, and began sucking the juice from it. Others followed suit. I looked about at the ludicrous sight of soldiers voraciously eating green apples while in an attack. Were we at last becoming nonchalant "veterans" as the newspapers might call them, or were we combat fatigue cases?

In the meantime, Lt. Jack Grimshaw, our plump platoon leader, was playing tag with an enemy half track a few yards ahead of us. He got within 25 feet of the armored vehicle, according to reports we got later, and missed it with two bazooka rounds. He was roundly kidded about the incident, but he succeeded in forcing the half-track to withdraw, but not until it had sent a few rounds of direct fire at us.

One of these hit the hedgerow we were behind and knocked some more apples out of the trees behind us. I picked up a few and began chewing them as well.

This turned out to be the last bit of resistance, for a few minutes later we were swarming over the tiny hamlet. Our machine gun was tied in with the mortar section in another orchard next to the village's main street.

Darkness had now fallen, and, since I was dying of thirst, I thought I'd try to find some water by the light of a burning building. I rummaged around some of the wrecked homes and sheds for a half hour without success.

As I returned in the darkness to the orchard, I was given an abrupt order to halt by Lt. Hunn.

I identified myself.

"Be careful about wandering around in the dark," Lt. Hunn said.

"There's still lots of Jerries around. You don't know how close I came to plugging you."

Back at the orchard I learned that a can of water had arrived in the meantime. I fumbled in the darkness with the can and my cup, and had my fill of water. I didn't care for food.

My next concern was sleep. I began to dig a hole, but gave it up. If they want to get me tonight, they can have me, I thought, as I fell flat on the ground. Within seconds, I passed out. A light rain which fell that night didn't disturb me, nor the other exhausted men.

On the morning of August 16, we had our breakfast early and at 7:00a.m. began to advance north of St. Bomer-les-Forges.

A subtle change in demeanor was taking place. There was now a note of relaxation, even a touch of holiday spirit. Although we sensed a German catastrophe, we did not know about the terrible Jerry losses in the Falaise Gap which was called the greatest "killing ground" of any area in the war, nor did we realize that our worst fighting was now behind us and that we were headed for days of easy triumph and cheering multitudes of French civilians.

I was not able to share completely the new feeling of victory, for my feet were beginning to hurt. Every step was becoming more painful. After we pulled off the road and set up a defense behind a hedgerow, I looked up the medics. They daubed a purple ointment on my toes to combat athlete's foot, and I hobbled back to the two-man trench Gibson and I had built.

While waiting here, a sergeant from company headquarters came to the haystack on our left and, using field glasses, examined the hills north of us. He was a scout and sharpshooter. He said he was from North Carolina where he had been a great lover of guns and hunting before entering the war.

"Now, if Ah ever git out of this 'live, Ah don't evah wanta see anotha gun, " he told me fervently.

We were not left at our leisure long. Another order was received to move out and away we went leaving our holes for someone else to use. We often said that these seemingly capricious moves were calculated to save the rear echelon troops the bother of digging in.

On this second march, my feet troubled me so much that I was unable to keep up with the column. They didn't wait, and I was passed by other riflemen and squads of heavy machine gunners as well. I began to think that our once full-strength machine gun section, now consisting of myself and Gibson, was going to be reduced to one man, commanded by Sgt. Horne. In due time, though, I caught up with the column when it stopped in a new green pasture, where we were soon again hard at work digging, always digging.

The next day, August 17, we received replacements, the first time since August 1 at Tessy-sur-Vire. Most of the men who came up went into the badly depleted rifle platoons, but our mortar section got a few new faces.

The machine gun section, all two of us with our one remaining gun and Sgt. Horne as our cheerleader, received Sgt. O'Brien back with open arms. O'Brien had been wounded slightly in the chest about thirty days before during the first attack I was in, July 16. We were also joined by La Voie, our Canadian-born, French-speaking runner, who was now drafted to carry ammunition.

O'Brien seemed happy to be back and not at all chagrined by the many missing faces in our section. He was very much interested in the new type machine gun we had been carrying since first issued after Tessy. As previously described, it had no tripod, just a couple of legs at the end of the barrel so that one man could carry it and easily set it in place for action. O'Brien tried the gun out by shooting a few bursts into the hedgerow behind us. Some of the rounds cleared the bank and caused anxious cries from men who were in the line of fire.

O'Brien laughed and said, "Well, the darn thing has got lots of dispersion."

Mail and packages were distributed. I hit the jackpot with several boxes of candy and cookies. We all dipped in and finished the contents in no time, for we seemed to have developed an insatiable appetite for sweets and rich foods of all kinds.

The next day was bath day. A group of us rode in a truck back through some of the areas we had fought for and which were now peaceful and serene. Again, as at Tessy, the shower service was operated by Blacks. I had hoped to get some clean clothes, but none was issued, so my clean body was re-clothed with dirty garments and exposed to the dust of the return ride.

Upon alighting from the truck at the Company headquarters area, I was astonished to see my cousin, Lt. Col. Devere Armstrong, who was in the Artillery Section, 1st Army. He had driven up to see if I was O.K. and was questioning Captain Pulver when I arrived.

The Captain very graciously invited us all to lunch with the other officers of the Company. What we ate, I can't remember, but I do recall a flaming dessert concoction. The flames were provided by dousing the dish with Calvados and touching it off with a match.

I remember more about our conversation. My cousin was interested in the effectiveness of artillery and asked if we had any idea of the number of casualties it was causing.

Lt. Hunn replied that it was difficult to ascertain, since the Germans were efficient at picking up their dead and wounded before we arrived on the scene.

I ventured the opinion that German artillery caused about eighty per cent of our casualties. Lt. Hunn fingered the bandage on his chin and said emphatically that the percentage would be nearly ninety.

We talked about an hour. Col. Armstrong said that our Division had gone through some exceptionally heavy fighting and that we would probably be due some easier assignments now.

I invited my cousin to see the hole Gibson and I had dug, for it was a masterpiece of its kind. It was large and roomy, had a very solid top, and was blessed with plenty of hay in the bottom. We sat in the grass for another half hour talking. My cousin said that he had been very worried about me, since he was well aware of what our Division was doing, and he expressed great relief at finding me unharmed and still healthy.

As he prepared to leave, he asked if there was anything he could do for me. I couldn't think of anything, but thanked him for looking me up.

His visit was a touch of home, and I began to think of the now distant civilian life that I had known myriads of bullets and shells ago.

Northern France, Belgium, Holland

August 19 through October 7, 1944

On August 19, our regiment left its rural diggings, mounted trucks and began a 118-mile triumphal procession across France. Native men and women greeted us deliriously in every town we passed through. They threw flowers and apples into our trucks, and offered wine and Calvados when the column paused for a moment. The day was a blur of faces, happy and joyous. An old man in one village seemed to be more pleased than the others. He shouted, threw kisses, and tried to shake our hands. No one in our truck paid any attention to him, however, so I nodded in his direction, and generously waved my carbine in salute, a gesture which made him all the happier. We all felt like royalty bestowing favors when we smiled or otherwise acknowledged the plaudits. It was a heady day, and there was more to come.

The glory ride ended at dusk in the center of a flat farming area. Looking about, I was alarmed at the lack of hedgerows which had been our comfort and protection for so long.

We were led to a small woods where our kitchen was set up and served a hot meal out of mess kits, an indication that we were still well behind the lines. After eating, our machine gun squad returned to a freshly cut grain field and dug some holes near the highway, which carried a constant stream of truck traffic all night. We slept well despite the noise and bustle.

We were in an assembly area near Dreux, which was 42 miles west of Paris. We had thought we were going to take Paris, but it was not necessary, since French troops had reclaimed the city for themselves. Our job was to break up the enemy retirement across the Seine to the north of Paris.

The next morning, August 20, we set out on the first of several day-long marches across the new style French countryside, the flatness of which continued to worry me.

Toward dusk we stopped at a French farmhouse where, it was reported, the chickens had been stolen by the Germans the night before. Our gun was set up in a hedge, not a hedgerow, but simply a row of bushes. For the first time, we were told to dig foxholes instead of slit trenches. The latter you can lie down in, but the foxhole is designed for stand-up protection. Since there were no hedgerows and the terrain was flat, we were more vulnerable to tank attack now. The foxhole, with its smaller opening, was theoretically better protection should a tank roll over your position.

The owner of the farm watched us dig. He saw that the ground was hard and dry, so he loaned us a pick to hack with. After the holes were dug, we refused to sleep in them, preferring to stretch out on the grass with a raincoat for protection. During the night it rained lightly, but none of us lost any sleep.

On the morning of August 21, we again set out toward the north. We learned that other troops had been making contact with the enemy even if we hadn't and already had captured a town to the north on the Avre River. The Germans had planted mines, one of which had blown up a jeep, and they had felled trees over the town's bridge. This didn't stop the infantry, but it did delay our tanks. Once in the town, we had our first contact with English-speaking French civilians. They had learned the language in school, they told us. Apparently, the closer we got to Paris the nearer we were coming to culture and education.

After we had passed through the village, I found the war dull enough to allow my mind to wander. I reflected that I had been in the fighting for better than a month and that I still carried the rank of Private. I decided to make a bold appeal for advancement to Private First Class, so I asked Sgt. O'Brien how long a man had to remain a Private in this army. He expressed great astonishment at my lowly station and said that he would see that I was promoted right away. With that taken care of, we went back to the tiresome business of marching and looking for the enemy.

That afternoon we learned that there were still some Jerries about. We were approaching a large and important airfield, defended by artillery and mortar fire. We didn't attempt to take the airfield frontally. We simply went around it to trap the defenders in a flanking movement. But this meant extra miles of hard marching well into the night. The men in the mortar and machine gun sections, especially those who carried ammunition, complained loudly of their fatigue and pain. Whenever we stopped, these men objected loudly. They wanted to get to the objective and get the agony over with.

The complaints did no good of course, but made us all feel cantankerous. Some GIs discarded gas masks and even ammo, for which they were roundly chastised by the officers next day. Eventually, we arrived at another French hamlet in the dead of night and set up a perimeter defense. Our gun was mounted on the ground near a rich-smelling horse barn. I dug a shallow hole beside the gun, flopped into it, and slept like a dead man.

The morning of August 22 was cool and foggy. I ate my K ration in the horse barn with the others and within a few hours we were on the march. My feet were beginning to hurt again, but I was not the only one who was suffering. To relieve our pain throughout the day, we were given turns riding on the ammunition jeep which now traveled with us to lighten the load. Finally, we got the idea of mounting the gun on the standard attached to the jeep.

"If we run into trouble," O'Brien said, "the guy who is riding at the time will have to get the gun off the mount."

It turned out that I was to be the one riding at the time. We surprised ourselves and a battalion of the enemy withdrawing in a wooded ravine.

The first sign of trouble was the sudden rattle of machine gun fire and the appearance of tracers emerging from the draw and zipping over our heads. The men quickly hit the ground and scurried to whatever cover they could find. The driver of the jeep jumped out and crouched behind the vehicle. I was forced to remain exposed while I unloaded the machine gun, or thought I did, took it from its mount and grabbed several boxes of ammo. I struggled with this heavy load about 25 yards to a small dirt road where I thought I might find O'Brien and Gibson. It was getting dark now and I could not see the men I was searching for, since they were doing a good job of remaining invisible. By calling O'Brien's name several times, I finally got a response and a reading as to where they were hidden.

"Good," said O'Brien, when he saw what I had brought. "We'll set up behind one of those shocks of wheat." He pointed to a spot about 25 yards to the east of the road in a flat, open field. The growing darkness was our only protection.

Gibson took the gun and inadvertently pressed the trigger. A red tracer round was discharged over O'Brien's head and high into the air. It must have looked to the Germans like a signal. To us it seemed as though we had telegraphed our exact location to the enemy.

We also were shocked at O'Brien's close call.

"I thought you unloaded this thing," Gibson said sharply.

"I thought I did, too," I replied with a sick feeling in my stomach. When was I ever going to be a competent soldier? I had forgotten the round in the chamber that needed ejecting.

The brief battle which took place in the valley on our left was dubbed "Lightning Boulevard." The Germans fired 20mm anti-aircraft shells down a roadway, creating a lightning bolt effect, to cover their retreat of men, vehicles, and some horse-drawn carts. Up till then, we had not been aware that the Jerries were using horses.

There was no action on our flat, recently cut, grain field. Our squad dug in behind some grain shocks and waited for the night to spend itself. I drew a two-hour guard. When I was through, I shook Gibson, my relief, gave him the watch, and told him it was his turn.

"O.K.," he said. I went to my slit trench for some sleep. I should have remembered that Gibson had a hard time waking once asleep and I should have stayed with him until he was surely with this world. But I didn't, Gibson never truly woke up, and our machine gun unit was without a watch for the remainder of the night.

Ordinarily, this lapse would be considered a serious offense, but O'Brien and the rest of us were so happy that nothing occurred during the night that we laughed it off. O'Brien, of course, issued a warning not to let it happen again if we wanted to stay alive.

August 23 was another pleasant summer's day of wandering around the countryside in search of lost enemy pockets. If you ever want to see a country thoroughly, I highly recommend cross-country travel. This part of France was rolling, and little patches of carefully tended woods added to the interest. During these marches I noticed strips of tin foil which appeared almost everywhere we went, no matter how remote. I later learned that the strips had been dropped by our planes to interfere with German radar.

Later in the morning we emerged from a dense woods and hiked down-hill into another French hamlet. On the edge of the town, we came upon an attractive, well-dressed French girl on a bicycle. She spoke good English and was sexy enough looking to intrigue our boys.

She said that she had seen our column from a distance coming down the hillside and had presumed that we were Germans on maneuvers. Then she naively asked if there were many of us and if we had taken Evereux yet. None of us knew the answers to her questions, but we made out as though we did and said that to tell her would be to give out military secrets.

She was amused and replied gaily that she had cycled from Evereux this morning to buy food and that she didn't want to go back if there was fighting there.

"What did you buy?" we asked.

She showed us several boxes of cheese, one of which she generously gave us. We tried to eat it later, but it was so strong that none of us could stomach it.

Suddenly the stutter of automatic fire was heard on our right to the east of the village, and our conversation was ended. We advanced through the town cautiously, but there was no more firing.

Meanwhile, a French girl, probably in her 20s, who had been too friendly with the Germans, had been corralled, and a swarthy Frenchman, wearing a beret, was kicking her along the highway to the vocal approval of the townspeople who lined the street.

Apples, coffee, and more apples were offered to us. A butcher gave us strips of ham, which we ate with small biscuits. An old woman burst out of her home in the first delirium of surprise and joy and greeted each one of us who passed with a kiss and expressions of gratitude. I don't know how long she was able to keep kissing so many stubbly faces, but she was still doing it when I rounded a bend in the street.

On the northern outskirts of the town we stopped while a squad of riflemen followed up a lead given by a member of the Maquis, the French resistance organization, as to the location of some Germans. I rolled into the ditch, and, warmed by the sun, quickly went to sleep.

Within an hour, we were once more on the move, this time uphill. My sore feet and I began to wish that something would happen to stop this relentless marching.

At the top of the hill, we came upon a Red Cross unit encamped to the rear of another small village. This gave us pause for we had thought we were among the lead elements. Perhaps we were and were now headed back into some of the rear positions. War is always confusion for the infantryman.

While slowly approaching this new village, I had my first drink of milk since leaving Camp Shanks, near New York. A milkmaid was so pleased at seeing us that she poured glasses of milk from a small metal bottle. I gratefully accepted and enjoyed the sweet taste of the fresh cool liquid.

The village was called Sassy. It was to be a luxurious home to us for several days, for we were now in Corps Reserve.

Our squad was assigned a pile of straw in a substantial stone barn. Blankets were brought up and we used them to keep warm and to shield our faces from the rats at night. The rats were friendly rascals who checked us out regularly after dark. Some of the men slept under a beam and woke up the next morning with pigeon dung on their blankets. We had humor, too, the greatest luxury of all.

During our first evening in the barn, a French youth of about thirteen or fourteen years brought a portable phonograph and played popular French fox trots. He smoked a cigarette and danced by himself with one arm encircling an imaginary partner. He also sang, in better voice than the singers on the recordings. We had real French flavor in addition to our stone barn, our straw, our rats, and our pigeons.

110

Our stay at Sassy, which had included such pleasures as eating from a chow line at our kitchen, seeing a few movies in a barn, reading letters from home, writing to family and friends, and generally loafing and resting, was interrupted on August 27 when we mounted trucks again and rode to Mantes on the Seine River. Our big guns were stationed in or near this town. Their noise was deafening as we drove through.

Crossing the Seine was a simple matter. Our trucks completed this historic moment by driving over a cement bridge that somehow had been left intact. A few blocks beyond the bridge, we were put on foot again.

A short hike got us out of town and into some woods and fields on the outskirts. Our kitchen was established in a patch of woods, and our machine gun and mortar sections selected another patch of dense, spindly second-growth saplings as suitable concealment.

The concealment was so good that during the night I had difficulty with guard duty because of the darkness and density of the thicket. LaVoie woke me, gave me the watch, and said my turn would be for a half hour.

"You're supposed to go to the path and stand guard there," he said as he headed for bed.

I wandered in the woods, with branches slapping me in the face, for fifteen minutes without finding the path. Looking at the watch, I decided that if it had taken half of my assigned time to get where I was — and I wasn't sure where — I'd better spend the remainder of my guard duty trying to find my way back so that I could awaken my relief on time.

This I did. It was the most futile stretch of guard duty I had ever experienced. I warned the next man that he might as well stay where he was and concentrate on finding the man who was to relieve him.

It rained during the night. Water made the bottom of the straw-covered hole soggy and cold, but sleep was not to be denied.

The next day we were close support to the 3rd Battalion, which with a reconnaissance group and tanks, pushed the Germans back four and a half miles to the town of Meulan on the Seine. We were shouldering our way in the direction of Paris.

Meulan, a village built on the side of a hill, was being shelled sporadically. Nonetheless, French civilians lined our way and silently watched us march through their streets. At the top of the hill and before we had left the final protective line of buildings, a quick barrage of enemy 88s sent us scurrying for doorways. One shell struck a building near us, after which a woman screamed for minutes as we hurriedly left for the open ground on the eastern outskirts.

O'Brien and I dug in together in a garden. O'Brien was worried about his reaction to the shelling, his first since rejoining us.

"Parker," he said, "the noise of that stuff makes me wilt inside."

"What do you think it does to me?" I asked to comfort him.

"Yeah, I know," he said, "but it's not like how you feel after you've been hit once."

"You'll get used to it again," I said, and O'Brien looked at me as though I were a liar.

When we put a top on the hole, O'Brien seemed obsessed about determining its strength. To my horror, he walked on the top and caved it in. This resulted in another hour of hard work, cleaning out the hole and building a stronger top.

The next morning, August 29, Company C was put in the lead in the continuing chore of pushing the Germans around. We were behind this company in reserve.

In the next town, some English-speaking French youths asked the now familiar questions:

"Are there many of you?"

"Have you taken this town or that town?"

"Je ne sais pas," I replied to all questions. (I don't know.)

An advance of about four miles was made before stiff resistance was encountered at Villette. We were up against elements of the 6th Parachute Division and the 18th GAF Division. They put up a hard fight with heavy artillery, mortar, anti-tank, and small arms fire.

Our Battalion commander, Lt. Col. Bradford, was wounded in the arm, and two of Company C's platoon leaders were lost as were several of our tanks. Direct anti-tank fire caused most of the damage.

During the early part of this action, our unit was in the village before Villette. We watched 81mm mortar squads set up hurriedly in gardens or yards to deliver supporting fire, and we got out of the way of ambulances and jeeps scurrying back and forth.

ABOVE — View of Condecourt from high ground during peacetime in 1962. On August 29, 1944, corps artillery made a tossed salad out of the village area while infantrymen watched from this high point. Beyond, on open ground, the Germans could be seen recapturing some American troops. BELOW — Barn at Sassy — It was in this barn that a French youth entertained us by playing records of popular music while dancing with an imaginary partner and singing the French words.

While enemy artillery was shaking the ground ahead of us, a Parisian engaged us in conversation. He seemed highly educated, for he spoke English easily and precisely.

"The Germans are finished," he said. "They know they are defeated, too," he added, and he told us about a group of Germans who had sought a good cellar for protection against our artillery in this village the previous night. I had noticed the evidence of heavy shelling, including a badly damaged church and spire.

"They were terribly afraid of your artillery," the Parisian said with disgust. "I served in the first war myself, and artillery was much heavier then than it is this time. Yet we weren't as afraid as these men were."

It was small comfort to me or the others to learn that the Germans were afraid. We were all afraid. I would have done the same as they did to save myself from artillery fire.

This conversation was ended by the ritualistic, fear-instilling order: "We're moving out." Men picked up their equipment as the order was repeated down the line. The enemy artillery was still whamming the ground as we slowly began to advance toward this meat grinder.

The battle for Villette, France, was unique since it was our last stiff engagement with the enemy on French soil.

Vilette was reputed to be a stockyard town where buyers from Paris came to look over the animals brought in for auction. We became aware of the sheds in which they were kept, first by the noise of something beating on tin roofs and then by the appearance of some GIs who had escaped from a prison camp at a chateau nearby. They had clambered across the metal sheds to reach the higher ground upon which we were advancing west of the village. The escapees chattered a bit and then vanished to our rear. Below us the town appeared as a mass of trees with here and there an occasional house or barn roof protruding.

Soon our column sank into the valley of trees and moved along the comforting side of a stone wall. Elements of Company C were still holding a sunken road which intersected at the end of the wall we were hugging. The wall enclosed the chateau and courtyard where the American prisoners had been.

114

By moving to the right flank of the village we had avoided walking into the beaten zone of the artillery barrages. But, when we were about 100 yards from the end of the wall, two things happened. It started to rain in sheets and the enemy began shelling the area. We ran through the rain to the end of the wall, veered right and climbed a hill into a patch of woods. The shells were exploding about us, but the rain was so heavy that we could not be observed for accurate firing.

At the top of the hill we came to a small dirt road which wound around the crest of the elevation. Here we stopped. The rain had ceased and we could clearly see a vast stretch of terrain below us. It seemed like a diorama of the battlefield and that we were now spectators and not participants. Green tree branches and leaves were erupting here and there as shells plummeted into the wooded villages of Villette and Condecourt, the latter almost being a continuation of the former. To the south, toward Paris, the ground was an extensive open greensward, made more green by the soft half light of the still storm-clouded sky. Far to our rear we could see our artillery pieces firing on still another front to the east. An observation plane hung like a soaring vulture looking for victims. We could also see two broken forms prone on the edge of the green carpet to the south. Apparently they were the first casualties in the enemy counterthrust.

Meanwhile, one of our artillery observers appeared with his radioman and began to adjust his battery on the valley. He used the church steeple in Condecourt as an aiming point, and once he had adjusted to that point he switched to our front and had his guns throw a few close rounds over our heads into a patch of woods about 300 yards to our right front. Then he said, "That's all."

Even his radioman was disgusted. We thought he should pound the German-held area, whether he could see any specific targets or not. We didn't realize that corps artillery was focusing on just such a mission, for within a few minutes the valley below began to erupt as hordes of shells hissed and whistled in like an angry swarm of death-dealing insects. It was like watching a huge bowl of salad being tossed as the green stuff leaped and twisted in the air and fell back again.

"Our third platoon is down there helping Company C," someone said. I felt sorry for anyone that close to the barrage. Before it had stopped, another man shouted excitedly: "Look, there's a bunch of GIs surrendering."

He pointed to the green carpet. About a dozen miniature brown-clad figures walked in a column toward the middle of the open field.

"They've got their hands over their heads. They ain't got no weapons," another GI, who was looking through glasses, said.

We saw two dark-uniformed men come into the field to meet the Americans. One of the Germans seemed to move in an agitated way.

"Well, lookit that," the GI with the field glasses said. "That Kraut is jumping up and down like he was tickled to death."

"What they givin' up for anyway?"

"Maybe they got cut off and didn't see how they could come back through that barrage."

"They ain't got helmets."

"Maybe they threw them away before they quit."

"Naw, I'll bet they was prisoners that the Krauts had before this and they got caught in the middle in this fight and didn't know where to go."

The latter guess turned out to be correct. None of our troops surrendered. Getting some of their prisoners back was a cheap victory for the Jerries.

Just as dusk was falling our artillery searched out the field in which the Americans had been recaptured and succeeded in hitting a hay barn and setting it afire. As a result the sky was illuminated most of the night.

We were told to dig in on the hillside. In doing so, we found a chalk bed about a foot under the topsoil. Every hole was a white-rimmed dot on the hill signaling our positions even in the darkness.

The next morning was clear and warm and, since the Germans had withdrawn, the war once again became a walking marathon, with a holiday mood prevailing.

Each French town that we "liberated" celebrated by ringing the church bell, treating us with apples, bread and jam, or whatever was available.

For two days, August 30 and 31, the latter my 30th birthday, we walked south along the Seine until we hit the Oise River. Then we swung northward. No need to go to Paris. The French were taking care of that. Furthermore, we had other work to do.

On the morning of September 1, Capt. Pulver and what was left of his company assembled in an apple orchard where he told us that we were going to take another truck ride and go as far as we could. We did not know, of course, that within two days we would be in Belgium and that the battle for France was over, for us anyway.

In the afternoon, after our Captain's morning speech, the 120th Regiment began an historic truck ride of 180 miles across the old World War I battlegrounds of northeastern France. The enemy was thoroughly routed now, but there was opposition at several points along the way. A task force at the head of our column took care of these stubborn pockets while we waited at leisure in our trucks.

Our tour at first was a lark, but it later became very uncomfortable. There were frequent stops and starts, and finally an hours-long stop in the countryside while "the point" dealt with the enemy at Cambrai. Meanwhile, the weather suddenly became cold, wet, and windy. We were not only shivering, but were unable to sleep.

The next morning the column started moving again. We had the canvas over the ribs of the truck, to keep the wind and rain out and so could not see much of the country that we passed through. In a large town, probably Cambrai, a French woman approached the rear of our truck and offered us eggs. I got one and put it in my pocket. Some of the men punched holes in their eggs and sucked them, but I decided to wait until I could cook mine.

Early in the morning of the next day, September 3, we finally arrived at Tournai, Belgium and accordingly, were probably the first American troops to reach Belgian soil in the mad rush to pursue the fleeing Germans. We dragged our weary selves out of the trucks which had been our homes for three days and unlimbered our cramped muscles. It was still pitch dark, but we succeeded in spreading out on the ground behind some buildings.

To protect myself from the still chilling wind, I snuggled down on the side of a terrace. I was so exhausted that I slept with my face in some nettles and didn't know it until daylight.

Upon awakening, my first concern was the egg. Miraculously, it was still intact; I had not tossed and turned in my sleep and rolled on it. I discovered that members of a cannon company unit near us were frying eggs. My immediate thought was to toss my egg into the same frying pan, but then I decided to trade it for a box of synthetic breakfast food, a ration that never reached us at the front but which the cannon company had in abundance. By adding water, the ration became a cereal with sugar and milk. I made the deal, put the cereal in my canteen cup and ate my breakfast.

Later in the day, we marched the streets of Tournai to take up defense positions. The civilians were delighted. German prisoners were being marched out of the city while we were marching in. Gramophones in the houses were playing "It's a Long Way to Tipperary," showing the influence of the British who had been in this sector in World War I.

At one point in the march, civilians handed out bottles of vile-tasting beer, which the troops eagerly drank. About a block beyond, a boy collected the bottles and put them in cases. It was the best organized hand-out I saw during the war.

The next five days in Tournai had a delirious peace-time quality. Our bedding rolls were brought up, the first we had seen of them since Tessy. We lived in shallow holes under our shelter halves; letters were received and written; the division band arrived and played; movies were shown; our kitchen joined us and served hot food in our mess kits again; and Belgian civilians hung around to talk with us. But the final sign of peace was an order to go through two half-hour sessions of close order drill each day. When we were informed that the battle-hardened remnants of Company B were to take up the formalized habits of barracks soldiers, Captain Pulver tried to make the order palatable by stating that in preference to combat he would be willing to do close order drill for the rest of the war.

Once again, we were hopefully looking for an end to the fighting. The Germans must surely give up now, we felt. The British had driven past us to take Brussels and had left an anti-aircraft unit near our position, and we got quite friendly with the crew. They had been in the war much longer than we, and had no illusions about the Germans. They liked our C rations, so we gave them what we had. In return we got some tea and a few interesting tales about their experiences in Africa.

On September 7 the division had accumulated enough motor fuel to resume the pursuit. During the early morning hours, some replacements were brought up to fill our many vacancies. It was raining hard, and I felt sorry for them as they put up their shelter halves in the mud and rain. It was still raining when daylight presented us with a gloomy morning. I then felt sorry for myself as I rolled up blankets, clothes, and shelter half in the mire.

The trucks gave us an 80-mile lift before running out of gas in the afternoon. The mud-spattered trucks pulled to the side of the road and let us off near the Waterloo battlefield south of Brussels. Our column headed into a well-kept forest belonging to some wealthy family, and we bedded down for the night. The grooming was so good that all the leaves were carefully stacked in uniform piles, and few, if any, shrubs could be seen on the floor of the woods.

I began to get acquainted with the new men assigned to our machine gun section. They asked many questions about combat, and we tried to answer them, knowing that experience would be their best teacher. The new men seemed strangely foreign to us. Some, until recently, had been civilians in that distant almost forgotten U.S.A. One explained that he had been in the heavy mortar company, but that he had screwed up in some way, and, as punishment, had been sent to our rifle company. Apparently it was not an honor to fight for one's country.

On the morning of the 8th, we began the first day of a three-day march to the Meuse River. We plodded 27 miles to Jadoigne, Belgium, and stopped for a time in the village park. Sgt. O'Brien got angry with his bayonet because it would not come off easily when he wanted to show it to some of the teen-age boys who crowded around. When he finally detached it, he gave it to one of the youngsters, who received it ecstatically. The rest of us had long ago discarded bayonets as useless equipment.

We moved to the outskirts of the town and occupied some V-trenches dug by the Germans. I chatted with a young girl who lived in a nearby house, using some of my fractured French and showing photos of my wife and baby girl. To my astonishment, she asked if I would like to sleep in her house that night, but I declined pointing to our trenches and the mounted machine gun which I would help tend during the night. Later, when we reached Germany, we gave up much of our outdoor life and stayed in houses, basements, and barns almost exclusively, but there were no civilians around then and weather and shelling dictated more secure quarters.

In the early morning hours of September 9 we began another day-long march. At the eastern edge of Jadoigne, the column stopped for a long time enabling some of our men to get cups of hot water at an adjacent house. They were thus enjoying their morning coffee, synthetic though it might be. I called at the kitchen of this house to try my luck. I was cordially greeted and given a chair to sit on while a new batch of water heated on the wood stove. When the kettle was ready, a Belgian lady who looked as though she might be a secretary with her tailored clothes and up hair-do, poured the water into my cup, pinned a bit of cloth representing the Belgian colors on my field jacket, and planted a kiss on each of my bewhiskered cheeks.

"Belgium is a great country," I declared to Sgt. O'Brien when I returned with my cup of hot water, the bit of Belgian flag, and my uplifted spirits. I put some boullion powder in the hot water and drank it down while on the march.

The remainder of the day was ponderous with slow-moving advances, which, however, were enlivened when we approached and passed through each new Belgian town. The Belgians gave us apples, bread, and even ice cream in one of the larger centers, and the boys returned greetings in crude French. It was a holiday, but a laborious one, for we marched about thirty miles.

When we finally halted at dusk, my feet were so sore I could hardly stand on them. That night, while bedded down on some straw on top of a bank by a railroad track, I made the mistake of taking my shoes off in the hope of getting some relief. The cool night air dried the skin and made my blistered feet seem brittle and more sensitive than ever. To get my shoes on in the morning, I felt as though I were cracking the skin of my feet to bend them into place. When I started to walk, I discovered another problem: my hip sockets seemed to have tightened and were difficult to move.

I doggedly started this third day's march with my head down and only a faint hope of keeping up with my younger companions. In a short time it was apparent that I could not maintain their pace. When they were taking a ten minute break, I was plodding along trying to catch up.

Sgt. Barnett walked by me during the next marching period and saw my plight. He told me to get a ride on the ammunition jeep the next time it leapfrogged past us. When the jeep came long, I hailed it, told the driver of Sgt. Barnett's approval, and hopped aboard.

The driver was the Polish boy who had kidded me about ducking mortar shells at Mortain. He said that he had been transferred from the rifle platoon after that battle to his present luxurious position as a jeep driver.

Our progress ended this day in a small village near Fort Eben Emael, a bastion which the Germans took early in the war with specially trained troops and which a unit of our Division captured without firing a shot, although it was held by 300 Germans.

We stayed in this village for two days and then crossed the Albert Canal and the Meuse River, entering Holland for the first time. During this advance, the main topic of discussion was not this new historic military achievement, but the recently announced point system for discharge from the Army. Winning the war went on the back burner, while getting out of the service moved front and center. Most of us were dissatisfied with the details of the system. Length of service and medals were worth lots of points, and none of us had any medals to show for our months of combat experience. Furthermore, the combat badge wasn't worth any points at all.

The reception given by the Dutch people was highly pleasing and unexpected. They cheered the loudest, were more friendly, gave us as much in the way of tokens and gifts, and helped us more in actions against the enemy than the French or Belgians. We had been told to be more suspicious the closer we came to Germany, for it was felt that there would be more German sympathizers the closer we got to the enemy homeland. Our intelligence in this respect proved to be far off the mark.

On the evening of September 13 we entrenched in an apple orchard near Gulpen, Holland. We were to remain there for three days before attacking a prepared system of trenches between us and the Siegfried Line.

The next day our machine gun section was ordered to march four miles forward to an outpost position on a hill overlooking the enemy held trenches. It was a chilling sight to see this forbidding defense line, prepared by forced Dutch labor, which we knew we would have to take later.

I went looking for hay or straw to line my hole. Halfway down the hill I came across some Dutch people who, I thought, might be able to tell me where I could get some hay. They didn't understand my charades, so I used some French (morte vert) and pulled strands of field grass. They then understood and directed my to a barn.

The next day we returned to our encampment, and there we were told by our Colonel, speaking to the assembled company, that we would attack soon and that our Division would crack the Siegfried Line. The

Colonel then asked for the hands of those who had been original members of the Regiment when it landed. Four or five hands went up. (Our Regiment in the end suffered about 200 per cent casualties.) The Colonel then asked what ranks they held. All were Sergeants and squad leaders with the exception of Pfc. Wisnewski.

"Why aren't you a Sergeant?" the Colonel demanded. Wisnewski mumbled that he didn't know. The Colonel turned to Capt. Pulver and said, "Captain, I want you to see that this man is taken care of."

"Yes, sir," said the Captain. But for some reason, Pfc. Wisnewski remained at his lowly station, and, it was said that he was the only original private in the company to go unscathed through the entire combat experience from St. Lo to the Elbe River and Magdeburg.

About this time, I began to feel rather lowly myself. In one of my letters home, I complained that I was nothing but a "pack horse" and wished that the Army could find a job for me in line with my capabilities. Maybe I planted an idea that was later to bear fruit, for all of our letters were read and censored by our officers.

On the morning of September 16 we enjoyed hot cakes and maple syrup at our field kitchen and then, well fed, set out in a light rain on our mission of breaking through the German trenches east of Gulpen.

I had just received about a dozen letters, which I read on the march. I couldn't keep them, so I wadded them into a ball and gave them to a GI standing by the roadside and asked him to burn them for me.

"Sure, I'll take care of 'em," he said. I sensed that he felt sorry for me. I did too.

By the time we reached Gulpen, it had stopped drizzling. The column halted and I rested my boxes of ammo on a low stone wall in front of a well above-average Dutch home.

A few shells began to hiss over our heads as a light artillery barrage was directed at the enemy trenches to the east of the village. Our approach to the town had been concealed by a continuous line of trees hovering over the road and town.

As I rested I reflected that this would be the 13th attack our unit had participated in, offensively and defensively, since I joined the outfit July

16. Would 13 be lucky or unlucky?

I was interrupted in my thoughts by a smiling Dutch matron coming from her comfortable-looking brick house with a wooden bowl full of fruit. We helped ourselves and thanked her. She asked questions about our mission. I evaded them by saying I didn't know, which was more or less the truth, but when she asked if there would be any enemy shelling, and her eyes were wide with anxiety as she asked, I told her that it would be a good idea to keep under cover. If I had been in her shoes, I would have tucked the bowl under my arm and headed for the basement.

Generally, civilians thought our presence represented safety from the Germans. Conversely, we knew that wherever we went there would be trouble, and why anyone would want to watch us while we went into an attack when they could be in a safe place never failed to confound us.

Within a few minutes the men shouldered equipment and moved through the remainder of Gulpen, while townspeople stood quietly by to watch. On the eastern edge of the village, we crossed a crudely reconstructed bridge and hit some gently rolling pasture and orchard country. I noticed with relief that we still could not be observed from the enemy trenches.

Our route was along a small wagon trail which brought us to a group of farm buildings. Then the rattle of enemy small arms and machine gun fire began as bullets sang and cracked in the air about us. The advance continued as though nothing had happened.

We followed the dirt road which, much to our pleasure, was concealed by a hedge on the enemy side and which, furthermore, began to recede gradually into the ground and become a familiar sunken road similar to those in Normandy.

We were now climbing up the hill and approaching the enemy lines. Some of our riflemen were peering over the edge of the embankment and taking up temporary positions. One of our machine gun squads was ordered to join them. The other squad of which I was a member continued to follow the attacking riflemen along the twisting roadway.

"Here comes a Jerry prisoner," someone said.

A tall, white-haired German who must have been in his late forties walked toward us with his hands upraised. He was wearing a long overcoat that almost reached his ankles.

As he neared me, he began to speak in perfect English: "There's nothing to worry about. There aren't very many of us."

"That's good," I murmured in surprise.

As he passed he said to others behind me: "Just a bunch of old men up ahead. I was in the first war. Now they got me in this one."

Soon this talkative German was followed by a motley array of silent German infantrymen, dressed in assorted uniforms. There were about 30 over-age Jerries holding their hands overhead and marching to our rear. I think they were glad it was over.

They had given up their trenches, which we were shelling too accurately for their taste, preferring the sunken road a few yards in front of the entrenchments. They had been lined up along the road watching for us to attack from their front and were caught napping when we casually walked into their position from their right flank via the same road.

We now waited while elements on our left, who were having a stiff fire fight, caught up with us. One of our mortars was set up in the sunken road and shells were dropped on an enemy machine gun about fifty yards ahead in an orchard, knocking it our of action.

I was curious as to the reaction of some of the new men in our squad to this fight. I asked one of them how he liked it.

"Not bad," he said nonchalantly, as he wandered about searching through abandoned German paraphernalia on the ground. He picked up several leather items as souvenirs. He would learn in time, I mused, that all of this was junk, an extra burden to be carried and guarded.

Where I was lying, I noticed several "V for Victory" matches bearing the slogan, "Buy Bonds." These Jerries must have had contact with Americans somewhere before to get our matches.

After about a half hour, we boldly arose from the sunken road and walked a few yards to the trench, which had seemed such an obstacle and which was now just another gash in the earth. We crossed a main highway a few feet beyond and reached the top of the hill.

One of the rifle platoons had cleared out the enemy resistance and was now enjoying target practice from a railroad embankment about 100 yards to our left. They were spaced at intervals and were firing as though on a rifle range at fleeing Germans in the flat below.

"Good work, Captain," said Colonel Birks, our regimental commander. I breathed easier. The appearance of brass at the front always gave us a lift, although mostly for cynical reasons. If it was safe for them, it couldn't be too bad for us. Not that our commanders did not take risks, oftentimes unnecessarily, but it was also a reality that they did not expose themselves to areas that were obviously a bad risk, and should not, I might add.

We began to move downhill to a railroad underpass. Our tanks were now rumbling up to support us, and a heavy machine gun company had set up on the railroad embankment and was enjoying a shooting party at the little town of Eijs which lay below us.

(In 1962 when I revisited this area I found that a beautiful monument commemorating the Dutch war dead had been placed almost on the ground where I had observed the "V for Victory" matches.)

Before our infantry and tanks went through the underpass, we were stopped by a loyal Dutchman who told us that there were two German 88mm guns lying in wait for our tanks to appear at the underpass. Our heavy machine guns directed their fire on the gun emplacements, pointed out by the Dutchman, while our infantry moved ahead. The tactic resulted in the capture of the guns and their crews before they were able to fire a shot, a most remarkable coordinating of machine gun fire and infantry daring.

The Dutchman whose information had helped us so much had run across the open ground between Eijs and the underpass to meet us, a risky venture in view of the gun emplacements behind him. He said that he had been a bicycle racer and had taken part in some of the six-day races at Madison Square Gardens, New York, before the war.

"Holy Smokes," he said," your artillery had me pinned down for a long time."

We walked through Eijs to its eastern outskirts and waited there while patrols of riflemen probed the front and our flanks. While pausing here, an elderly, white-haired Dutchman, followed by several children who had been sheltered in his manor-like home, jovially greeted us in English.

"Only a few hours ago," he said, "the arrogant Germans left here. One of their officers told us that they would be back, that this was only a temporary retirement. How many of you are there?"

Sgt. O'Brien gave what I thought must have been later regarded by the Dutch as a classic answer. He said: "Don't worry. Within a few hours there will be so many GIs here you'll wish to God you'd never seen any."

"No, no," said the Dutchman. "That is not possible. Not after the

Germans."

(Major Ellis W. Williamson, then Regimental S-3 and later 1st Battalion commander, was largely responsible for our successful attack with a minimum of casualties. He had patrols explore the area, studied available maps, and devised the approach via the folds and gentle rolls in the ground so that we were able to get close to the enemy without being seen and even outflank their lines.)

In further discussion with the white-haired, distinguished-looking Dutchman, we learned that Aachen, or Aix-la-Chapelle, was only a few kilometers further east, that our informant was a wealthy man in the community, and that his home had indeed been used as a shelter for the children, more of whom now dared come out on the street to see us.

While our patrols continued to search our flanks, one of our tanks proceeded east a few yards on the road to Aachen to fire a few rounds at real or imaginary targets. When we hit the road again, we passed a brick barn which was burning. Apparently it had been the target of the tank's shells. A lone Dutch farmer was forlornly inspecting the damage.

We turned off the highway and headed north over hilly open country to begin what was eventually to be a pincer movement aimed at Aachen, the first important German city our Army was to encounter.

After wandering for several hours over the countryside, we stopped below a hill upon which a Dutch hamlet was situated. Our tanks held back, too, while some American planes strafed. We could not see what they were attacking, but obviously they had come across enemy elements and were shooting them up.

A friendly round of artillery gave us a start by dropping about 200 yards behind us in an open field, digging a large hole, and sending metal fragments whining over our heads. An artillery observer corrected the range and we were not bothered again with short rounds.

We entered the village and, since it was growing dusk, we set up a defense line on another hill overlooking a spacious valley in which many fires had been started and which burned throughout the night.

It was here that we got our first taste of Dutch hospitality. Two Dutch youths watched while we were digging in. When one of the men

126

leaned on his shovel and complained that he was tired, one of the boys grabbed his shovel, told the GI to take a rest, and dug the hole for him. They also brought us fresh drinking water and straw for our holes.

After I had made my preparations for the evening, I noticed a familiar face on my right. It belonged to the stubby little runner who ran through the rain to Paige and me when we were placed like sore thumbs in an exposed position in Normandy just before the St. Lo breakthrough. He had brought the welcome news that we could pull back to a better position. At that time, I must have been near hysteria for I kidded the runner about being lucky to be still alive. This night, when I remembered who he was, I referred to the incident and noted that he had survived to this point. He was now a BAR man. I don't imagine that he thought survival was much of a joke, since BAR men had notably short careers. I never saw the man again after this encounter.

On the morning of September 17, we shoved off again and passed through several more small Dutch towns which fervently welcomed us. At about noon, we halted at the outskirts of Spekholzerheide, while one of our tanks traded fire with a German machine gun nest, a vastly unequal contest. As we passed the knocked out gun emplacement, I saw that two of our medics were working over one of the Germans who had been hit three or four times with 50 caliber bullets. It was ironic that our Army contained forces of destruction and healing in the same package.

When our riflemen first became visible to the residents of Spekholzerheide, a tremendous roar went up from the town as from a football stadium. Crowds of people who had been lined on the street to witness our arrival now surged across lots to greet us. One Dutchman got down to business right away and asked me for cigarettes. I had a small K-ration package and gave it to him.

Our column slid down the side of an embankment onto a right-of-way for three or four railroad tracks. The rails led to some coal mines in the town. The sunken road position of the tracks afforded a safe approach to and through the town in case things were not as they seemed.

Along a retaining wall at one of the coal mine buildings, a crowd of young people was perched on top to watch and cheer. One buxom blonde girl, trying out her English, yelled as I passed: "Hey, I love you."

I shouted back: "This is so sudden."

A foxhole near the base of this tree was home during several weeks in September, 1944, on the outskirts of Spekholzerheide, Holland. The owner of the farm and orchard, Mathieu Sleipen, is shown here with his daughters in 1962.

Everyone laughed.

Beyond the building, we turned left up a steep incline and over a wall and into the town. The maneuver was difficult for we who had to carry heavy equipment, but there were so many helping Dutch hands that it turned out to be no problem. We were lifted bodily over the hurdle.

So these were the people of whose loyalty we were to be skeptical? How could we mistrust them?

An old man with a pail of apples distributed them among us when we halted momentarily. It was the first of many apples I was to eat for the next ten days, for our infantry and tanks churned into a ripening apple orchard on the eastern edge of town and there we were ordered to dig in.

Behind us were a large Dutch farmhouse and outbuildings, behind which our kitchen crew brought up and served a hot dinner that evening. While we were eating quietly in this peaceful atmosphere, two rounds of enemy 88 fire dropped in wounding two men in the mortar section. Despite the glorious welcome we had had from the Dutch, the Jerries still didn't want us around.

Sgt. O'Brien studied the sloping terrain in the orchard and designated the places for the members of his squad. He placed our gun at the crest of the slope and had two gunners entrench themselves next to it. He dug a hole for himself about ten yards back of the gun emplacement. Finally, I was placed about fifty yards further to the rear near a wooden tool shed, which I noticed had American-made farm equipment in it. Beyond the tool shed was the combination Dutch home and barn.

"If we get a counterattack," O'Brien said, "you're supposed to come running forward to the gun with your ammunition and then take off to the rear behind the house and barn and back up the road where you'll find our ammo dump. Then you bring up more ammunition."

"If Jerry tanks come in," he added, "just take off and watch out for me or I'll knock you down in the rush."

O'Brien cussed the lack of tank support, which had moved out after the brief enemy shelling.

"We can't possibly hold out against a tank attack without some anti-tank weapons," he pointed out. "So if they come at us with tanks, just get the hell out of here."

I remembered O'Brien's Purple Heart which had been earned when he helped stop an enemy tank by firing an anti-tank grenade during the hedgerow fighting on July 16. He had been so close to the tank that a metal fragment had struck him in the chest. Our squad leader was the kind of man who admitted he was afraid, but who behaved with courage and distinction in battle.

While digging next to an apple tree, I ran into a root which wouldn't yield to my entrenching tool. I went to the farmhouse and asked the lady of the house for an axe and made motions as though chopping to help her understand my request. She nodded agreeably and came back in a moment with an egg. I laughed, shook my head, and improved my pantomime with an imaginary axe. This time she understood and came back with the tool I needed.

When I returned to my excavation I found several Dutchmen crowded around examining my equipment. One of them offered to dig the hole, and I accepted. On my left, Sgt. Sparks, a colorful individualistic infantry squad leader, had two men hacking away at the earth, while he complacently smoked a pipe and talked with a member of the Dutch underground resistance.

The youthful and eager Dutchman was urging that we move east into Kerkrade since it was virtually undefended. Sparks had already been on patrol in the town and knew that this was substantially true, but he said simply that we had orders to "set here."

When the Dutchman became more insistent, Sparks responded with irritation: "Don't worry about us, Bub. We'll give those Jerries a fight soon enough. We ain't turned 'em down yet when they asked for it."

One of the native spectators asked me for cigarettes. "I don't have any," I said. He pointed to a box of K rations on the ground and read from the list of contents: "One package of Lucky Strikes." Then he looked at me expectantly.

"O.K.," I laughed. I opened the box and gave him the cigarettes.

"You nix smoken?" he queried, when I refused to smoke with him.

"That's right," I replied. Cigarettes were only a medium of exchange for me. He insisted on giving me a Dutch bank note which I finally accepted as a "souvenir."

The second day in our orchard position some German infantrymen on patrol came out of Kerkrade (a city which was almost a continuation of Spekholzerheide being separated from us only by a shallow wooded valley), and came within about 200 yards of our guns.

Our machine gun opened up with a few bursts of fire, and riflemen around us joined in trying to pick off the fleet Jerries.

During this minor action I was interested in the behavior of a man who had been wounded by shellfire in Normandy and who hadn't been able to overcome a debilitating fear of enemy artillery since. During subsequent fighting, after his return to our unit, he had repeatedly been unable to continue as soon as the German artillery opened up. His fear was open and unashamed. He went to pieces without any semblance of pride.

Of late we had not experienced much German artillery and this man's confidence had been returning. In the minor engagement described, he clearly showed that in a small arms fight he was unafraid, even jubilant. He stood in the open in the orchard and fired several rounds from his rifle, and, when the Germans got out of range behind a hedge running perpendicular to our lines, he whooped and ran to the hedge to get a better view and continue firing.

When the incident was over, Sgt. Horne came out from the brick barn behind us and reprimanded the machine gunners for firing on such a minor target.

"You've just gone an' revealed your position," he scolded. "Save the gun for bigger targets. That's what it's for."

That night we were pleased to be joined by an anti-tank company which tugged in an anti-tank gun and set it up under one of the apple trees. More holes were dug and our orchard took on the now familiar look of a rabbit warren.

During the previous night we had been disturbed by a noise coming from Kerkrade which sounded like enemy tanks moving around. One of the natives told us later that the noise was the motors at the mine in Kerkrade. The water pumps were still going even if other activity had been interrupted.

Life began to take on a humdrum aspect during the next few days. (Our machine gun section remained in this location for ten days.) I came to count on the daily appearance of a lame Dutch boy of about ten, who gathered fallen apples in a basket, often going well beyond our guns. Even though we were usually in our holes, exposing only our heads and shoulders, he was completely unafraid. Once, after a few enemy shells had fallen in our midst, he appeared as usual, examined some of the damaged branches and waved his hand deprecatingly toward Kerkrade and the enemy.

During this lull, we wrote letters, slept, ate everything we could get our hands on (packages from home were most welcome), went to the rear for showers in the mine facilities at Spekholzerheide, and on September 25 we saw a movie at a local beer hall.

The show was "Standing Room Only," a comedy about the housing shortage in Washington, D.C. I was besieged by a small Dutch boy and a Dutch girl, aged about six or seven, who both wanted to sit on my lap during the movie. I laid my rifle aside and put one on each knee. The war no longer existed for a time but, after the movie was over, I stepped outside into the darkness and heard again the familiar hissing of shells headed toward German-held territory. The war was still on and I must return to my "standing room" foxhole.

On September 28, our machine gun squad was moved to a new location on the southern outskirts of Spekholzerheide. It was to be the beginning of a new military life for me. The rifle platoons we joined had their quarters in a large barn on the defilade side of a gentle knoll which extended into relatively flat and open country. The open-sided barn was filled almost to the ceiling with neatly piled bales of straw. Most of the men were living in and around the barn. Some had used the bales to construct small homes to keep out the cold September winds and rain. From the top of the barn, where we posted sentries, it was possible to see the dragons' teeth of the Siegfried Line. We also had sentries at the crest of the gentle slope in front of the barn.

During this period our rations were at a low ebb. The somewhat skimpy food brought up from the kitchens did not satisfy our appetites. As a result a few of the men at the barn had taken matters into their own hands and were making strews, hobo style, in tin pails over small fires. Potatoes and other vegetables were available in the fields nearby, and a chicken or two, bought or stolen, from the farmhouse beyond the orchard added flavor to their conglomerations.

I dug four holes in the next two days while my superiors tried to make up their minds where our machine gun should be situated. On the fourth try I was under an apple tree in an orchard again, with a cow to keep me company. I worried about the cow stepping into my hole while I slept, and this nearly happened once. The dumb brute walked on the cover and caved it in, forcing me to reconstruct my earthen home.

About October 1, I received news which gave me joy and some chagrin. The man whom I had replaced on July 14 had now recovered from his sprained ankle and was to be given his old job back. This meant that our machine gun section was overstrength, a problem we had not had before during the days when we were down to two or three men and I was one of them each time. I had previously asked for transfer to the mortar section if an opportunity should ever come, and here it was. I had become acquainted with the men in the mortar squads and liked them. Furthermore, I understood the mortar better than I did the complicated machine gun and thought I might be of more use with the former weapon. However, I disliked leaving the men with whom I had been associated, especially our squad leader, Sgt. O'Brien. He apologized to me for making me move out to make room for the returned soldier, and almost had me feeling it was a tough break to leave the machine gun section. I was aware, however, that O'Brien had known the returnee from early training days in the United States and wanted him back rather badly. Thus, I was a bit miffed that despite my more than sixty days of combat time I was easily sluffed off. My annoyance wasn't reasonable, nor in my own interest. All the same, when I walked back through the orchard to another field where the mortarmen were located I was feeling a bit low.

I started to dig another hole, this time in the rain. While I worked, one of my new associates in the mortar squad — a man by the name of Kennedy — watched me shoveling the sodden masses of clay and mud. Kennedy had a round, ruddy Irish face, and his helmet covered an early baldness.

"Parker," Kennedy finally interrupted, after solemnly watching me work, "I hear that you are a graduate of the University of Michigan. Is that right?"

"Yeah, that's right," I grunted as I heaved some more slop out of the hole.

"Gad," said Kennedy in wonderment and with an Irish twinkle in his eyes, "what the Army doesn't do to a man with a college education."

This was the beginning of a friendship which lasted through the war and many years after. We exchanged Christmas cards and occasional letters and saw each other twice when I visited him in the East.

Kennedy had been educated at a business college in Pennsylvania, and had later established a taxi cab business in Newburgh, New York. He said he had learned the business by playing poker regularly with the boys in the call room at another taxi cab firm. When he had learned enough, he started a business of his own and succeeded by providing more services than his rivals, he told us.

On October 4, Companies C and A attacked Kerkrade, while Company B made a feint in our sector to confuse the enemy. Our mortars were fired in this action. Toward evening, we were ordered to pack up and march back to Spekholzerheide and into the former positions of Company A in a beet field to the east of town.

The next morning we walked back into the town while it was still dark and were issued extra hand grenades.

"You'll need these for house-to-house fighting," we were told. "Company C just got to the edge of Kerkrade yesterday. We're going through them."

Our march route took us back to the first orchard in which we had spent so many days. We paused here awhile and then slipped down into the wooded valley. After a short distance, we climbed a steep bank to the railroad track on the edge of the city. Now we began to see the debris of battle. I picked up a new shovel. My own had broken recently. On the tracks we walked past the body of one of our officers who had been shot in the head. There were also some German dead. We edged our way through a cemetery and past a hospital, where some live GIs of Company A were preparing their breakfasts. They seemed indifferent to our presence. The road ahead led straight into the heart of the city and enemy territory, and that's where we headed.

Kerkrade was deserted. The Germans had evacuated the civilian population of about 30,000 on September 25 by simply sending them through our lines. Now on October 5 as our rifle company advanced through the deserted streets we gradually came to realize that the Germans had left, too. We were much relieved. The enemy had probably withdrawn to meet the main thrust of a breakthrough in the Siegfried Line at Ubach, a few miles north of Kerkrade.

We stopped near a jewelry store window which still had valuables, including lace, on display. Sgt. Kirk, one of the veterans from Normandy days, pointed to the articles and laughingly remarked that here was a chance for "souvenirs."

Asked if he wanted any, the sergeant replied that he was through trying to accumulate souvenirs.

"You guard something with your life for weeks; then one day some-one hollers 'chow,' and you leave it layin' on the ground and when you come back it's gone," he growled.

Lt. Hunn was worried about the locked houses flush on the streets, so he forcibly entered some to see if they held Germans. He smashed down doors and broke windows, but found the homes empty in every instance.

We were met at a major street intersection by a Catholic priest with two young girls, indicating that not all civilians had left. The girls showed their gratitude by kissing the riflemen as they passed. After a few brushes at the scraggly faces, they gave up bussing for waving and smiling at the boys.

As usual we headed for the outskirts of the city. At its eastern edge we passed through a wire mesh fence, about fifteen feet high, which separated Holland from Germany, and stepped for the first time on enemy soil. We set up shop under a wooden stadium used as a bicycle rink.

I wanted to dig a hole, but my new shovel had been painted shut and I couldn't budge the folding joint. I stepped through the fence-opening into Kerkrade with a companion to see if I could find a civilian who had a vise and some oil with which to loosen the mechanism.

We found a helpful elderly man, who recognized the problem. He led us through a labyrinth of back yards and alleys into a small tool shed where he was quickly able to fix the shovel.

Upon our return, we found that someone had "liberated" a keg of beer from a nearby tavern. The beer had an overly sweet taste, but we drank it all the same.

135

While we were enjoying ourselves, a terrific battle to break the Siegfried Line was going on directly north at Ubach. The noise of artillery, both American and German, was almost constant. In our sector, however, all was quiet and we spent a peaceful, beer-soaked night under the bicycle arena.

The next day the sounds of battle were closer — a sign that our troops were having success. We had direct evidence that the battle was closer when a burst of spent machine gun bullets splattered against the wooden rink, sending us scurrying for cover.

That evening we were ordered to get ready to leave. As soon as it was dark enough we began what turned out to be a long night march to get into position to go through the Siegfried Line the next day. We were not informed as to where we were going or why. But it was a clear night, and we could tell by the North Star that we were moving north. Late that night we reached our objective and stopped in still another orchard to sleep. Before we had a chance to dig in an enemy plane droned over and dropped a flare. Kennedy and I froze in position and held our breaths. The plane strafed and dropped some butterfly bombs, which wounded a couple of men.

Someone in our mortar section spoke a little Dutch and succeeded in getting permission for us to sleep in the basement of a nearby farm house. The owners didn't think it was right that we should bed down in the basement — they had better quarters upstairs — but we assured them that we had a great love for basements.

The next morning observers with field glasses reported two or three pillboxes to the east with brown-colored bodies spilled around them.

"Boy, it cost us plenty to get those pillboxes," one of the GIs remarked.

That afternoon we left the orchard and began a slow advance east along a dirt road leading to Ubach. As we passed the machine gun section I saw a familiar face that had been missing for more than two months. It was Barth, who had been wounded in the back on July 16 in the hedgerow fighting. He was very glum. He said his back still bothered him and that he didn't "have any business being in the infantry."

In Ubach we saw the horrifying evidence of a terrible battle. The buildings were more severely damaged than any we had previously seen, and the corpses lying about were badly shattered. All that remained of one man were his dust-covered hips and legs.

136

About 300 yards south of Ubach our company settled in a flat field, spotted with haycocks and containing two captured pillboxes. We arrived at dusk just as an enemy observation plane flew over and drew ack-ack fire from our guns. The enemy flier had a good look at our troops scattered about the field.

The pillboxes were quickly occupied as command posts and the rest of us dug holes around them and in the hayfield. A body removing detail cleaned up a depressing total of twelve dead Americans on the west side of the pillboxes.

After I had made a slit trench, I moved a haycock near it with the idea of pulling it over the hole as a disguise when I went to sleep. I soon was forced to use my camouflage, for enemy planes appeared, dropped flares and began strafing and bombing us. Some ran into the shelter of the pillboxes, but it was too far and too late for me to reach their protection. I sweated out the air attack with my head as close to the bottom of the hole as I could get it.

Since our rations had not arrived and I was starving, I had earlier eaten my emergency ration, the D Bar. This was a large solid piece of chocolate, and I made the mistake of eating the whole bar. The dismal consequences of such uncontrolled greed for chocolate became apparent during the air raid. My shorts were soiled, no doubt about it.

Fortunately, I carried extra shorts and socks in my gas mask container. But I realized with disgust that in order to change I would have to strip nearly all of my clothes off. I first removed the gas mask container, then my ammo belt and field jacket. Next I had to unlace my leggings and remove my shoes before I could take off my pants. This done I was able to gingerly slip off the shorts and bury them. Now, almost naked and drawing the curious gaze and unkind remarks of my fellow soldiers, I began to put my wardrobe back together. The leggings were the most time consuming and troublesome. I had barely finished my toilet when another air raid caused me to plunge into my hole and draw the haycock over me again. Despite more bullets and bombs, I managed to stay clean this time.

The next morning Kennedy came to me with the intelligence that we were going to attack again.

"How do you know?" I asked.

"Well, I practically stood guard at one of the pillboxes last night, and the Captain called the officers in for a conference," Kennedy said. "I heard them discussing objectives."

He was right. October 8 was our first battle on German soil, and it was a long day.

Germany,
The Cesspool
October 8 through November 1, 1944

At about 8:30 a.m. we shouldered our equipment and began to move southward in an attack which was to take us along the axis of the Siegfried Line.

I passed Lt. Hunn while a rifleman was talking to him in pleading tones: "I'm not tryin' to get out of going in the attack. But I'm sick. I was sick all night. I ain't in no shape to attack. I'm not trying to get out of goin' though. If you say so, I'll go."

The lieutenant looked at the rifleman carefully a moment, then said, "O.K., go back and join the kitchen until you feel better."

This part of Germany was mining country, even more so than in the Netherlands. Consequently, it was heavily built up with brick homes, mining structures, and huge slag piles. These piles towered over the area and provided excellent observation points for the enemy. Water towers were used, too. Our artillery and tanks fired at these points frequently to make them untenable.

We walked down a railroad which was flanked on one side by large mounds of earth, or old slag piles which had grown over with grass. We flushed out several groups of German soldiers who quickly surrendered. German civilians, quiet and sullen, watched us outside their air raid shelters.

Leaving the railroad, we sneaked around a group of brick houses and came out at the top of a bare hill which sloped gently toward Zopp, a little town about 500 yards away.

Suddenly a light tank on our left began to draw enemy artillery rounds. There was a slag pile directly in front of us and to the rear of Zopp. An observer on the pile could have counted us and reported whether we had brushed our teeth this morning. The shells, apparently fired from but one 88 gun, fell to the front and left of us about 150 to 200 yards. We could hear the report of the gun and the whistle of the shell and then see the explosion and the upthrust of earth, accompanied by the singing of the metal fragments.

Our troops had to advance toward the artillery bursts, but they were glad to do so in this case, for a scant fifty yards ahead was a group of air raid bunkers. Some men dived into them. Others dropped on the ground behind them. By the time I got to the bunkers, the column was moving to the right into a housing development. Here we stopped in the shelter of the houses and some began to dig holes in an orchard anticipating a long wait.

But we soon resumed the attack. Now the terrain dropped off sharply into a heavily wooded valley which was damp and chilly. On a road completely covered by large trees closely spaced, we came upon a platoon of Germans still in their holes. As our lead riflemen approached, they popped up from the ground and surrendered. Many were in camouflage suits. Most seemed well into their forties. At the end of the road, our mortar squad was ordered to set up its weapon in a farm complex partially up the side of a hill. After the mortar had been established behind a shed, we reconnoitered the adjacent barn and farmhouse.

The four or five persons living in the house provided our first contact with German civilians. We had been ordered not to fraternize with Germans, but we had to converse with them some to search the house and determine if there were any Jerries around. The occupants said that there had been three German soldiers in their basement last night, but that they had left. We learned this through a ten-year-old boy who had studied English at school.

The kitchen range was fired up, so we put our K-ration cans and coffee water on the stove to heat and enjoyed a well-prepared hot lunch. In the meantime, Kennedy was amusing himself by convincing the lady of the house, who looked something like the mama in the Katzenjammer Kids, that she had nothing to fear from the Americans.

"Eisenhower ist Deutsch. Spaatz ist Deutsch. Ach! Roosevelt ist Deutsch," Kennedy told her. He became quite popular with mama and others in the family. They were very much interested in the contents of our K-ration boxes, and it pleased them when we gave gum to the children.

Meanwhile, heavy German shelling was hitting the area we had recently passed through. Most of it was skimming the tops of the trees and smashing onto the hillside. The concussion could be felt in the buildings. Despite this shelling, the grandfather of the family, a man who must have been in his 70s, dropped the book he was reading and went into the orchard in the direction of the shelling to gather apples. When he had enough, he brought them inside and presented them to us, after which he returned to his reading as though he had done his duty and could now forget us.

At midafternoon, the ten-year-old boy called our attention to a cloud of black smoke on a hill to the south of us. It was one of our tanks burning. We didn't know what to make of it. Sgt. Proffitt tried to contact the rifle platoon we were supposed to be supporting and found that it had disappeared.

"Fine," said Kennedy. "Now we can stay here indefinitely. We're lost."

Sgt. Proffitt, however, was angry and disturbed that the rifle platoon leader hadn't notified him, and he set out immediately to learn where Company B had gone. After a bit he came back and told us to pack up, that we were going to the hill where the tank was burning.

So the five of us said farewell to the German civilians and marched back into the war.

Our column of five men, led by the sergeant, returned to the canopied road, crossed it, and set out over open ground toward the base of the hill with the burning tank on it. To our left, a cannon company crew was firing its artillery piece to the east. The noise was deafening.

The field we crossed was peppered with small, shallow shell holes, indicating a recent mortar barrage and suggesting that it could happen again before we cleared this exposed terrain. But it didn't, and we began to climb the hill. Near the top the land was terraced. We scrambled over two terraces and at the last one came upon a group of riflemen.

"What's happened?" we asked.

"A Jerry anti-tank gun just knocked out two of our tanks," was the reply.

I peered over the terrace edge and saw that one of the tanks, although it had been hit, had not caught fire. The crew had backed it down the hill to a defilade position. The motor was still running. The burning tank could not be seen from our position.

Someone noticed troops moving on a hill about a mile to the north. The soldiers were visible as they walked in single file past a break in the trees on the crest of the hill.

One of our men turned a pair of field glasses on them. After some study he reported: "Those poor guys are so loaded down with equipment they couldn't be anything else but American GIs." We turned our attention to the front again.

After a few more minutes of waiting, Sgt. Proffitt had us scale the last terrace to pass behind the tank and into an orchard adjoining a farm-house on the left. We picked our way through a tangle of fallen branches, around large shell holes and neat German V-trenches, and into a garden. On the other side of a bordering wire fence was a small, winding dirt road with an orchard on the other side. In the dirt road, lying flat on the ground, were troops of Company B.

"Get down, you guys. They's a machine gun firing over here."

We quickly scrambled through or over the fence and prostrated our-selves in the dirt road.

As I listened to the occasional bursts of the enemy machine gun coming from the orchard to the south, I marveled at how quickly we had changed from a peaceful and happy situation at the farmhouse in the valley to a machine-gunned road, all in a matter of a few minutes.

While we were prone, Lt. Jack Grimshaw, whom I hadn't seen since

Mortain days, walked by us very erect and nonchalant.

"Watch out for that Jerry machine gun, Jack," someone warned.

Jack approached the garden gate, opened it, and was about to step through when a prolonged burst of enemy fire enveloped him. Jack had an astonished look on his face as the tracers created a random pattern about his body. I expected him to fall dead on the spot. But, through a miracle, none of the bullets hit him. He darted through the garden after a backward glance and a puzzled frown in the direction of the firing.

We remained in the road for a spell before being ordered to return to the orchard in back of the farmhouse. We were to set up our weapon and make our quarters here for the night. We were delighted, for Jerry had very obligingly dug us deep V-trenches which we could easily convert for our use. We needed only to add tops to make them complete.

The V-trench consisted of two slit trenches coming together at a point. They were deeper than the shallow diggings we were able to excavate with the entrenching tool, and the sides were neatly squared off. The Jerries obviously had more time and better tools than we did in creating such professional holes. All of this admirable work had been done to defend Reifeld, a very small hamlet of which our farmhouse was a part.

The other mortar squad had distinguished itself during the day by setting up in the courtyard of the farm complex and dropping a direct hit into an enemy trench to knock out a machine gun. This accurate round had broken the back of enemy resistance forcing other Germans in the sector to retreat to the safety of a pillbox where they were later surrounded and captured. By contrast, our mortar squad had got itself lost and accomplished nothing. However, we did not begrudge the other squad its glory.

The next morning, October 9, we found that the Germans had pulled back. Accordingly, our riflemen began to probe for the new defense line. We climbed fences, skirted houses, entered one house for a time, passed the entrance to a mine, crossed more roads and open fields, and came to a stop at a railroad embankment. Here our troops were setting up a defense line. The Germans had armor in Birk, a little crossroads village on the outskirts of a large town called Bardenberg, and our boys were meeting stiff resistance.

We sneaked across the open field, which was under observation from a church steeple in Bardenberg, and dug holes in the soft ground of a plowed field about five yards behind the embankment. Both of our mortars were ordered to fire at Birk. We got off about three rounds from each gun before the Jerries decided that that was a lot of nonsense and directed tank fire at us. One shell grazed the top of the bank and sent up a cloud of yellow dust. Our mortars stopped firing, for our observers had to peer over the bank to direct our range and could not continue without danger of having their heads blown off.

Shortly after this action, an American tank began to maneuver into position in an orchard to the rear of the open field behind us. The roar of its motor caught the attention of the armor in Birk and direct tank fire was aimed in its vicinity. These rounds skimmed over the edge of the bank. One hit in the middle of the field, threw up a cloud of dust, and caromed into the distance with the peculiar noise that an armor-piercing shell going end-over-end makes.

Small arms and mortar action took place at an overpass where the tracks spanned a small road. Soon Skeeter, our Mexican-American runner, came trotting by, holding a wounded hand. This was his second Purple Heart and better than the first since it knocked him out of the war. We joshed him about his good fortune.

Where the time went, I didn't know, for it was getting dusk. We were ordered to backtrack with the intention of approaching Bardenberg from another direction. As we walked in single file across open terrain, our heavy machine guns began to fire at Birk. Almost immediately the Germans returned this fire with machine guns and 20mm anti-aircraft shells in the direction of Bardenberg, where Company A was attacking.

The conflict was intensified as a German counterattack on Bardenberg went into high gear. As we approached this city, we became aware that the Germans were shooting at us, too, for the air began to buzz and crack with bullets.

While our column clumsily double-timed toward the protection of a small road with a ditch running beside it, I was curious about the use of enemy anti-aircraft fire against our infantry. The shells were exploding about 1,000 yards away over Bardenberg and the growing dusk served to give the firing a Fourth of July effect in white. The elevation of the guns was low, but when the trajectory had reached the height of a high power line between us and the enemy, it would appear to glance downward as though ricocheting off an object in the sky.

My interest in this evening illusion was cooled in the next few seconds as the intensity of the bullets flying about increased. When the column stopped moving on the road, I and others dropped into the shallow ditch for protection. I was tired and, not knowing how long we would be halted, I shouted ahead to Kennedy to wake me up when we moved on again.

I didn't sleep, but I didn't want to be left in case I did doze off. Someone ahead of us must have fallen asleep, however, for the chain of troops was broken, and in a minute or so Rish called back: "Where did they go?"

"Weren't you watching?" I shouted at Rish.

"I told 'em to let me know when they pulled out," Rish replied.

"They probably went on into Bardenberg," someone said. "Keep going. We can't stay here." Bardenberg was about 500 yards ahead where all the action was.

The fact was that the rifle platoon we had been following had turned back to seek the protection of a small housing development about 100 yards distant. Behind us was another platoon of riflemen who also wanted to keep moving.

"Let's go!" Rish and Kennedy shouted as they jumped up to dash toward Bardenberg where we thought our troops had gone.

I struggled up from the ditch and as I did so a bullet passed within an inch or so of my head, causing me to hunch my shoulders, put on a sprint, and hope that another bullet wouldn't hit its mark.

The other men must have felt as I did, for they were running as fast as their heavily loaded bodies would permit. We came to a main road skirting Bardenberg on the south and leading east to Birk where the heavy fighting was taking place. The road was alive with bullets and tracers, but we ran through them to reach the shelter of the first brick building in the city.

Silver, one of our ammo bearers, fell down while crossing the road. Sgt. Bahylle, of the rifle platoon behind us, raced to the fallen man, scooped him up with one arm, and assisted him to safety.

Kennedy and I entered the rear door of one of the houses. We found the basement entrance from which came a faint light. In the cellar was an

ABOVE — The Cesspool revisited in 1962 was repaired and cleaned up. This photo was taken through the gateway looking into the courtyard. The manure pile, which was in the center, had been removed and the area paved over.

old man and a young girl huddled around a candle. When we appeared, the old man got up and offered a chair for one of us to sit on. We didn't stay. We were looking for the rest of our Company.

Lt. Franklin of another Battalion came from somewhere. He, too, was lost in the growing darkness. However, he found a telephone line in the garden behind the buildings, and we followed the wire, knowing that it would lead us to some sort of headquarters. We ended in the center of the city at a large hospital, loaded with German civilians.

The 119th Regiment had headquarters in the city. This unit had been the object of the German counteroffensive, which had started at the same time as our attack on Birk. Casualties were heavy in Company A, which had been in the lead, and now many of us who were supporting them were lost from our Company.

The local commanders were happy to have us to help blunt the German offensive, so we were assigned a defensive sector. Our mortar squads were glad to get a house with a cellar. Our guards were posted, and the rest of us made ourselves comfortable with an old quilt or two thrown over the floor for bedding. Groping about in the darkness I discovered a can of cherries on a shelf. I sweetened the tart cherries with sugar from two small boxes I had been saving and wolfed down the entire contents in no time.

We were beginning to feel at home, when one of the men called down the stairway: "Get your equipment together quick if you want to live. The Germans are sneaking up with tanks."

There was much cursing and fuming as we fumbled about in the pitch black to roll up blankets and find our weapons and equipment.

Jake Haglebarger refused to get excited: "Nuts," he said. "I've heard that so many times. Let the Germans get me!"

Outside, we heard a tank roaring about, but it turned out to be our own. The panic was over and we were about to return to our cellar, but then Lt. Hunn showed up.

"Come on you guys," he said. "I'm taking you back to Company B." The lost were to be reclaimed.

We marched through the night over the same route we had taken in the daytime, but now all was quiet. We reached a shed at the mine by the railroad track, and there we were permitted to end our day with merciful sleep, which was not to be denied even though we knew the war would start over again in the morning.

In the wee hours of October 10, our troops caught the Jerries napping at Birk by silently slipping up on them under cover of fog and darkness while most of them were sleeping. We got about fifty prisoners, who looked as dog-tired and ragged as we did and who probably thought it was a terrible time of day for combat. Or perhaps they thought that two days of hard fighting to fend us off was enough. Anyway, we didn't fire a shot and neither did they. Jerry always quit when we were close enough to use bayonets, which was the main reason for getting rid of them. Neither side was bayonet-bitter.

The fog had lifted and daylight returned when our mortar platoon joined the lead riflemen and machine gunners. The day was to be another cloudy and bleak one. The trees and shrubs hadn't fired up with color, and never would, we later noted.

We crossed a solidly-built stone bridge with a water-filled moat on each side and entered a massive rectangle of stone and brick farm buildings. Near the center of the cobblestoned quad was a huge manure pile, contained by a cement curb. It had the rich not unpleasant smell of fertility. Still, it was manure and it was to be a symbol of the quality of life for us for more than thirty days in the hottest spot we had ever held during the war. (Being bombed by our own planes in Normandy was bad, but it lasted only minutes and it wasn't done by the enemy.)

Our Company was involved in the capture of Aachen, but our ant-like view didn't give us much of the big picture. As it turned out, the complex of farm buildings was called Pfaffenholz, which was only a few yards from Birk, an important road junction on high ground. Birk, as previously mentioned, was a suburb of Bardenberg, now in our hands. For us it was a confusion of names, with farms and settlements seeming to run together. The upshot was that we were astride the main highway connecting Altdorf and Aachen and were facing Euchen, a village which lay about 900 very flat yards to the east. In subsequent days on guard duty, I got sick of looking at that ominously open ground and picturing the heavy price we would pay to cross it.

On this morning, however, we were a complacent bunch enjoying the prospect of a comfortable and secure stay. The buildings were like a fort. They would protect us. The hay in the barn would warm and comfort us, and the tree "killers" would be heavenly sanctuaries from the perils and inconveniences of ugly war.

Our squad clanked across the courtyard and through the hay barn, another substantial structure. On the other side was a garden area that had been mostly harvested. The Krauts tried not to leave many goodies behind. Beyond the garden was another ditch, a dry moat adjacent to the highway. A German self-propelled gun had been abandoned in the ditch. In the days that followed we climbed over it constantly to bridge the moat. On the other side of the brick road and throughout this area were a number of V-trenches near a well-fortified ack-ack gun emplacement. We took over this strong point, and all guns were then aimed in the opposite direction.

Deciding to set up our two mortars in the garden so that they could fire over the trees lining the highway, we then proceeded to dig holes in the soft earth. It was good soil for a garden, rich and loamy, but it didn't make for a firm foxhole as the sides caved in easily. I fashioned one that would serve and covered it by placing a metal wheelbarrow upside down over it. I also got some hay and upholstered my new home.

At this point, for the first time in my hectic association with the 30th Division, I heard the long hissing sound of a very heavy round from a big German mortar, or perhaps a railroad gun. I had the impression that if I had looked up in time I might have seen a barrel-like object lazily soaring over our heads. Several rounds hissed over. None were accompanied by the report of the weapon firing it. Hence, the conclusion that they came from a big mortar, or a miles-distant railroad gun. The rounds cleared our buildings and fell in an orchard behind us where our 81mm mortars were set up. So it wasn't going to be so peaceful after all. Did Jerry have us where he wanted us?

I huddled under my wheelbarrow, but Kennedy wandered about by the highway, perhaps confident that the shells were all going to pass us by. If so, he was wrong. One did crash in the highway trees, creating a truly terrific concussion and showering us with metal, bits of wood, and a confetti of leaves.

Kennedy returned dazed and staggering somewhat, but otherwise unharmed. "Jeez! That was a close one!" he said, blinking his eyes as though trying to come back to his senses.

After this alarming flurry, our squad leaders decided that our holes would not be sufficient cover. To their dismay and ours, they discovered that Captain Pulver had taken over one basement as his CP for Company B, and that two other kellers which joined each other were occupied by Company D, the heavy weapons men. It was like musical chairs.

We settled for a small room off the horse stables. A hay loft and the clay shingles of the roof would give some protection. The place was warm and dry, and there was just enough room for all of us to bed down. Here we spent the night taking our usual turns at guard. During my stretch, an enemy plane droned over and dropped flares to the southeast. They also dropped a few bombs, calling cards to tell us we weren't welcome in our new neighborhood. Meanwhile, our artillery hammered out occasional barrages to discourage prowling patrols.

On the second morning in this location, October 12, the Germans launched a heavy counterattack with tanks and infantry a few hundred yards to the south of us, mostly at the sector held by Company A. Some heroic work by artillery observers who stuck to exposed observation posts to bring down effective concentrations of artillery helped greatly in avoiding a breach of our lines. The enemy left eight disabled tanks on the field.

Although on the periphery of this action, we got a share of the German barrages. I was in a V-trench near the highway in an orchard adjacent to our farm buildings. One of our tanks was about thirty yards behind me. As it fired to help repulse the enemy, it drew several rounds of armor-piercing shells, forcing me to dive into my hole. The shells missed their mark, but they made the ground shudder as they buried themselves in the earth. I got an attack of vigorous gum chewing, so much so that one of my gold inlays came out.

The next morning we were awakened early by some mortar rounds crashing into the roof over our stables and setting the hay on fire. Loath to see our quarters burn down, we quickly organized a bucket brigade from the moat and succeeded in putting the blaze out. Company D personnel, who had been holding the two basements and kicking out anyone who dared seek shelter with them, decided prematurely that the whole place was going up in flames. They didn't want to fry. They panicked and fled, and we gleefully filled the vacancy. We now had found our "home."

The cellars, constructed with low arched ceilings, each had a small window, but these were blocked with material to keep flying shell fragments out. A small shaft of light was permitted to avoid total darkness. About eighteen to twenty men could lie down in the basement in which I lived. Each prone position was owned by someone and carefully guarded. Two or three spots were on a rather flattened pile of apples, a rough bed, but, then, soldiers can sleep anywhere.

At night we burned candles and enjoyed a social hour. It was a rarity in war for a large group of men to get to know each other. Many were newcomers, replacements who caused me to lose my rank as the oldest man in the outfit. I was thirty, but a replacement known as Texas, who was later chided for noisily grinding his teeth while sleeping, was thirty-eight. Others were not that old, but mature enough to show us that America was getting to the bottom of the Selective Service barrel.

A man by the name of Silver wore glasses. I hadn't seen that since early Normandy days. Another GI of Portuguese descent was the butt of pretended envy because he was so well hung. "Are you guys from Portugal all like that?" he was asked. "We pretty good," he grinned in his somewhat fractured English.

The men swapped stories of narrow escapes, a favorite source of humor among combat troops. They also discussed home and girl friends, or estranged wives, and we eventually got into politics since we were to be allowed to vote by absentee ballot in the Presidential election. Kennedy and I were the only ones in favor of Dewey. Kennedy was fervently anti-FDR.

No one questioned why we were there, living like sewer rats and putting our lives on the line every day. Nor did I observe anyone offering prayers, or making special deals with the Deity. It was a time of trust in each other, our officers, our government, our country, the people back home, and silently, without ostentation, in God.

A bit of culture also permeated our keller. I recited some poetry to offset the bawdy offerings of others. One that became an immediate hit with my next door bedmate from New York City was A.E. Housman's "When I Was One-and-Twenty." He identified with the sentiment, and he made me repeat it every night. Finally, he, too, memorized it.

To my astonishment, when I dared to sing some popular songs, the men became quiet and let me be solo entertainment. Apparently my tenor range and soft crooning style suited them, for it became ritual as night after night passed in this basement for me to sing the "taps," as it were. When the evening's conversation had dwindled and sleepy time was upon us, I was asked to sing "Just a Gigolo." Why was this number popular? Certainly not for the words, nor the sad plight of the gigolo. They liked the melody, its plaintive tone, and its back-home feeling, I suppose. I was able to give the song a pure and lilting tonal quality as well as a somnolent nostalgic mood that helped them sleep.

Our idyllic evenings were not matched by the days. The weather grew colder and wetter. The shelling became constant and unpredictable, so much so that we started calling the place Club 88. Later, as the heavy stuff from afar continued to cause havoc, we changed the name to The 240 Club. Men were being torn asunder — legs and arms blown off, or killed as they stood outside, or crossed the quad. Our kitchen crew members always had a terrified look on their faces when they drove the chow jeep into our yard. Often they were shelled as they approached from the rear. Once inside our rectangle they dashed to unload as soon as possible and they always served us inside. One day, Lt. Jack Grimshaw, long-time platoon leader dating from Mortain days, caught some shrapnel in his chest while standing in the kitchen doorway. He died later in the hospital.

The sudden hellish shriek and blast of a shell that streaks in and explodes a safe distance away can instill abject and cowering fear. But when a blast is near enough to cause casualties the survivors can be stunned by the concussion and shaken to their roots. Some, but not as many as might be expected, simply go to pieces, hopefully temporarily.

The unpredictable shelling at Pfaffenholz generated pessimism and fear we had not known before. The dark mood was reinforced by the bleak weather and our increasingly limited freedom of movement. We burrowed deeper. The floor boards in the dining room, for example, were torn up so that a hole could be dug in the ground below. Guards on the perimeter of the open ground to the east could only be changed after dark. Since the men were forced to stay in their holes all day, they found a new use for the K-ration box. They urinated in them and dumped the contents outside. This box, which contained breakfasts, lunches, and dinners in concentrated form, was heavily coated with wax. When torn into small pieces and burned, the box provided just enough heat to warm a canteen cup of water for instant coffee, cocoa, or bouillon. Lemonade could be made with cold water, but most GIs didn't like this drink. The lemonade packets were strewn on the ground all the way from St. Lo to the Elbe River. The natives picked them up and thought they were very tasty.

Some men preferred the south side of the house to the courtyard, which appeared to be an enemy aiming point. But these men did not take time to cover their leavings. Eventually, Capt. Pulver ordered a detail, including me, to go into the exposed area and clean up the mess. It was shortly after this distasteful episode that we began calling the place The Cesspool.

One day — about the middle of October — we received word that mortarmen would take turns with the machine gunners in standing guard in the front-line holes on the east side of the highway. We didn't like this decision one bit. Our mortars were still set up in the garden in front of the hay barn. While on sentry duty, we stood under cover in the barn on the ready to man our weapons if necessary.

I and another man were assigned a spell of guard duty at one of the frontline machine guns. It was a long and tedious stretch. As I stood in the darkness seeing nothing and hearing nothing, I began thinking of the recent past, the glory days in Normandy, northern France, Belgium, and Holland. It had been hard fighting in Normandy, but after that the war had seemed won. Church bells pealed in each village as we approached. Natives handed out apples, cidre, even champagne, and sometimes cheese and meat.

"Alles kaput" was the cry. The enemy had been on the run and we were chasing him. But how different it was now. Not only were we at a standstill, but even German shelling was more intense, as though the enemy was showing his wares for the first time. German civilians were not glad to see us. They stood silent and glum as we passed. We had thought Jerry was whipped, but he most certainly was not. It was a depressing time. How much longer could a veteran expect his luck to hold? The Army would indeed move again, and the only way to move was forward, across the murderous-looking open ground facing Euchen, deeper and deeper into the unknown and dark fortress of Germany.

As the time for our guard relief approached — just before dawn — we became concerned that the new men were five minutes late. We became irritated when fifteen minutes had elapsed and still no one was in sight.

"Let's give them a half hour and then find out what's wrong," I said. "We could get stuck out here all day."

The darkness was beginning to recede. Where little had been visible to the front before, we could now see shadowy shapes of buildings in Euchen, even the church spire. Still no one appeared. Forty-five minutes late now!

"Let's go," I said disgustedly. The other man demurred. "Gosh, I don't know," he said.

"I know the sergeant in charge of this machine gun squad," I explained. "He has a terrible time waking up. One time in Normandy I tried to get him up to take my place and he came out of his hole swinging at me and dropped right back into it. He was so drugged with sleep he didn't know what he was doing. He never did get up for guard duty. I'll go. He's probably so far gone he'll never wake up."

I clambered out of the hole, crossed the highway, and started climbing over the derelict German armored vehicle. Suddenly out of the gloom came a snarly command: "Get back to your post! Where the hell you think you're going!"

It was Sgt. Gibson arriving with our relief at last.

"Where the hell you been! You're an hour late!" I countered, as I ignored his order and returned to my basement bed.

The next day I heard that I was going to be reported for insubordination and leaving a guard post. I didn't doubt it.

"What a way to end my fabulous career in the Army," I said to Kennedy. "The Army is going to do what the enemy couldn't. I'm going to be shot as a deserter."

"Those machine gunners are unhappy with all of us," Kennedy said. "They think we've got it too easy, and that they're doing all the dirty work."

I had to admit they were right. I had been in a machine gun squad too long not to know that it was much harder duty than the mortarmen experienced. Still, I had done my stint, especially back in those hedgerow days, I reasoned, knowing that even that could not save me from the Army's need to maintain discipline.

Two days later I got my special summons to go to headquarters.

"Parker," the sergeant said, "we're sending you back to Valkenberg for a three-day rest."

"How come?" I stupidly responded, being unable to adjust to such lenient treatment.

"You've got over 100 days of front-line time. Other guys are going to Paris. But they've got more combat time than you." He seemed to be apologizing.

As a July 14 replacement, I couldn't equal the combat days of the original troops, but apparently I was the only man to qualify for second best in our unit.

What happened to my court martial? I didn't dare ask.

At Valkenberg, the Army, USO and Red Cross had collaborated to set up an Army Recreation Center. We got a glimpse of girls again, but they weren't for us. American girls were in Army or Red Cross uniforms, and the Dutch girls had learned how to avoid GIs. During my three days there, I was amused at the effort to get us to relax and sleep at night. At bedcheck, an Army nurse would drop by with sleeping pills and a cup of water. She would watch to make sure we swallowed them. I complained that I didn't need the pills, that I was an accomplished sleeper, but it was Army regulation. I presume they believed we would have nightmares about combat experiences, or would be too tense to unwind.

Eating was my greatest pleasure during this stay. We were served family style in the hotel dining room. After the others had left the table, I cleaned up the leftovers in the serving dishes. I couldn't explain the sudden insatiable desire for food, for I had felt no pangs of hunger while existing on the concentrated energy intake from K and C-rations at The Cesspool.

My roommate, a first scout with a rifle platoon, said he had spotted a bakery a short distance from our hotel. He suggested we share a pie. Together we entered the shop to be greeted by a young Dutch girl who asked if we had ration stamps. We said that we did not, but that we had cigarettes. A package of smokes was accepted, and we had an apple pie. We left the bakery and began eating as we walked down the street. At the first bite, we knew what was wrong with it. There was no sugar. All the same, we ate it ravenously.

I knew that my friend had a highly dangerous job as lead scout. He talked about it one day. "I kind of like it," he said. When he saw disbelief on my face, he explained: "Well, you may be out in front that's for sure and you may be trying to draw fire to see where the enemy is, but, you know, that fire is usually small arms stuff, and the Krauts aren't very good shots. Meanwhile, they start throwing artillery and mortars, but not at the lead scout because he's not a big enough target. All that stuff goes over my head to the rear where most of the troops are. Besides, the minute you draw small arms fire, you hit the ground or find cover somewhere, and you aren't the target you were before. Yeah, I like it. I think I know how to do it now. I'd like to stick with it."

After the three days were up, I never saw this man again. One was always making an acquaintance in the Army and then realizing some time later that you are still here and the acquaintance is gone for any number of causes that warfare provides.

We spent our time wandering around the small city, climbing an ancient tower once visited by Napoleon, attending movies in the evenings, and quaffing a drink or two in a local tavern. I even made an appointment with an Army dentist to get my tooth fixed. He refused to replace the gold inlay, but he did put in an amalgam which would last until I could find a better time and place to have a substantial job done.

The morning we were loaded into trucks preparatory to returning to the front, the owner of the hotel and his daughter showed European hospitality and manners by remaining outdoors in the chilly air to wave us farewell.

"Come back again," the hotel owner said. His business in the past had been to some extent with English resorters. Most of the Dutch could speak English. It was a required subject in their high schools. Over all, the Dutch proved to be the most hospitable of all the peoples whose countries we fought through.

I rejoined my outfit, which by then was in a housing development in the rear of the front lines. Our Division was being relieved for a few days by a new Division which had been sent forward to get a taste of shellfire in our defense line. I noticed that the rifle platoons in our Division were practicing advances in spread formations across open ground.

While gazing out the window of one of these shattered and looted houses, I saw a soldier who had come over on the boat in the same replacement package with me. He was riding a bicycle he had found somewhere. He told me that he had been hit once and had just recently returned. What had happened to the many other faces I had not seen for so long? It was dawning on me that I was the only one remaining of the original replacement group sent to Company B on July 14.

The next day we returned to our basements in the farmhouse near Birk to begin again the front-line life. While moving in we encountered the troops being relieved as they trudged to the rear. Much banter was aimed their way: "How did you like being in the real Army? How come your uniforms got all dirty?"

The following morning — I think it was October 30 — I was dozing in a corner of our dungeon, trying to forget everything — the peace and contentment of life in the rear as well as the dreary fearsome future. My nirvana state was interrupted by a call to report to Company headquarters. There the 1st sergeant told me I was to go back to 1st Battalion headquarters. Here comes my court martial, I thought.

I didn't relish leaving the basement to venture into the shell-torn outdoors, but it must be done. I slogged through the mud, noting ravaged trees and holes full of water, as I walked to Battalion Rear, as it was called, about a half mile northwest of the front. Here I was interviewed by Tech Sgt. Speed. He said the Battalion wanted a man to write up combat and service awards for our men, and he had noticed from my personnel record that I had writing experience. Would I be interested?

Suppressing a whoop of joy, I replied that I would consider the offer a great opportunity. When did I start?

"Right now," Sgt. Speed said. "You better go back and get your gear and move in with us."

I hiked back to The Cesspool with something of a spring in my steps. I ran into the basement, gathered my equipment, and announced to those present that I was leaving and that I bequeathed my spot in the corner to Kennedy, who had lately been crowded out of the basement and was sleeping again in the horse barn.

I found Kennedy in the stables. He was sitting on a milk can reading a newspaper.

"No court martial, eh," he said after he learned of my good fortune. He called me a "lucky stiff" and wished me well. I warned that I might not make the grade and, in such event, would be back fairly soon.

"No," Kennedy said, "you'll never have to come back." He refused my offer of the basement sleeping spot. "This may be a horse barn, but it's healthier than that basement," he said, wryly looking overhead at the hole in the roof which allowed plenty of fresh air.

Kennedy was a free spirit. Later, after many of our medics were killed or wounded by our own planes bombing Malmedy while we held this city during the Battle of the Bulge, Kennedy volunteered to become a medic. In this role he earned several medals, something he couldn't have done as an under-orders ammo grunt in the mortar section.

I remember an incident during the wild truck wide across Germany to the Elbe. One April night the men had to sleep on the ground or in a nearby barn. The next morning Kennedy, bleary-eyed, unshaven and weary, was sitting on a truck tailgate eating his breakfast, a piece of cheese. A GI came up to him and in solemn tones said: "You know what's happened? Roosevelt just died!"

Kennedy took another bite of cheese and replied: "Tough shit!"

As I bade goodby to Kennedy I did so with mixed feelings of relief, sorrow, and anxiety. I hated to leave my friends at the front. I felt somehow that I was letting them down. Yet, I was relieved to be leaving the sink hole, the constant shelling, the dismal prospect of attacking Euchen. In fact, I was so relieved that I began to worry that some quirk of fate, so prevalent in war, might yet deprive me of the better life ahead. Nothing happened, however, as I hiked back to the Battalion CP, and I reached my new home without a shell to disturb my progress.

On November 16 I was sheltered in a farm building at the front waiting for the attack that I had dreaded and which my buddies could not avoid. Some of our planes bombed the enemy lines, and our artillery and mortars opened up. I knew that there was no substitute for sending in the infantry for another "nakedness of the battlefield" exposure. But I also knew that Major Ellis Williamson, commander of the 1st Battalion, had laid careful plans for this venture. He had talked to the men of the entire Battalion in the courtyard of the "monastery" rest area in Kerkrade several days earlier. He compared the 900 yards of terrain they were to cross to the flat, tarvia courtyard on which they stood. He said that several fake attacks showed that it took the enemy twelve to fifteen minutes to react with artillery and mortar fire. He asked the men: "Can you advance in a fast walk, not a run, over that 900 yards of ground within twelve minutes?"

Now our troops were to attack at 1:00 o'clock, or 1300 hours. Could they do it? The answer came as in a field-manual writer's dream. A constant pounding of enemy positions proceeded as the men rapidly walked under the umbrella of fire, while at the same time firing their weapons. The effect was to keep the Germans down in their holes, so that when the barrage was lifted at the precise moment our troops arrived at the enemy lines our GIs were looking down their throats. Euchen was quickly overrun, 164 prisoners were taken, and an enemy 75mm gun emplacement was overwhelmed after it had time to fire but two shots.

News of this astounding success spread quickly to the rear, and the elation was heartfelt, especially by me when I later looked up my friends to ask details for possible awards. Further pride in the operation came when it was learned that correspondents at higher headquarters described the action as the "Perfect Infantry Attack," which it was.

This breakout instilled high morale for the extensive fighting still ahead. These troops were destined to complete many successful night attacks in the Ruhr area heading for the Rhine crossing, and were to be labeled Roosevelt's Lightning SS Troops by German radio newscasters. The Battle of the Bulge was a cold and bloody interruption, after which the invasion of Germany continued to the banks of the Elbe River in Magdeburg, where on May 5 we formally shook hands with the Russians. The war was over.

Meanwhile, our Battalion Commander became Lt. Col. Williamson and he devised several more maneuvers to outwit the enemy in battle. I wrote him up for three of the five Silver Stars he earned. I also wrote the awards for men involved in heroic actions at Birk and The Cesspool. The investigation of the actions for these honors may have provided some of the basis for the Unit Citation given the 1st Battalion by the War Department for capturing and holding the ground at Birk from October 8-12, 1944.

In 1965, while an editor of a Michigan daily newspaper, the

Major General Ellis W. Williamson, commander of the first U.S. combat troops in Vietnam, formerly commanded the 1st Battalion, 30th Division, in WWII as a Lt. Col.

Traverse City Record-Eagle, I noticed a picture of my old boss coming on the transmitter. It was Col. Williamson, but now he was Brigadier General Williamson in command of the 173rd Airborne Brigade, the first combat troops introduced in Vietnam. His professionalism as a military leader had been graphically revealed on that November day in 1944 when he got our troops out of the depressing sinkhole of Pfaffenholz across what could have been a murderous killing ground, and into a new phase of movement and victory. The manure pile had been left behind never to be seen again, even by me when eighteen years later I visited the place and found the manure gone and the entire courtyard paved over. All of West Germany had been reborn by then — out of the odious cesspool of war into a new and prosperous era of sanity and peace.

ABOVE — After transfer from the front in November, 1944, to write awards and decorations with Special Service in Kerkrade, Holland. The author is kneeling at the extreme right. BELOW — On the way home at Camp Lucky Strike outside Paris, the author is shown with a friend, Lt. George Ennis of Rochester, Michigan.

The author is shown in this 1962 photo with Dr. Gilles Buisson, a Mortain physician who survived the battle, and who later became mayor of the village and wrote a book about the fighting there. The extended arm points to the place where a shell destroyed machine gun ammo carried by the author.

Epilogue

The war in Germany lasted until the Nazi capitulation May 8, 1945. The author served as awards and decorations non-com through those months (November through April), including the Battle of the Bulge interruption in Belgium.

He continued writing awards and some of the regimental history during occupation duty in Wernigerode in the Harz Mountains region and at Plauen, near the Czechoslovakian border.

Since the 30th Division was scheduled for the assault on Japan, it was moved in stages from Germany to Camp Lucky Strike outside Paris, and then from Le Havre to England, where, after a brief stay, (during which time the atomic bomb was dropped on Japan) units were put aboard the Queen Mary in August for shipment to the United States. The Japanese surrender was announced before the liner reached New York.

Meanwhile, the author had contracted infectious hepatitis and was hospitalized at New Brunswick, New Jersey. After his recovery, he was discharged from service, October 8, 1945, in Chicago, and sent to Detroit, where he had been inducted October 9, 1943 thus completing two years of military service to the day.

Additions to Second Edition

Why add the following three chapters? Because the opportunity came with the publication of this second edition of "Civilian at War."

Also it has become increasingly obvious since publication of the original book in 1984 that more of the author's experiences after being pulled from the front lines needed telling.

The author was in battalion rear, usually a few hundred yards behind the front, during the Battle of the Bulge as well as the Rhine river crossing and other engagements in Germany.

Later he had the thrill of revisiting old battle sites and finding some of them undisturbed by time. Also much later Company B, the author's rifle company, began holding reunions at which new information about what happened in various combat situations became available.

Finally, in Post War Talk the author finds a soap box upon which to vent his opinions.

Voila! Bon appetit!

Ken Parker
February, 2002

The Battalion Rear War

The first order given me at Battalion rear in my new job as awards and decorations non-com was startling. I was told to get a shower, a shave and some new clothes. I must have looked like one of Mauldin's cartoons. I rode in a jeep back to Spekholzerheide where I showered at one of the coal mines. The facility consisted of a large room with about 30 shower heads mounted in two overhead rows. It seemed primitive and public but it cleaned a lot of bodies at once. The new clothing included a fresh jacket to replace the filthy and torn old one.

Now presentable as a barracks-type soldier I was jeeped to regimental headquarters in Kerkrade and more specifically to the Special Service section. Here I met a group of men not only responsible for churning out recommendations for awards for the three infantry battalions that make up a regiment, but also soldiers who specialized as typists, historians, and even movie projectionists. A tall rather paternalistic Captain Jackson presided over this menage which lived and worked in a commandeered house in Kerkrade. I was assigned a second floor room where I slept on the floor.

At my first opportunity I typed a letter to my wife who was now living with my parents. I knew that receipt of a typed letter would astonish them, since my previous communications had been penciled scribblings on pieces of paper scavenged from wrecked houses or industrial sites. I also knew that the contents of the letter informing them of my deliverance, as it were, would give them the same joy and relief I was feeling. I learned later that it did, including whoops and hollers.

I was informed that the Division brass was concerned that its men were not being as recognized with awards as those in other infantry units. Writers were needed to interview candidates and witnesses right after an action so that prompt recommendations could be made and awards approved for the men while memories of the action were still vivid and witnesses still alive.

Each of the three battalions now had an awards man responsible for interviewing and writing. My battalion was the 1st, including men in companies A, B, C, and D, the latter our heavy weapons company. I got to know the officers and some of the non-coms fairly well in these units and since I was treated warmly and with respect by my superiors I began to take on a more understanding feeling toward them.

One day after lunch at a headquarter's kitchen, I was accosted on the street by two Dutch girls about 8 or 9 years old. Although underfed, they were vivacious and attractive. Poor nourishment brought out the delicate features in their faces and gave their eyes a mature look beyond their years.

Hands in fur muffs to protect against the early December cold, they happily joined me on the street giggling nervously as they hooked an arm on each side of me. One held up some coins. I said, "money, money, money." The musical sound of these words made a big hit. They laughed and repeated, "monee, monee, monee." They intended of course to exchange souvenirs. I could take the coins for my collection, and they would gladly accept a piece of chocolate or a cigarette as a token. But I had none to give. They skipped along with me for a block or so before giving up. Then they good-naturedly slapped me on the rump and shouted goodbye. They still were shrieking their farewell when they disappeared around a corner.

I returned to my "office" in the living room of our Dutch house. I felt good. There was no war for me. I liked my work. And Hitler's Germany was no longer a personal problem. Even while at the front, I hadn't thought of Germans as much different from us --guys suffering through the same

God-awful experience, but getting the worst of it.

There were some in our office, however, who still bore a cold hatred of Germany. The degree of animosity seemed to correlate with distance from the front. The best spokesman against the Germans was a bespectacled officer who served as regimental historian. He sat in a dingy corner smoking a pipe and recording the various actions. While the war was stagnant (the Battle of the Bulge was yet to come) he rapped with the rest of us at the end of the working day. I learned that this mild man had some ferocious opinions.

I had read about the proposed plans for post-war Germany advanced by a member of the Roosevelt administration. He wanted to turn Germany into an agricultural nation, virtually without industry or machinery with which to make war again. I also knew that the Allies would accept nothing less than unconditional surrender from the Germans. The criminal leaders were to have no rights of negotiation and, as it turned out, they were to be tried as war criminals if still alive.

Our historian, however, topped them all. He seriously advocated killing all Germans. He didn't seem to realize that his policy was even more monstrous than Hitler's death camps and other atrocities. But then this was just talk, a privilege that we were fighting for -- the right of free and ridiculous speech.

Then came the Battle of the Bulge, December 16, and all of us were suddenly thrust into a new kind of war, albeit for us from a comfortable distance.

I was abruptly switched from regimental headquarters to 1st Battalion headquarters for the night truck ride to the Ardennes. The carrier was canvas-covered and it was also a very dark night so we saw little of the terrain. Furthermore, we were told little about precisely where we were going.

Eventually we reached city streets on the outskirts of a center we later learned was Malmedy. We didn't stop there. We headed into the hills east and south of the city. Our final resting place was a stone and brick farmhouse in a small settlement called Arimont. I was assigned the kitchen area which had a wood-fired range and a table for my typewriter. I slept on the tiled floor.

When morning came, I saw a spectacularly beautiful scene. Farm buildings dotted the hillsides and smoke curled up from chimneys. Pristine white snow blanketed everything and hung in soft cotton billows from trees and shrubs. Carefully planted evergreens were everywhere running up the mountain sides, row on row. It did not seem possible that deadly combat was going on in this innocent looking terrain. No soldiers were visible on either side nor could one see any evidence of a defense line. Winter, with its snow and cold, had swallowed us. As we were to learn later the severe winter weather was to become a second enemy force. Movement was hampered by the depth of the snow, and minor wounds were to turn into amputations because of the below freezing cold.

We shared our new quarters with a grandfather figure who had remained behind while the remainder of the family sought a safer location. He seemed to be in his late 60s or early 70s. He spoke French and German, and admitted that he had served in the German army on the Russian front during World War I. However, he was a great rooter for the Americans this time. During our stay, he never failed to study the maps in our copies of the Stars and Stripes, the official GI newspaper.

The old man gave us our first word of the later-called Malmedy Massacre. He pantomimed "les Americains" with their hands in the air, and then created the sound of a machine gun while clutching his middle and pretending to fall forward. We got the idea. Later a New Year's eve patrol by Company B under the leadership of my old boss, Captain Murray Pulver, stumbled over the bodies, mostly snowcovered by then. They also captured a German sentinel who was asleep in his hole.

The actual location of the massacre was at Baugnez, a road junction with sparse population. We called it Five Points after the number of routes connected there. The site is now a tourist attraction with the names on an outdoor brick and cement wall of all the GIs killed there. An American flag flies over the memorial to further honor and mark the place.

It was while at the Belgian farmhouse that I first learned that Walter Paige's parents were trying to learn more about the circumstances of his death. I was sitting at my typewriter in the kitchen when Tom Mock, a sergeant in the mortar section of Company B, came out of Capt. Starling's office. I heard them talking about Walter Paige. Naturally I asked what was

ABOVE — The old man at Arimont, Belgium, whom I promised to look up sometime after the war. When I finally did in 1962 I learned that he had died. BELOW — The author is shown in 1962 enjoying a celebratory drink with the resident of the farm home which provided shelter during the Malmedy part of the Battle of the Bulge. The host, Jules Gabriel, told the author that the "old man," his father, had died a few years earlier.

up. They explained that Walter's parents had written, but so far they hadn't found anyone who knew him. Whereupon I volunteered that I had known him fairly well as a result of conversations in the kitchen area before we were fed into the front lines.

They turned the letter over to me and I wrote extensively of our visits, the significance of the actions he had been in, and his death at Tessy-sur-Vire on August 1. This started a correspondence that culminated a few years later with my visiting Walt's parents (with my family) in New Bedford, Massachusetts. Mr. Paige died a few years later. He was so taken with our then five-year-old- daughter Marilyn that he left a small bequest to her to help with her college education.

I had no bed while at the farmhouse. I slept on the tiled floor each night while the old man slept fitfully in a chair by the kitchen range which he tended during the night. He said he had a heart condition which forced him to sleep upright.

Unexpectedly, one day, I was loaned out to an armored battalion that needed help in writing up awards for its men. Since this was my specialty, I was dispatched via an open-air jeep to another part of the snow-covered Ardennes. I was provided space in still another farmhouse and had started work there when, lo, another order came down from on high: get ready to move out in ten minutes. The battalion was to make a night march to another defense sector.

I did not know where I was nor where I was going, and I was inadequately dressed for a lengthy open-air drive in freezing weather. Sympathy and aid, however, came from a young somewhat attractive Belgian miss who fetched a woolen Army scarf and draped it around my neck. How she got it, I didn't ask. However, I deduced that she had been somewhat friendly with the GIs from the banter I had heard previously between her and one of the men. He was bluntly asking for sexual favors to which she replied: "Good for you. Not good for me." Sensible girl.

Our new location, after a very frigid ride, was in another farmhouse, but not nearly as comfortably heated as the other. I was forced to sleep, not next to the stove in the downstairs area, but on an icy floor in an unheated bedroom.

That night was one of interminable agony, not so much for the hardness of the floor as for the impossibility of sleeping through the cold.

My body kept jerking awake, seeking new positions, and squeezing itself into a ball in the hope of finding warmth.

I marveled at the stamina of the men standing guard in the open foxholes. It was the longest night I ever endured, and also the shortest, since I beat the sun by several hours in returning to the downstairs heat-center. I wanted to get to work and get out of there.

I had several interviews, wrote up some awards and instructed my replacement, a former lawyer who had been handling courts-martial cases for the battalion.

While there I picked up a new army expletive, unique to this outfit, many of whom were from New York City. Men coming in from the cold would say, "Mink, but it's cold."

Massacre site is now a memorial at Baugnez, or Five Points, Belgium. Plaques on the wall record the names of all the victims.

Agreement could be expressed by simply saying "mink." The same word, given proper emphasis, expressed some sort of curse.

My deliverance from this location came when the colonel of my battalion discovered I was missing and ordered that I be returned immediately, to which I fervently said, "mink."

Christmas in the Ardennes was both beautiful and bleak. It's bleakness, of course, was provided by the Germans, who made a major mistake as it turned out in launching a winter offensive. Our side had to make some fast adjustments to stop the attack and suffered many casualties, some self-imflicted. All the same the enemy was the big loser in the end.

Although Malmedy was in our hands, our planes were sent to bomb it because of poor communications at Army headquarters. Four bombing raids were made in three days, beginning December 23 and continuing through Christmas Eve and Christmas Day. GI and civilian casualties were heavy. Men I had barely got to know at Special Services were killed. The projectionist was one. Medics, cooks, and bakers were wiped out. The need for medics was so severe afterward that appeals for volunteers from frontline personnel went out. My friend Warren Kennedy responded and spent the rest of the war as a medic, a decision he often regretted since tending the wounded often meant exposing himself to some of the fire that had felled his patients.

Frustration at being constantly hit by friendly aircraft resulted in one of our anti-aircraft units shooting down an American plane. After the pilot drifted down in his parachute, he was queried as to his mistake. He then showed the maps he had been issued indicating that our territory was in enemy hands. It was not until the Rhine river crossing that ground-to-air radio communication was finally established to avoid such tragedies in the future.

When Christmas Day dawned, American GIs at the front were living in holes in the ground, somehow surviving the cold and snow. Some GIs cut pine trees and decorated them with anti-radar foil that had been dropped by our planes.

I was grateful to be in the farmhouse at Arimont with the old Belgian farmer to tend our wood range and keep us warm. The old man was invited to help us eat a sumptuous turkey dinner served at our headquarters on Christmas Day. Men were brought in rotation from the forward foxholes to share in the feast. The old man stood in line with us for a liberal serving of turkey, mashed potatoes and gravy and other goodies.

Our Christmas good will was extended further through a suggestion from Lt. Col. Howard Greer, formerly captain of Co. B. He was now commander of the 2nd Battalion. He thought we should take up a collection of candy and other gifts for the youngsters in Children's Hospital, Malmedy, an unfortunate target of American bombings. A large cardboard box appeared at our farmhouse. It already contained quantities of candy, fruit, nuts, chewing gum and other items, some of which had come in Christmas packages from home. We added more from our riches.

Col. Greer acted as Santa, and the children got their gifts and the implied message of cheer from the men at the front. Thinking of others less fortunate than we helped wipe out the war for a day. The Christmas spirit was powerful enough to rise from the deep freeze of death and devastation.

The breakout from our positions toward Thirimont and other objectives aimed at trapping the enemy in the bulge began the morning of January 13 with a terrific shelling by our artillery. Some of the canons were located so close to our farmhouse as to crack the plaster in places.

The attacking units soon verified the Malmedy Massacre site which a Company B patrol had stumbled on January 1 in a night raid. The location on the map is called Baugnez, but we referred to it as Five Points, as previously noted. Our battalion executive officer described this spot as Five Points to Major General Leland S. Hobbs, our division commander, when he dropped in at our command post during the battle.

This visit came on either Jan. 14 or 15, and it was far from social. Our regiment was having extreme difficulties in seizing Thirimont. Gen. Hobbs rebuked the Major immediately by saying: "Five Points? I don't know what you're talking about. Be more explicit."

By Jan. 17, it was time to say goodbye to the old Belgian. I promised him that I would be back some day and I would look him up. (I kept the promise with a visit many years later, but by that time the old man was deceased.) I rode in an open jeep down the winding mountain road with its vistas of snow-covered hills and pine trees, and passed through Five Points on my way south to Thirimont.

At the massacre site, I saw a group of black troops, members of First Army graves registration, gathering up the remaining bodies. I gave the spot a good look, but as is usually the case it failed to match my preconceived "map" picture. It belongs now with many other previously little-known dots on the map which wars have made famous and even sanctified.

The battle for Thirimont was made extremely difficult by the deep snow and sub-zero temperature as well as the village's stone and brick houses which were spaced well apart from each other, thus creating a series of forts that were able to support each other with crossing machine gun and rifle fire, not to mention artillery and mortar barrages.

As stated before, wounds that would have been minor under normal conditions caused legs and arms to freeze due to loss of blood. Many wounded suffered amputations as a result. One young man in battalion rear had recently been promoted, at his request, to lieutenant to serve with a combat unit, namely Co. B. In his first battle at Thirimont he and his men succeeded in taking one of the heavily fortified houses, but the newly commissioned officer suffered an arm wound and eventually the loss of this limb.

I first saw these blackened houses, set afire by sulphur grenades, from a comfortable seat in a jeep. There were frozen corpses in the snow, most of them German. That night I slept in the basement of one of the captured houses.

After our battalion captured its final objective, Nieder Emmels, and the Bulge battle was nearly over, I visited the front to gather material for awards. There was so much to do that I was forced to stay overnight with men of Co. B in still another basement. Bodies were bedded down all over the floor, many of them being Belgian citizens. I suspected that some of the Belgian misses, in a generous and celebrative mood, had paired off with some of our GIs.

Later in the evening of the next day, I walked back to battalion rear headquarters located in another basement sanctuary. Before I got there, some army brass drove up in a jeep and asked if we were receiving much interdictory artillery fire. I said not much, and they motored on.

My new night quarters had been made especially comfortable by the spreading of hay across the floor. It was while I was arranging my bed for the night that I had a curious premonition of another man's death that became the subject for a column many years later in the Traverse City Record-Eagle. I prefaced it with a quote from "The Killer Angels" by Michael Shaara: "Freemantle had a sudden numbing thought: by evening this man could be dead. Freemantle stared at him transfixed, trying to sense a premonition. He had never had a premoniti;on, but he had heard of them happening, particularly on the battlefield. Men often knew..." the column reads as follows:

The sergeant handed me the letter from the parents.

"There's another camera in it for you," he said. "I don't know how to handle this."

We were in battalion headquarters somewhere in Holland. Troops of the 30th Division were practicing river crossings, getting ready for the Rhine River action to come the last week in March 1945. I was busy writing recommendations for military awards, but occasionally was asked by headquarters personnel to do some writing for them. The sergeant was the only one who offered to pay. I had learned some time ago that although many were willing to recognize writing ability, few thought it was worth remuneration.

The sergeant was an exception. He had a black-sheep reputation, but he knew values and men's motives. He was the wheeler and dealer found in most outfits. He had about a dozen cameras and several watches and pistols obtained through barter, exchange of favors and outright looting.

I already had one of his cameras, a small cheap affair that he had given me for doing one of his reports. Now he wanted to make another deal.

"What's this about," I asked, without reading the letter.

"The parents want their son's watch back," he said. "They don't believe it was destroyed when he was hit. I suppose they think a bullet couldn't have killed him and wrecked his watch at the same time."

"How was he killed?"

"It was at night. He went outside to relieve himself and a shell came in. It wasn't just his watch that got torn up."

I looked at the name on the letter: Stevens — a headquarters man I had seen from time to time. Death, of course, was common, but this shocked me, for I hadn't known the man was dead, but I did know he was dead.

My mind flashed back to the closing week in January when the Battle of the Bulge was coming to an end. We had taken our last objective in that deadly and terrible action and were bedded down for the night in Nieder Emmels, a Belgian village.

I was in the basement of a stone and brick house with many other headquarters men who were spreading hay for their beds. Candles were burning to light our efforts. I looked up and saw Stevens crawling to his blanket. His face was illuminated by the flickering light. Suddenly it took on the pale, greenish look that I had observed so often — a death mask. Was it the half light that was creating this dreadful image? If so, why weren't other faces in the crowded room showing the same macabre reflection? The verdigris sheen then disappeared from his face. I dis-

177

missed what I had seen as perhaps caused by something inside me — fatigue colored by too much exposure to suffering and death, as well as constant gnawing fear.

I hadn't seen Stevens since, which was not unusual, as our duties did not bring us together often. But I remembered the death mask.

"Where was Stevens killed?" I asked.

"At Nieder Emmels, the latter part of January," the sergeant said.

Good Lord, I thought to myself, it must have happened right after I saw the fatal image on his face.

In answering the letter from the parents, I did not mention my premonition. No need to add more to their grief. I can't remember exactly what I wrote, but I do know there was no way of convincing them that the watch was destroyed — not stolen— without stating that the young man was killed by a shell, even though in setting their minds to rest on the possible theft, I undoubtedly created a vision of horror that their imaginations might build on.

The sergeant offered one of his cameras when I had finished my ghoulish work. But I refused. The sergeant read my letter and grinned at the line that said, "You can be sure that anything of value was sent to you."

That leer in the sergeant's eyes gave me another premonition. Was the watch really destroyed? I hoped I was reading too much into his grin. In any event, the watch wouldn't matter to Stevens.

****

"Hood took the hand, held it for a moment. Sometimes you touched a man like this, and it was the last time, and the next time you saw him he was cold and white and bloodless, and the warmth was gone forever. ." — "The Killer Angels," Shaara.

After the Bulge battle had been won and the Ruhr and Rhine rivers had been crossed, the war became mostly a truck ride for me as German resistance crumbled and forward movement was swift and decisive.

However, our troops got ambushed in Germany's Teutoburger Wald on April 3. This was a somewhat mountainous heavily wooded park-like region revered by the Germans as the site of a victory over the Romans in AD 11 or 9 — accounts vary — under the leadership of a German chieftan named Hermann. A huge statue of Hermann stands on the site to honor the German "liberator."

However, some historians believe that the defeat of the Romans cut off most of what is now Germany from the mainstream of European civilization for centuries and laid the seeds for many later German and European problems.

The ambush cost us some good men who should have survived the nearly-ended war. We assumed that the stiff resistance was attributable to SS leadership of above-average soldiers being trained as officers at a camp in that area, as well as the inspiration of Hermann and his 174-foot-high monument. Picture, if you will, crack American troops in similar circumstances at Valley Forge, let us say.

But if we thought these Germans were fighting only for home, country, and honor on sacred home soil, we found later that we were mistaken. Our troops discovered a large quantity of booze in a warehouse after the Germans had finally given up. Naturally, our GIs wasted no time in drinking toasts to Hermann, way up there in the sky.

When I came on the scene a few hours later in Hiddesen, the village on the other side of the Teutoburger Wald, the American Army, as represented by some of the men of the 1st Battalion, was in a highly festive and friendly mood, flushed with victory and alcohol, and ready to forgive the townspeople, especially if they were pretty and wore skirts.

I did not realize how close our outfit was to dissolving into an orgy until I attempted to interview one of the officers about some of the heroic actions which had just taken place. This officer was seated in a dining room with a bottle on the table. It was Cherry Heering, a powerful liqueur, which the men had been gulping as though it were pop.

The officer had it clear in his mind what he wanted to tell me, hic, but he had difficulty, hic, in getting it out in intelligible form. I asked that he draw a map. He sketched the terrain and enemy strong points, accompanied by vocally slurred identifications, and when he finished he handed me a piece of paper that looked as though a chicken had stepped in some ink and walked about indiscriminately.

I gave up and went out into the street to see what else was going on. By that time, fortunately, the Army had regrouped and order had been restored.

The battalion commander showed great humanity. No one was arrested. Instead, believing that the men had paid in blood for this alcoholic treasure, and also believing that the booze, served in reasonable amounts, could be a just reward for valor, he ordered the spirits to be seized as "enemy war material" and carried with us for subsequent consumption. By April 19 our unit had fought its last battle, and another liquor warehouse at Magdeburg on the Elbe had been seized to add to our store of booze. It was time for cocktails.

The bottles were divided evenly among the various units in the battalion. To create a proper nightclub environment, the battalion headquarters artist, a young man who could duplicate a Petty drawing, was called upon to decorate the walls of an abandoned home with a number of these striking females. Operation of the bar was then delegated to completely trustworthy men, with or without bartending experience, and free liquor was served each evening, but only for an hour, after which everyone was thrown out.

Since the battalion moved about frequently, it was necessary to recreate the bars and call again and again upon the skill of the artist. He never failed us. In this manner, the entire contents of the Teutoburger Wald and Magdeburg warehouses was consumed within about a month without serious violations of proper deportment. All of this was accomplished, too, without asking the men to check their weapons at the door.

Hermann, on that day in April 40 years ago, may have been saddened to see his native soldiers taking a licking on the very ground where he had won almost 2000 years earlier. And the loss of such a vast quantity of spirits must have been disheartening, too. But the captured booze made at least a part of the U.S. Army of occupation more tractable and amenable as it spread the benefits of the Western civilization denied so many centuries before.

Our last battle in Germany saw me riding in a truck while our troops were knocking out roadblocks and tank traps ahead in the city of Magdeburg. One sight I remember is seeing a wounded medic being jeeped to the rear for treatment. His was a familiar face and this time it bore the look of surprise that most wounded men showed as though wondering how this could have happened.

During one prolonged truck stop in the city I got out to rummage around in the porch area of an apartment building. Here I noticed the case of a German typewriter almost buried in junk and debris. I pulled it out, opened the case, and found a portable typewriter of most unusual quality. I can't remember the trade name, but the machine was a beauty. The keys were spring-action and many of the parts were chrome-plated. I immediately drafted this piece of German craftsmanship to help me in my job of writing awards recommendations for our troops. My old typewriter, an obsolete and wheezy mechanism, was happily dumped.

The war did not formally end until May 8, but in our sector it was over after Magdeburg was taken. Patrols were sent across the river to explore enemy territory. They came back to report many tanks, artillery pieces, and troops, none of which would fire at them. It was obvious that we were being invited to take over so that the German troops could avoid capture by the Russians. But we stayed where we were. Once the enemy sensed that we were not moving, many of their troops deserted at night to swim or raft their way across the river and surrender to us in the morning.

Meanwhile the pace of my work on awards stepped up dramatically as the men had more time to think about past actions and report until-then unrecognized heroic deeds. Their memories became sharper with the realization that every award was worth several points toward determining discharge from the Army.

And so my new typewriter had a smoking inauguration into the world of red tape including the preparation of affidavits and certificates to be signed by witnesses of past military actions as well as summary statements of the deeds that had earned Bronze Stars, Silver Stars, Distinguished Service Crosses and, rarely, the Congressional Medal of Honor. The latter, incidentally, is the only award given for action "above and beyond the call of duty."

My new "liberated" typewriter pleased me mightily for its ease of operation and the high quality work it churned out. But it had one slight fault. The letters "x" and "z" were transposed. Where the "x" is on an American typewriter, the "z" appears on the German model, and vice versa. Some of the army clerks who had also acquired German typewriters found a mechanic to change the letters to the normal American placement. But I elected to simply train my fingers to adjust to the change. I hated the idea of tampering with something that was already nearly perfect.

When the time came to leave Europe and embark for the United States, I longed to keep it in my personal possession enroute, but we were warned that taking such contraband home would not be allowed.

Accordingly, I reluctantly consigned my paragon to the regimental box for shipment to the States, where we would be reunited.

But on the way home I came down with infectious hepatitus (yellow jaundice), was hospitalized on the Queen Mary, and transferred to an Army hospital in New Brunswick, New Jersey, for a six-week recovery period. Meanwhile, Japan surrendered, and when I was well I was discharged and never rejoined my unit.

I knew where my division was camped, so I wrote a letter to my superior officer in the awards section, enclosing a five dollar bill, and asking that he ship my typewriter to me. It was the only souvenir I had of the war, I said. The officer replied by returning my money and stating that the typewriter had been smashed aboard ship during a rough crossing. I didn't believe a word of it.

However, that was not the end of that beautiful typewriter's influence. About 15 years later, while working at the Traverse City Record-Eagle, some irate shuffleboard officials descended on the editorial department outraged at a typographical error in the report of the national championship competition at the courts, which still exist at the Senior Citizen Center on Front Street.

Since I had written the story, I was interested in the nature of the complaint. It seems that the winner in the men's division was called Dixie something-or-other, but our paper had printed his first name as "Dizie."

I realized immediately what had happened. My fingers had absent-mindedly reverted to their memory of the German keyboard. I watched quietly as a search was made for the original copy, but it had been thrown away. I didn't say a word, for I couldn't betray my German typewriter for something as ordinary as a shuffleboard title.

One sunny day back in the middle of April, 1945, a large group of first battalion soldiers, including me and my typewriter (the old one), were riding in trucks, comfortable in the assumption that the war was nearly over and that we had survived when suddenly we were faced with the possibility of being casualties, almost as the war's curtain was coming down.

Ahead of the motorized column was armor and infantry serving as "point," breaking up whatever slight resistance remained as we headed toward Magdeburg and perhaps even Berlin, as we thought then.

Our column stopped and started often. Finally we halted near a complex of farm buildings, which we found to be still occupied by foreign labor, some of them French. The men got off the trucks to strike up conversations and search for eggs in the henhouses. Some even visited kitchens looking for goodies that could spice up our rather flat-tasting rations.

One of our group, a reprobate even we — living as rough as we did — could hardly tolerate, found time to seduce one of the farm girls. We learned of this because a farmhand who had been her boyfriend began to berate her publicly. She screamed back at him while our reprobate smiled and quietly slipped away. He had such a history of fast conquests that in an effort to humiliate him I wrote him up for a "servicing" award, lauding his brave performance despite enemy shelling, machine guns, and mortars. I typed this on a formal Bronze Star certificate to make it look official. But he chose to be proud of the award and did not view it as a reprimand.

During this interlude, we heard several nearby explosions. They startled us, and we didn't learn what they were until our column pulled out again. Near the highway and concealed by trees was a newly created ack-ack gun emplacement. The GI crew had used dynamite to excavate a hole quickly. Sandbags were stacked around the circle and they were in business should anything happen. We thought of it as a routine precaution. I had once observed a crew firing well behind a German plane, which turned out to be one of the first jets to fly in combat. Our gunners couldn't adjust to its extraordinary speed.

After about a thousand yards, our truck column stopped again under a slight covering of trees. Although many flowers were blooming, the trees hadn't leafed out much yet. Suddenly there was a drone of planes approaching from the east. We thought nothing of it — the sky belonged to us. American planes dominated during the day. But one of our men exclaimed that this time it was different. "Those are Jerry planes!"

There were five fighters flying overhead. We expected they would pass by, but instead they broke formation to circle us. Then we knew we were in for it. The men scrambled out of the trucks and headed across an open field toward a small forest about 500 yards away. I scrambled with them.

At the halfway point, I stopped, realizing I could not reach the imperfect protection of the woods in time. I also reasoned the planes would be looking for major targets, the stationary trucks or a mass of military personnel. I was far enough from the trucks to be safe. If I stopped where I was I would be separated from the other men, a lone target in an empty field. In addition to further excuse myself as a worthy victim, I plopped on the ground and hoped my brown uniform would blend with the brown soil so I might also be virtually invisible.

All the same, I had regrets, after so many deliverances from death, that I should be vulnerable to a senseless end by some Nazi planes that had no business being in the air.

I watched over my shoulder while prone as the lead plane got into position for strafing. Just as it was about to make its run, however, it exploded into flame and quickly crashed to the ground. Then another plane was hit and trailed black smoke as it struggled away for a probable crash landing. The other fighters turned tail and flew away.

The ack-ack gunners had done their job superbly. I had forgotten them completely and I think from their actions all the other men had as well. The ack-ack crew's preparedness on that day, plus its accuracy, saved many lives that could have been sacrificed tragically, for nothing.

By April 19 we had fought our last battle and rested on the Elbe River at Magdeburg waiting for the Russians and collecting prisoners as they crossed the river at night. I thank those ack-ack gunners for the many bonus years they granted all of us that day.

When the war in Europe ended in 1945, peace was greeted by the beautiful and balmy month of May. Flowers bloomed, trees leafed out, sun-drenched days stretched into soft and scented evenings.

The infantry units that had been making war were now assigned occupational duty in villages and cities throughout the U.S. zone in Germany. I was alternately stationed at Wernigerode, Barleben, Halberstadt, and Plauen.

To recall those days of immense relief in such idyllic surroundings I consulted letters I wrote home during that month. Although there were a few references to the joys of peace and the strikingly beautiful scenery, most of my thoughts then were about the Army's point system for return to the states and the unworkable non-fraternization policy regarding the German people.

At Halberstadt I had a large room of my own with a grand piano in it. My thumping out a few tunes on the piano encouraged an accomplished pianist from the adjoining flat to ask if she could entertain us, which she did with a thundering rendition of several classical numbers. Ironically, she demeaned herself later by taking up with our previously mentioned sergeant major reprobate. So much in that instance for non-fraternization!

On this topic I was moved to write: "Several attempts have been made in our *Stars and Stripes* newspaper to show that the Germans are hopelessly militaristic by telling how some German children were playing war, or perhaps admiring our guns. I remember playing war as a kid. I notice out my window that a couple of German boys are draped over an empty GI trailer. One is inside the thing, flat on his back, while the other is sitting on the sideboard. If they are thinking dark thoughts, I have no way of knowing it, or doing anything about it.

"The army wants none of its personnel to be missionaries. While the idea has merit, my response is that we are perhaps missing an opportunity. Education is the generally recognized cure for what is wrong over here. There is firmness and justice in our present policy, but there is nothing on which to build for the future. I suppose, though, there have been plans laid for this phase of the job, too, and the army is considered out of its sphere to dabble in this part of the problem."

A few weeks later I was in Wernigerode in the Harz mountains. This was a resort village with a picturesque square and a park with trails leading into the foothills on the outskirts. The weather continued balmy. "It's odd," I wrote, "but I think the cessation of hostilities combined with the wonderful weather has taken the sting of defeat from the native Germans, if indeed there was any sting to begin with. One feels that they were numb from the long years of war, and had been hopeless for some time."

I then commented somewhat bitterly on the point system for determining who should go home. More weight was given to length of service than to combat time. "I know of very few combat men, that is men who actually did the fighting," I wrote, "who are qualifying, for the simple reason that it is rare that a combat man lasts long enough to compete in respect to months of service with the more secure GI who has a clerical job, like myself.

To my way of thinking the man who spends three or four months fighting has gone through hell and back, but his combat time is rated no higher than the rear echelon Joe who rarely knows what an artillery shell sounds like." That was the opinion of someone who did not have enough points.

Every award was worth five points. Accordingly, as awards and decorations non-com for an entire battalion I was kept extremely busy during occupation, for there was now time for the men to recall past actions and put me to work to see if they couldn't get an extra five points on their record.

I spent most of my time near the Czechoslovakian border at Plauen in luxurious quarters on the perimeter of the city. The inner city had been flattened. I was told that 15,000 people were still unaccounted for. Gangs of prisoners worked at cleaning up the rubble. I talked to one of the guards one day. He said they had uncovered two bodies the previous day.

Many German soldiers roamed the countryside free. None of them looked like soldiers except for their uniforms. "They are either too young or too old," I wrote. "They are probably farmers or miners. It does seem strange to see them loose. Most of them are quiet and docile." Prisoners were delegated to clean our rooms, do KP and even to develop film from our liberated cameras. Some also did guard duty in residential areas, perhaps to guard against foreign prisoners released from German camps. These made no bones about their desire to kill SS troopers.

Again commenting on non-fraternization, I said: "The German women have been without men for so long and our GIs of course have been without women for so long that relations are rather promiscuous among certain classes on both sides. I've been arguing against the non-fraternization policy with my officers for some time now. It's just like prohibition. It will never work."

I also declared against hating Germans: "(Hate) is a very exhausting process. You've known someone in civilian life whom you didn't like and perhaps hated legitimately. Yet how long could you stand it to be around him and keep pouring on your hate. People aren't built that way."

My conclusion: "As policy to follow over the long run with the expectation of getting what we want from these people, it is asinine and highly impractical. I think that our only concern over here, after shooting the flagrantly guilty, is simply to watch these people help themselves back to a civilized state and to make sure that they never have another opportunity to upset the world."

In time, Parker's foreign policy prevailed with a big assist from the intransigent behavior of the Russians. As for the point system and getting back to the States, rather than going to the war against Japan, Truman's decision to drop the bomb took care of that.

Staying physically clean in the wartime army was always a problem. Thousands like me struggled through dirt, rain, mud, sleet and snow with little or no opportunity to clean up. We had no time to think, or do, anything about personal hygiene. Furthermore, before entering a town, we systematically wrecked it, including its plumbing system.

I recall four showers that were worked in during lulls on our almost-daily-jousts with the enemy. But a bath? That was something dimly remembered from stateside.

Two of the showers, enjoyed in August, were in outdoor portable units operated by a special detail in the rear.

Two more showers came in coal mine facilities in Spekholzerheide, Holland — one in the middle of September and the other at the end of October.

These cleansing events were so rare that I have no trouble remembering them.

As for the bath — immersion in a hot and healing pool of water — there is no way I can forget it.

Preparation for my one-and-only bath was begun in October and culminated October 21, 1944, when American forces finally took Aachen, or Aix-la-Chapelle, after 19 days of seige and house-to-house fighting.

Two young men from Traverse City, Michigan, helped secure my bath by taking part in that engagement. They were Dick Weiler, Grand Traverse County Sheriff for many years, and Francis (Fuzz) McCall, long-time city clerk. According to a story told me by Fuzz years later when our paths crossed at City Hall, Dick and Fuzz met accidentally in Aachen during the battle near the Hotel Quellenhof, a hostelry that I later bedded in during a return trip to this spa city.

Despite the stalwart efforts of the American Army, including my two Traverse City cohorts, I wasn't able to enjoy a bath in Aachen until several months later, sometime in May, after the war was over.

Aix-la-Chapelle is famous as Charlemagne's city in the 8th century when it became the coronation site for the Holy Roman Empire. The city continued to host this event into the 16th century. But it also was revered for its hot sulphur springs, which have made it a mecca for seekers of curative baths.

It was my good fortune to be sent back to 120th Regiment headquarters in Aachen for a short time in May to help write the regimental history. While there, one of my buddies, who already had been initiated into the secrets of a bath in Aachen, invited me to join him in one of these ecstatic immersions.

Aachen was in ruins. The few upright buildings left were hollow, blackened shells. As we drove to our destination, several tanks in an extensive hollow area open to the sky practiced gunnery against an embankment, giving us an auditory and visual demonstration of the cause of such devastation.

Our jeep slowed for a pile of bricks, one mound among many. But there was an opening in this pile, and the breach, cave-like, descended into a subterranean wonderland. The walls and ceilings were of brown marble, and a native attendant with a white jacket and towels guided us to our separate compartments opening off a long hallway. I believe I paid the attendant a mark or two.

My bath was a miniature swimming pool, about twice as large as the whirlpool bath at a typical resort. There were no windows. The floor and walls also were brown marble. The electric lighting was subdued and seductive enough to suggest a seraglio.

I don't recall a strong scent of sulphur. But it was indeed hot water. I quickly drew back upon first sampling with a toe. I tried again, but couldn't stand it. I was so close to getting my one and only bath in Europe and I couldn't handle it. But I persisted. Gradually, by submitting to what was close to lobster-boiling treatment, I eventually dunked myself. Once in I didn't want to get out. All the dirt, pain and tension of the previous months were dissolved and rinsed away. When I finally crawled out I was a vitiated heap, barely able to dress myself. However, I felt that I had been born again.

I staggered out of the room and back to the jeep. That afternoon I was no good to the regimental history section, since I repeatedly dozed over my typewriter.

There was never again to be a bath like that for me. I came close at Banff, Canada, years later in a public hot springs pool. But the water wasn't nearly as hot, and it was far too populous a setting — nothing exclusive and private as in Aachen.

My lone bath during the European campaigns also was singular in that the Army, normally an organization devoted to togetherness with no provision for private sleeping quarters, dining alcoves, enclosed toilets or exclusive health spas had at last been the instrument for a world-class bath in complete seclusion — but it took one long belligerent year to do it.

I've had the rug pulled out from under me many times, but only once was it a 100-yard bolt of white silk.

On that occasion, the rug-yanking took some dreams with it — dreams of silk curtains, silk bedspreads, silk shirts, silk dresses, even the possibility of smooth silk sheets and silk underwear. But the Great Silk Heist was discovered, and a regiment of GIs was bitterly disappointed.

It happened when our troops discovered a parachute factory loaded with bolts of silk that had not yet been processed.

Our regimental commander was noted for thinking of the welfare of his men. These were guys who had won the war in the mud, snow, sleet, and shell-torn terrains of France, Belgium, Holland, and Germany. Now the shooting was over. A little reward — not loot — would be appropriate.

So the parachute cloth was declared "captured enemy war material." Thus each man was issued 50 yards of silk. Somehow, without intending to be greedy, I acquired a full bolt, or 100 yards of the stuff that had been shunted aside in the confusion of distributing so much material. I put the cloth in the bottom of my barracks bag and began to imagine how to use the silk, once I got home. It appeared that our return would be rather soon, since the Army wanted us to help out in Japan after a brief visit to the United States.

One of our stops during the leap-frogging pull-out from Germany was at a camp called Oklahoma City, near Rheims, France. While there, the men began to receive passes to Paris, only a short distance away. One day I was among a truckload of GIs transported to this fabulous city. I had thought I was going to miss Gay Paree. Once during the war, we were slated to take Paris, but these plans were changed at the last moment to turn the job over to the Free French and General Charles De Gaulle. Later, when a few passes were issued to veterans during a lull in the fighting near Aachen, I narrowly missed qualifying for a trip to Paris. I went to Valkenburg, Holland, instead.

The Paris I saw on a bright, sunny day in July 1945 was intact, having escaped the destruction of war. Its people were friendly and bustling about their daily tasks. We soon became aware, however, that they were hungry. Some wanted to buy our K-ration boxes (our food for the day), and others — young brash girls — wanted our money in exchange for the usual favors that such women have to offer.

A friend and I opted for a bus tour as the best way to quickly see the main attractions, such as Notre Dame cathedral, the Eiffel Tower, Champs Elysees, the boats on the Seine, Napoleon's Tomb, and many other famous sights.

The matronly lady who arranged our bus trip first asked if we would prefer having two sisters from a respected family show us around. The girls wanted to practice their English, we were told. We turned the offer down, fearing that it might be too restrictive, or a subterfuge to get us involved in something worse. We wanted to wander on our own after the bus tour. I think now we may have made a big mistake.

While my friend and I were riding a bus and later the Metro subway, as well as simply strolling the lovely streets of Paris, some of our fellow soldiers were visiting Parisian dress shops — not to buy, but to sell. They offered the silk they carried wrapped around their bodies and under their field jackets. The silk sold for up to $400 for 50 yards.

When these GIs got back to camp they promptly went to the Army post office and bought money orders for the equivalent dollars and mailed the money home. Thus they had neatly and quickly cashed in their silk and banked the money.

When word spread that our silk was worth so much money from ready buyers, many others cashed in as well. I gave a thought to the $800 worth of silk in my possession, but decided against liquidating. I wanted it as a present for my wife.

The bonanza was too good to last. Army inspectors began interviewing some of our entrepreneurs, and asked where they got so much money. They replied that they had won it at poker, but the inspectors were not satisfied. They continued to probe, and for good reason, since at least one of our silk dealers had been paid in counterfeit money and had innocently passed it on to the Army post office when he bought his money order.

Eventually the truth came out. No one was arrested, but the remedy hit all of us rather hard. We were ordered to give up our hoards of silk forthwith. We would be allowed to keep only a small piece, large enough for a scarf, as a souvenir.

The day that the trucks came around for our "captured enemy war material" was a dark and rainy one. No covers were on the trucks. The silk was tossed in helter-skelter while the rain pelted down. One would have thought it was a garbage pickup.

The trucks roared away with my $800 worth of silk among the forlorn bolts. I often have wondered what happened to this sudden treasure. Surely not the dump. Someone with authority must have dreamed as I did of silk drapes, dresses, curtains and the like, and acted accordingly. Usually one good heist begets another. On the other hand, maybe they made parachutes out of it.

"The biggest thrill of your life, when this thing is over, will be sailing back home into New York Harbor and seeing the Statue of Liberty."

So said Col. Hammond Birks on a hot July evening in 1944 in the Normandy hedgerow country. He was speaking to a group of replacements, who were to fill the infantry gaps in 1st Battalion ranks. The colonel, who was later to become a general and command troops in Korea, was in charge of the 120th Regiment of the 30th Infantry Division. He was trying to tell us what to expect and encouraging us to believe that we had a good chance of surviving.

I was more interested in survival than in seeing the Statue of Liberty, although I knew if I did view the old gal again, it might well be an emotional experience. She would be a symbol not only of liberty enlightening the world, but of triumph and good fortune for the GIs coming home after V-E Day.

When the war did end and our Division began the slow process of getting back to the states, I had plenty of time to think about home and the elation of being part of a troop ship hailing the Statue of Liberty as we arrived to the plaudits of home folks.

But this was not to be.

I was on a pass to London when it first struck me that something was wrong. I didn't have an appetite. At first I thought it was because of the wretched food that the English, still heavily rationed, were able to offer at the canteens and restaurants. But even the vegetables tended to nauseate me. A tomato ought to taste good, especially since I hadn't had one in about two years. I gradually began to look inward, and the more I examined my symptoms, of which there were several, the more I became convinced that I was sick.

I waited a few days to see if the illness was a temporary malady. But even breakfasts turned me off. Oatmeal with milk and sugar tasted like paste. When a soldier can't eat, he's in trouble.

Inasmuch as the Queen Mary, which was to take us home from Southhampton, was scheduled to sail within a few days, I decided to hold on a while before reporting to the medics. The last thing I wanted was to be detained in an English hospital while my buddies headed for the good old United States.

I was weak and haggard when I finally climbed the gangplank to the ship. I parked my barracks bag at my bunk somewhere in the innards of the stripped-down liner and headed for fresh air on deck. I leaned over the railing in the classic seasick pose, watching the water lap around the dock and the boat. As soon as the Queen Mary began to put some distance between itself and the moorings, I headed for the sick bay. Even so, I was worried that I might be checking in too soon. They might fly a helicopter to the ship to take away this infected body and isolate it somewhere.

The doctor examined my yellowish eyeballs, asked some questions and made some tests — all of which took a long enough time for the Queen to get farther and farther from shore — before concluding that I had infectious hepatitis, or yellow jaundice. I was ordered to the ship's hospital. Before I went there, however, I returned to my bunk to get my barracks bag, which in the meantime had been rifled. A camera with some pictures taken in Germany was gone. I felt so bad physically, though, that I didn't care.

Thoughts of getting home or of seeing Miss Liberty in New York evaporated as I wholeheartedly embraced one of the major cures for jaundice — bed rest. Even the half dozen or so nurses, the first real live American girls I had seen in a long time, failed to impress. Nor did the back rubs that these angels gave from time to time penetrate my devotion to supine relaxation. I was really sick.

I heard about the excitement topside as our ship sailed past the Statue, but none of it was for me.

I and others in the sick bay were the first off the liner when it docked. Ambulances took us to an army hospital at New Brunswick, New Jersey. It was night when we were bedded down again in a large ward.

The next morning one of the ambulatory cases came to my bed with a look of alarm on his face. What had happened? "They've put us in a ward with blacks," he said, actually using a word to designate race that I won't repeat here.

I had encountered this prejudice before in the army. Some of those from the Deep South were especially bitter. All the same I always gave them an argument. In this case, I said: "So what. They're human beings. Wait until you get to know them. You'll see."

Before the morning was over this same GI was enjoying their company, as were others in the ward. One of the blacks was an accomplished musician and entertained on a piano.

But for a moment I thought my homecoming, sans the Statue of Liberty with stark racism as her replacement in a hospital ward with a bunch of sick men, was to be a baleful one indeed. What saved it was the humanity, no matter how much it may be repressed, that comes to the top most of the time in most Americans, with or without the Statue.

The War Revisited

I once searched for hell...failed...tried again and found it. But hell had become a bucolic scene — just as I had expected.

It took two trans-Atlantic flights to find my personal battlefield at St. Lo, first in 1962, followed by another visit in 1967.

My first search was a dream-like frustration, which I later recorded as follows:

The French gendarme walked toward our car, a rented Renault 4L touring model. Had we aroused suspicion? This was the fourth time we had ended at the intersection of the roads to St. Lo and St. Gilles. Perhaps the Frenchman trimming the hedge at the intersection had told the policeman about us.

"Go on; get out of the car," my wife said. "Tell him what you're trying to do."

So I did, with the history of the World War II exploits of the 120th Infantry, 30th Division, in my hand.

"J'etait un soldat Americain," I began, "ici en la guerre dix huit années passé'. " (I was an American soldier here in the war 18 years ago.)..."combattant...mitrailleuse...St. Lo," I continued hopefully.

The gendarme's face lit up with wonder. Apparently not many GIs had returned to France as yet, especially in this lonely countryside. There followed a wierd conversation in fragmented French and charades. I showed the regimental map of the area. Yes, we were in the right place; this is the hallowed ground, but I couldn't find the hedgerows with which I lived so intimately from July 16 to 25, 1944. They weren't there; the land was strange.

And yet I knew that this had to be where the thousand-plane bombing took place preceding the breakthrough; that here was where Lt. Gen. Lesley J. McNair and several hundred men from our regiment were killed by our own bombs; and that here Gen. George C. Patton's armored columns began the famous sweep that spelled the beginning of the end of the Battle of France on July 26, 18 years ago.,

I had long wanted to retrace the combat route of my outfit, because it had been involved in a great historical event, and so had I in a small way. But was my dream of returning to the site — hellish though it had been at the time — to remain a dream? The French sun, the birds singing, the general quiet of this lovely part of Normandy defied me to prove there ever had been conflict here, that I ever had seen men die here, gloriously, horribly and ludicrously. It defied me to prove that I ever had felt the shocks of fear and bravado, or ever had smelled the stench of death, for here was peace and contentment and hardly a scar. Our flight from Detroit to Glasgow, our journey via train and boat to Paris, where we rented a car to drive to this lonely, quiet place, seemed quite fruitless.

But yes, we were on the spot exactly, the gendarme agreed. I turned the car around and slowly tried again, via different trails and wagon tracks. The cross-country tour was beautiful and interesting, but I saw nothing that measured up to my memory of the region.

At last we gave up. However we were not completely bereft. We had had the satisfaction earlier in the day of visiting Omaha Beach, the great invasion landing point. I had landed at Omaha in 1944, with a replacement package and marched up the steep hill into St. Laurant. Also on this day, August 1, 1962, the exact anniversary of the death of my good friend Walter Paige Jr., I had found his cross among about 10,000 others.

On the southern side of the St. Lo-St. Gilles road intersection, I stopped the car. There was the double hedgerow that I had remembered so well from my first day of combat, July 16. It had then contained two knocked-out tanks, one German and the other ours. And here was the hedgerow on which the counterattack was met, although our machine gun was disabled. And that must be the barn, now in ruins, and the wrecked house on the other side; it hasn't been rebuilt.

I walked down a sunken road. If this is the place, I'll come out on high ground; there will be a ravine where we did outpost duty all night and where I lost all my equipment when the shelling started. But the sunken road leads me on and on, as in a dream, and leads to nothing. This can't be the place. The terrain is flat. The regimental map doesn't agree. I've been mistaken.

And so I gave up again, defeated at St. Lo. There was little doubt that this was the area, but the hedgerows had been changed, I thought, probably first by our bombing and later by the French farmers themselves. I felt disappointed and let down, but ahead were many exciting discoveries that would make this European trip memorable and hauntingly nostalgic. I did not know then that I was to return five years later and find with very little difficulty the geographic hell of the summer of 1944.

My second chance came in 1967 when my wife was accepted for an International Studies summer session at Exeter College in Oxford, England. I joined her in her third-floor apartment at the college during the last week of school. I listened to a few lectures (dons in flowing black robes eloquent-

ABOVE — NORMANDY HEDGEROW- Notice that out of these mounds of earth grew grass, shrubs and even trees. This photo was taken in August 1967. BELOW — This photo in 1999 shows how high the hedgerows usually are. The author's son Robert, who stands at 6' 4" is filming his father during a visit to the road intersection next to a shrine at Le Mesnil Raoult.

ly discoursing on various literary topics) before leaving for four days in France. I was aided by a tourist agency in Oxford, which arranged for a train to Southhampton, a plane to Cherbourg and a car in which to motor to St. Lo.

This was to be an in-depth search. That's why I allowed several days. However, I was better prepared this time, since I had maps of the region based on aerial photography, generously supplied by the U.S. Defense Department. I was aware of the existence of such maps, since I had seen officers carrying them with each hedgerow numbered for ease in directing artillery fire.

The plane at Southhampton was one designed for ferrying cars to the continent, consequently there was space only for about a dozen passengers. At the Cherbourg airport I had thought I would take a bus to the city to get a car, but the tourist guide said the car would be delivered to me instead. Thus I was spared city driving and went directly south in the lovely French countryside. Farmers were trimming hedges by the roadside, and householders had developed hydrangeas that bloomed blue and even purple, a specialty of the area I believe.

As I neared St. Lo, I began to consult my maps. Suddenly I saw a small arrow-sign pointing to the west and up a sharp grade. It said, "Ht. Vents," a name that rang a bell from 23 years ago. I turned on a road that wound its way to the top of a ridge and to a road intersection. I turned left toward St. Gilles and slowly motored through the hedgerows. Then, to my astonishment there it all was — the sunken road on the left, the field broken by three or four hedgerows, the stone barn (still in ruins), and the huge hedgerow on the right that had been shelter during the thousand-plane bombing raid.

What had escaped me during hours and days of search before was revealed within minutes. The aerial maps had brought me right on target.

I decided to drive on to St. Lo, get a hotel room, and return for more exploration the next day. After breakfast the next morning, I went to a grocery and bought a bottle of Beaujolais, cheese and crackers. I was ready for a tramp in Normandy country.

At the battle site, I approached the farmhouse next to the ruined barn. I would need permission to roam over their land. I explained to the French housewife who answered my knock that I had been a soldier there in the war and wanted to look about and take pictures. She understood and waved me on in a help-yourself gesture. A boy about ten had been watching an American cowboy thriller on TV. He turned the set off and gave me his full attention. I was really a soldier here? A machine gunner? After the excitement had worn off and I showed signs of leaving, he let me go and turned on the TV again.

I walked down an angled sunken hedgerow trail made dark and damp by a heavy cover of trees and shrubs. Actually I was approaching the battle area from the enemy side and seeing for the first time the route used to surprise us with flanking fire. At the end of this 100-yard trek, I broke into the open and saw the seven or eight hedgerows that had cost so much on a July day in 1944. There should have been shells whistling and exploding, tanks rumbling, machine guns chattering, and rifles firing. But my first and worst battle site offered no such dramatic effects — only a farmer raking, and a bull who threateningly looked me over in one of the fields.

All the same my blood was singing as I picked up on all the familiar terrain features. Even some large animal bones caused me to wonder if they belonged to one of the many dairy cows killed that day. A huge excavation behind one hedgerow told me where the enemy tank had been dug in. This weapon had caused much hell and many deaths before it, too, expired. Beyond was the double hedgerow, behind which one of our tanks fired to finally disable the enemy monster. I and others had cowered on the ground near the tank, shaken by its explosions and enveloped in the dust.

I returned via the highway and examined the thorn-infested ditch in which I had crawled. I was now enjoying the luxury of an upright advance. Opposite the farmhouse I looked for the cottage from which I had lifted part of a bedstead to cover my hole. But the cottage was gone. Only a gate and cement steps were left.

I headed then for the ravine where our squad had spent a night on outpost duty with a wire leading back to the main line. I descended via a heavily canopied path down the side of the ridge to its base. Along the way I spotted a German firing step which time had not eroded. At the site of our guard post, I found that my tunnel into the hedgerow had caved in. The tunnel had saved my life that day since it protected from overhead shell bursts while others about me were wounded.

I took many pictures, and I would have stayed longer, but it began to rain. Even the rain was nostalgic, however, for I had been drenched during some of my 1944 sojourn there.

My mission was complete. I had finally found what had been lost, and the hell of those distant days was now dissipated by the calm rusticity of the area. My wine and my cheese tasted good, as I reflected that battlefields are haunted, especially by returning survivors.

Now that I had found the battle area in which I had crouched, crawled, and squirmed several decades before, I had two extra days to spend in France before returning to Oxford, England, where my wife was finishing an international studies program. The next venture would have something to do with a book.

Should I motor to Gay Paree? I decided instead to revisit Mortain and Dr. Gilles Buisson. I first had met him in 1962. He was writing a history of the battle at Mortain and had asked me to send him a letter relating my experiences there. This I had done when I returned home in 1962.

On the road to Mortain I picked up two young men hitchhiking. They were German students on a holiday. They wanted to go further than Mortain, so I let them off there to fend for themselves. During the ride, I mentioned that I was a veteran revisiting old battle sites. They seemed amused by this, and I gathered that they had no knowledge that they were in an area where Germans and Americans had fiercely battled a little more than two decades before. I had a feeling they thought my remembering it was somehow gauche and out of keeping with the new-found peace and prosperity in Europe. If so, they may have had a point.

Mortain is a lovely village, noted for a cascading stream running through it, as well as for the high promontory from which pilgrims of the Middle Ages could get their first glimpse of Mont St. Michel on the west coast of France.

This vantage point became known in our regimental history as Hill 314. Our 2nd Battalion was surrounded on this hill by the Germans, but the unit held its ground throughout the six-day battle, and later was heralded as the "lost battalion" that stuck it out despite great hardships.

I put up at a hotel called Les Cascades and went to the dining room, where I ordered escargots, the day's special. But the snails had been too popular. "All gone," I was told. I can't remember what was substituted, but I do remember a fine bottle of "cidre," the local wine made from apple juice.

That evening I had a long visit with Dr. Buisson and his mother, a charming French lady who understood that my grasp of their language was meager, and made it possible to converse by speaking slowly and using simple words.

Dr. Buisson surprised me by stating, "You're in a book." He showed me "Stalingrad en Normandie," by Eddy Florentin. The author had drawn on my letter of five years ago to give me a page or two in his history of the Normandy campaign. I was told I could get a copy at the local book store, which was just around the corner from my hotel. I got a copy and found some material from my letter — all in French. This book later was translated into English and sold in this country. I have that volume as well.

The next day I drove to Mont St. Michel. I wanted to sample one of the famous omelets there. I climbed up and into the rocky monastery area and found a restaurant serving omelets at long tables at which the customers ate in common. I sat next to a Frenchman, who soon figured out that I was a returned veteran. He told me he had been a "prisonnier," liberated by General Patton. I enjoyed his conversation, as well as the omelet, which if my wife had prepared, I would have sent back to be finished. The omelet was a frothy, whipped delight, almost liquid in texture, but delicious.

I still had the afternoon and another day ahead of me. I knew that classes were ending at the Oxford program and that a sherry party was slated for that evening in one of the dormitories. The purpose of my visit seemed over. The party was attractive. Could I make it in time?

I drove back to the Cherbourg airport, turned in my car, and spoke to an airline official. My reservation wasn't until tomorrow. Could I step it up a day and get on the next flight to England? They would see. I was the only passenger on the plane. Since the stewardess didn't have much to do, we talked all the way back to Southampton.

Then I used the marvelous English train system to return to Oxford. A cab took me to Exeter College, and I walked in on the party at 11 p.m. It was still going strong, although a little short on sherry by then. I didn't need any. I had already had the heady experience of getting there and demonstrating how small Europe is and how efficient is its transportation system.

I showed the guests my book. An English instructor who knew French very well translated some of the rough spots for me.

In 1981, as part of a three-month tour of Europe, I visited Mortain again to find that it now had industry, and that one of the plant owners, apparently wealthy, had bought the land where my personal battle was fought, had bulldozed the hedgerows away and filled in the holes. Nothing remained to indicate that the land had been touched by war.

On this same visit Dr. Buisson gave me an autographed copy of his book, "Mortain dans la Bataille de Normandie." The entire contents of my letter were interspersed throughout the work.

Enough was enough. If the French were sufficiently interested in my experiences to put them in two books, it was time I got busy. "Civilian at War" came out in 1984. I mailed two copies to Dr. Buisson. He said he was going to put one in the little church on Hill 314. I presume he did.

In recent years, I have heard from a writer who has authored an account of the battle, which he thinks has been largely ignored by historians in this country. He was baffled as to how one infantry division could have stopped such a mighty surprise thrust. In addition to bravery and the high morale of the troops, I would say that the most important reason was that we were fighting *behind* hedgerows for a change, instead of *attacking* them. It was like Lee at Gettysburg. Then, for the first time, he went on the offensive against a nearly impregnable defense line, and paid the price. So it was at Mortain.

On a 1985 trip to West Germany, my host family in a Hannover suburb met my request for transportation to Bad Pyrmont by providing a company car and an employee as chauffeur. My host was manager of the Hannover branch of a large insurance company.

In Bad Pyrmont, a charming spa town, we looked up the local newspaper and I told my story. Toward the end of World War II (April 1954), my unit stayed overnight in Bad Pyrmont. Elements of my headquarters company took over a well-above-average home in the outskirts, giving the occupants a few minutes to get out. The home had wall-to-wall carpeting and expensive and luxurious furnishings — a bit too much for unshaven, unbathed, muddy-booted infantrymen, used to sleeping in basements or holes in the ground.

I staked out an upstairs bedroom for myself. Flowing white curtains covered the windows. The spacious bed was billowy white, and the furniture too, was blond. On the desk was a diary. I opened it and examined entries I could not read, since I did not understand German. I deduced that the room was occupied by a young girl, perhaps a counterpart to Anne Frank, of whom nothing was known at that time.

I had consumed some champagne, a gift that night from an officer in thanks for writing up an award that resulted in a Distinguished Service Cross and a trip home for him. The bubbly also celebrated the war's near-ending, about two weeks away.

Leafing through the diary, I began to feel the girl's presence, even though I could not decipher the words. I decided I must make an entry, and I did.

Now I was back at Bad Pyrmont — 40 years later. I couldn't place the house where I stayed nor could I remember what I wrote. The newspaper editor heard my story; the photographer took my picture. We hoped that publication would reveal that the young girl is now grown to her mid-50s, still living in Bad Pyrmont, and that we may meet at last. I will learn then what I wrote and apologize after all these years for invading her privacy.

What follows is fantasy:

I return to my host family's home. Two days later the telephone rings. She has been found! Her name is Wilhelmina Schulz. She wants to see me, and she still has the diary. I am driven back to Bad Pyrmont. The cameras click as we meet. She is an attractive matron with three grown children. Her husband is a prominent businessman. He is present, as is my wife.

"Everything you wrote was so true," she exclaims in very good English. "I never dreamed that I should ever meet you, but how glad I am that you have revealed yourself at last."

"I, too, am very happy to meet you," I say. "I also am grateful to have this belated opportunity to apologize for being so brash."

"Ah, no apology, please. To apologize for what you wrote would be very wrong." I blush.

Timidly I ask if she has the diary, and there it is before my eyes, already opened to my somewhat scraggly lines. I read:

"This is an American soldier who dares write in your diary, a book that should be for your eyes only, and that should contain only your thoughts and observations. But I already have invaded your privacy. I am in your room and I am about to sleep in your bed. Perhaps I can atone somewhat by communicating with you and speaking of the days to come.

"You probably think that this is a terrible time — the complete defeat and downfall of Germany. But I want you to know and feel that out of this will come much better days. Peace itself will be wonderful. And beyond that will be the rebirth of your country and of all Europe...a much improved world for all of us.

"Germans and Americans are much alike. Many of German origin live in America, and have contributed to its strength and culture. Indeed, many of German origin serve in the army that has conquered your country. We will see in the years ahead if together we do not forge a lasting peace and prosperity. — An American GI."

When I finish reading, she says: "See — you cannot apologize."

"You are very gracious," I respond.

With that, let us end this fantasy. The newspaper apparently did not publish the picture and story, or I would have received a copy, as arranged. They had warned that the picture might not come out. Therefore I never met the young girl, now a matron I presume, nor have I learned exactly what I wrote in her diary, although the words might have been similar to what is now imagined.

So, what you have read is largely a fairy tale. And perhaps the Bad Pyrmont editor was right in his decision. Let's leave the entire episode to imagination — it probably comes out better that way. Still there is that desire to know, to penetrate what is doomed to remain a personal mystery.

My first trip to Berlin was aborted in May 1945, when through a prior agreement between the Russians and the Allied forces, we shook hands with some Soviet soldiers at the Elbe River in Magdeburg, stopped where we were, and eventually returned home.

In November 1985, I finally made it to the former German capital. I'm glad it took so long, for I doubt that there would have been much to see in 1945 after the Russians were through wrecking it, nor would the Germans have been as receptive. Today Berlin is one of the great cities of the world — rebuilt, modern, prosperous, and complete with all the cultural and entertainment amenities.

Berlin had one problem then and it was a biggie: it was isolated from the free world, floating precariously in an ocean of paranoia. A constant reminder and symbol of this isolation was the Berlin Wall, built not to contain the free Berliners, so much as to keep the East Germans from escaping.

About 30 Americans, enrolled in the Experiment in International Living program, were housed in a dormitory-style building about 200 yards from the wall, which in this area was liberally decorated with graffiti, including the likenesses of males relieving themselves against the obstruction.

Our institute director, Dr. Eckardt Stratenschulte, freely admitted that West Berliners suffered from "wall sickness." But he and many other natives we met showed an admirable elan and warmth, which extended well beyond the spiritual limitations of the Communist concrete barrier.

One of the many speakers who told us about life "behind the wall" was Dr. Manfred Bahman, the pastor of St. Thomas Church, a red brick Lutheran Cathedral next door to our quarters. He told us a heart-warming story of defeat and triumph.

Before the wall was built, the St. Thomas parish included 18,000 souls. But the Red Barrier, erected on August 13, 1961, cut directly behind the church and abruptly cut off 4,000 members and dealt such a blow to the economy of the remaining free area that during the next 20 years about 70 percent more parishioners were lost. Finally the church was closed as a health hazard while some blue asbestos in the ceiling, installed during renovation in 1959-62 was removed.

But the work of the church did not stop. Kreuzberg, the area in which the parish is located, declined as a place to live. "Guest workers," mainly Turks, moved in. Although the Turks had their own culture and religion, Dr. Bahman saw a need for a day care center for their children. So one was established in the parish hall. "This program was good, but we don't have enough of this kind of thing," he said.

A larger challenge came when the city instituted urban renewal for some of the abandoned buildings in Kreusberg. Trouble developed, since squatters in these ancient structures refused to move. They weren't highly popular, for many of them were "punks," those free-living types who wear Mohican haircuts in bizarre colors and are equally uninhibited as to dress and choice of pets, which in this case included affectionate rats draped around their necks.

An eviction involving police was achieved in June 1983, with the punks jeering the law and TV cameras recording every gesture, many of which were probably unseemly. At this point, Dr. Bahman and the church entered the story. The young people had to have a place to stay. The parish hall provided accommodations for a few nights; then a tent city was established between the church and the wall. The punks and their rats, their dogs and their beer cans stayed for 10 weeks.

One day the tenters asked if they could attend church. Although the remaining members of his church were conservative people, the pastor said they were indeed welcome. But could they drink beer and smoke during the service? Well, if you must, but you'll have to sit in the balcony. How about our pets? Absolutely not! But aren't animals as sacred in the eyes of God as people? Yes, but in their own environment.

So the punks went to church, sat in the balcony, smoked and drank their beer, and shouted a few "right-ons" when the sermon dealt with relieving the oppressed.

Dr. Bahman even invited the punks to a church reception, a move which at first shocked his parishioners. But after these people from opposite cultural poles mingled and learned more about each other, some understanding began to develop. Most of the punks had neither homes nor parents, and they came off as human after all, as did the conservatives to the punks.

Our group was exposed to many other examples of the "humanity" of the West Germans: friendliness in giving directions, help in running the machines in the laundromats, speaking English to translate mysterious signs, and saying "Thank you" for being Americans. I had not expected the latter, but many went out of their way to express gratitude for their freedom, for President Kennedy's famous speech in Berlin, and the airlift during the infamous Berlin blockade.

A personal thank you came from a huge German worker encountered in a tavern near our institute. He didn't let his lack of English stop him. He made us understand that he was a temporary invalid because of a rupture, a disability that he showed by lowering his belt line, a la President Johnson's operation exhibit. And when we departed he insisted on taking my hand and putting it over his heart to feel his friendship and gratitude. He undoubtedly was tipsy and uninhibited, but this was proof, I thought, that he was really sincere.

I doubt that my first intended visit to Berlin, if successful, would have elicited such response.

The parts of Germany which units of the 30th Division occupied briefly at the end of World War II did not become available for tourism from the West for many decades.

I finally got a chance to revisit the quaint villages in East Germany in October of 1991. As it turned out I returned too soon for East Germany needed more time to become truly a part of Germany and attuned to tourists from the outside world.

My dream was to revisit a village with medieval half-timbered houses and a quaint square, all nestled at the foot of the Harz mountains — a town called Wernigerode. It had paths leading into the hills for spectacular views. I had been there for several days on occupation duty, after the war ended on May 8, 1945, and I wanted to renew the vision of this picturesque place and relate again with the elation of peace and life beginning anew in the then-burgeoning springtime.

My interest was further stimulated by the listing of Wernigerode in Frommer's 1991 travel guide as an attractive tourist objective.

We picked up our rental car at the Amsterdam airport and immediately got lost. After getting directions at a luxury hotel nearby, we were on our way along with hordes of other cars. About 50 miles short of Magdeburg, we ran out of time and left the highway to look for overnight accommodations in one of the villages.

We found Hattorf, a charming little town that looked as though it had been built for a movie set. (We were still in the former West Germany, but just barely.) An illuminated hotel sign stopped us. After making sure that we wanted to stay only one night, the innkeeper showed us a very spacious room with down comforters and French doors opening on an inner garden. We were bedded and breakfasted in unexpected luxury at a reasonable price.

The next morning our immediate goal was to find Barleben, a suburb of Magdeburg where my old unit, the 30th Division, fought its last battle. I was quartered in an upstairs bedroom in a house in Barleben when the war ended.

We missed the turn for Barleben and exited instead in an area called Industrial Magdeburg, but we must have been on the outskirts, for the region was bucolic. After some aimless driving, we came to a settlement where I asked directions. I then made a wrong turn and finished at the town dump. Backtracking, we got over a railroad crossing just before a train zoomed past. Finally, we encountered a more traveled street and spotted a sign for Barleben.

It was slow going, for the road to Barleben was peppered with traffic lights. When we reached the village, I had no idea where to find the house where I had stayed. Every structure looked the same — blocky and apparently smeared with an earth colored plaster. I took a picture of a shop which had a yellow "Barleben Video" awning on it, the only bit of color in town.

So much for Barleben, I thought. Let's go to Halberstadt, where I had stayed a few days before landing in nearby Wernigerode. We were now heading south on a secondary road system that soon ensnarled us in a 1 1/2 hour traffic jam about five miles long. We had no idea what was holding us up. The long line stretched in a curve over undulating terrain. The vast stretches of farmland had no fences, nor buildings. The driver ahead opened the trunk of his car and got food for lunch, something we had not thought about preparing for until then.

We eventually learned, after much bumper-to-bumper inching forward, that a Y intersection, regulated by an inadequate traffic light, was the problem, aggravated by cars turning left. When we burst into the open we sped to Halberstadt, stopped briefly for photos of houses which looked like those in which I had lived, and headed for Wernigerode and something to eat.

The approach to Wernigerode should have alerted me. The traffic, although moving rapidly, was too heavy for a road that I thought was leading to a modest little village. And the appearance of several high-rise apartment buildings in the distance at the foot of the hills should have set off an alarm. But it was not until we reached the town that the full impact of the awful changes hit me. This out-of-the-way paradise was now a tourist trap and a seedy one at that, not unlike the beauty spots we have ruined in America.

Traffic was dense, stoplights were everywhere, parking was nil, and one-way streets added to the confusion. There was no way I could drive to the square, park, and let nostalgia take over.

After a vain probing in the car, we returned to the outskirts and an unpaved parking lot which cost a mark or two for a day. Then we walked into the so-called village. I saw the paths, now black-topped, leading up the slopes, but I couldn't find the square. No one had heard of it, or they didn't know what I was asking about.

We ate a dull lunch in a fly-infested ice cream parlor and decided to give up and return to the car. But one last search on another street revealed the square — but not the one I had pictured from long ago. It was the place for sure, but there now were carnival-like booths scattered about selling ice cream, souvenirs, and the like. All the same, I took several pictures before we left. But I didn't even try to walk the hillside paths — we were too disappointed and tired.

A lengthy, twisting drive alongside the Harz mountains brought us to Ilfeld, a grayish town which, however, did have a massive hotel, restaurant, bar emporium. We stayed there overnight, the next morning we learned that the main dining room was closed. I asked about it and was told that it was "finished," a word that was appropriate for Wernigerode and my illusions.

Post-War Talk

Reconcilliation between the American GI and his counterpart in the German Army actually began during the final phases of the European campaign in 1944-45.

Why this was so may be hard to understand. But the evidence that it was happening is overwhelming.

I discussed this lack of animosity late in the war with T/5 Bernard Seidman, who was doing the same job I was — writing up awards and decorations for deserving heroes. Seidman had been wounded in the leg at Mortain by a shell fragment. The shell had been rammed into the breech of a gun miles away. Someone had given the "fire" order, and the projectile had been sent on its way. "I don't know who was responsible for my wound, and I never will know," he said. "It's such an impersonal thing. I can't be angry with anyone."

I took note of this feeling in a short story I wrote for "Yankee" magazine in its June 1979 issue. The yarn was called "West of St. Lo." In it I had

213

the narrator comment: "Then he (a new replacement) started on Hitler and the Nazis, and how the world had to be saved from tyranny. He sounded like one of the training films when he got going. I had been in it long enough to forget why we were there. Most of us didn't think of the Germans as bad guys anymore. We knew they were in this thing with us and if it rained they got as wet as we did and if it was hot they sweated as much, and we knew sure as hell that they had as much stuff, and more, shot at them as we did."

I received a congratulatory letter from a Raines Meyerowitz of Nova Scotia. "I'm German myself," he wrote, "spent the war years in Britain as a refugee from the Nazis. Despite what those criminals did to my family, my country and the world, my love and loyalty for my native country remains unshaken. It is good to see war described as lunacy, rather than as an epic battle between the good guys, the Allies, and the bad guys, the Germans."

Another factor in reconcilliation, I believe, was the American GI's respect for German technology. The American entrenching tool was patterned after the German version. The water and gasoline can was a duplicate of the enemy model and even was called a Jerry can. Some of their weapons were superior to ours, especially the 88mm gun. The Germans were first with jet planes and the buzz bombs. And to top it off, their plumbing was the best in Europe — almost like being at home.

To further document the identification of experiences between the opposing infantrymen, I took another look at "Bill Mauldin's Army," a collection of war-time cartoons. A dozen or more of those drawings depict the German soldier as human and even funny.

In one of the cartoons, a messenger tells Willie and Joe, bogged down in front of a house holding German soldiers, "We gotta blast 'em out. They found out we feed prisoners C-rations."

Another shows two Germans watching an Italian pouring a liquid into a barrel. One says to the other: "We must be retreating, Fritz. They're watering the vermouth."

In another, Willie and Joe are on night guard duty at the front, and

Joe is playing a mouth organ. Willie says, "Th' Krauts ain't followin' ya so good on 'Lili Marlene' tonight, Joe. Ya think maybe somethin' happened to their tenor?"

The nearest the cartoons came to outrage at the Germans is depicted in a panel showing a shot-up wine cask, draining its life forces on the ground, which is littered with broken bottles. One GI has his hands over his face in despair. The other vituperates: "Them rats! Them dirty, cold-blooded, soreheaded, stinkin' Huns. Them atrocity committin' skunks..."

What more is there to say about this early reconciliation? A whole lot more, for sure, during occupation duty.

A non-fraternization policy was announced and promptly ignored by the GIs. I won't go into details. Suffice it to say there were many German war brides who came to the United States, and that many American soldiers deeply regretted the end of occupation duty.

The military always likes to speak of casualties in terms of percentages. It's like calling taxes "enhancements." At the end of the war in Germany in World War II, I remember being told that our outfit, the 120th Infantry Regiment, had sustained 200 percent casualties over a 10-month period, which was an impersonal way of letting the survivors know how lucky they were.

But how could there be anything left of an outfit that was wasted twice? The replacement system. By feeding men in like replacement parts, combat units could be kept on the line longer without losing momentum. This system shortened the war and saved lives — but not the lives of those in the front-line units, of course.

All the same, there were some lucky survivors. Were they the dashing, strong macho types who knew little or no fear? The survivors I remember best were not like that at all.

Wally was a thin, wispy youngster with blond hair and a drooping moustache that may have been a humorous attempt to make himself look ferocious. He had a high-pitched voice, but it had authority all the same, for he was one of the smartest and quickest combat sergeants in Company B. He survived while others disappeared. Then came the Battle of the Bulge. After it was nearly over he got the shakes and was sent to the rear. Much to his disgust, he got well soon enough to return in time for the next offensive, but as usual he endured.

"Sparky," an incorrigible during training days, blossomed into a patrol expert in combat, a Daniel Boone type. His trademark was a green camouflage scarf tucked around his neck. It was not worn in a long Dr. Who dangle. His assignments were daring, but he accomplished them with stealth and careful maneuvering. He would not sit next to a window. "Ain't no use exposing yourself," he would say. He lived, too.

Kennedy, a balding mortarman of Irish descent, ran a taxi business before the Army selected him for the honor of fighting for his country. He found the war somewhat amusing — not hilarious mind you, but full of irony, sometimes cruelly so, but not so much that he couldn't find the ridiculous element. He enjoyed treating the constant narrow escapes as funny: "This armor-piercing shell went through the building and right between this guy's legs and wrapped itself in his raincoat, hanging down from his belt, and he didn't get a scratch." Kennedy became a medic during the Battle of the Bulge when a lot of vacancies for this kind of duty appeared after our own planes bombed us. "Those guys were supposed to be in a safer place behind our lines and look what happened," he said shaking his head at the irony. He then found that being a medic during a battle was highly dangerous duty. He won two Silver Stars, which, to him, definitely a non-hero type, was the funniest irony of all.

Among our officers were Capt. Pulver and Lt. Col. Williamson, both of whom believed in taking objectives with as few casualties as possible. They were good at outsmarting the enemy, falling back from beaten zones, decoying here and striking there, using protective terrain features, flanking

COMPANY B OFFICERS — Photo taken in March, 1945, before the Rhine River crossing. From the left, Lt. Frank Jarzabek, Capt. Pulver, Lt. Warren Charleston, Lt. Loshek, and Lt. Charles Barnett.

whenever possible and never charging with great elan at well-defended enemy positions. Our colonel was so good that he earned five Silver Stars, became a brigadier general and made a career of the Army, giving up his former job as a music teacher.

We had a few of the macho types, but for the life of me I can't remember seeing any of them around when it was over.

So who survives? Could it be the ones who helped make their luck with resiliency, with bending and weaving, with constant attention to the details of survival?

But enough of casualties. The best way to avoid them is to stay out of war entirely. This is agreed, but how to do it is still a subject for national debate.

Wars are won by a "few good men," as the television commercial suggests. It still astonishes me, as I think about my involvement in World War II, that one or two men can carry an entire company or battalion to success in battle.

It is extremely difficult to determine what actually happens in a major conflict because war itself is a deadly confusion that the men who are in it don't understand at the time. And often those who could testify are lost through death or wounds.

All the same, military historians have determined that although armies may number in the millions, only a few thousand men do the fighting. From Napoleon's time to the present this has been true. For example, only 14 percent of those in Vietnam were directly involved in combat.

Furthermore as the prominent military historian S.L.A. Marshall determined, only 15 percent of the infantrymen actually fired their weapons in World War II.

This figure is hotly contested by many infantrymen on the basis of their experience. I think the percentage must have been much higher in my company. On the other hand I recall that during more than 100 days of combat, my machine gun squad purposely fired its weapon at the enemy once and got bawled out for doing it since the target, a lone soldier, wasn't big enough. We had merely given away our position.

In my first battle in the hedgerows on July 16, 1944, I fired my pistol about five times, and a malfunctioning M-1 rifle that I found on the field, some six times. At Mortain I fired my carbine three times. After that, nothing.

There are several reasons for these statistics, I believe. Most civilians entering service have not been brought up to kill. They can't change overnight.

Also, it is natural to want to see a target to fire at. Most of the time the enemy is not visible. Another factor, according to my war experience in Europe, is that some 90 to 95 percent of casualties were caused by artillery. Small arms fire was considered merely a nuisance by comparison.

Returning to the thesis of a few good men, our company commander, Capt. Murray S. Pulver, was most certainly one. He fought from

July 16, 1944 to the end of the war in May 1945. In his first battle, he knocked out two tanks with a bazooka and won a Distinguished Service Cross, one step short of the top award — the Congressional Medal of Honor. He later received a Silver Star and two Bronze Stars. In my opinion, he should have had a Congressional at Mortain.

War talk by men who have been in a war is always interesting; whereas moon talk by a poet who has not been to the moon is likely to be dull.

—**Mark Twain**

I heard some war talk in 1989 at the second reunion of my old rifle company — Company B, 120th Infantry, 30th Division. Most of the talk was about combat in the European theater in 1944-45. And all of it had to be true because they were all witnesses as participants and thus kept each other honest.

Earl Johnson, our company's contribution to major league baseball as a pitcher for the Boston Red Sox, recalled that during the attack on Euchen over 900 yards of open ground, a rabbit ran across the front.

"All those expert riflemen took a shot at it, but the rabbit went unscathed," Johnson said.

This was the only blemish on what was later called "The Perfect Infantry Attack," in which a well-coordinated artillery barrage provided an umbrella for the infantrymen as they fired their small arms weapons while advancing at a fast walk. Casualties were few and the enemy never had a chance to react before being overrun by our troops. Only the rabbit got away.

Harold Chocklett, a soldier who went through all the campaigns from St. Lo to the Elbe River, told of a fellow GI's being depressed about going into another attack. He was sure he was going to get it this time. Chocklett fell back on his special brand of combat philosophy in an effort to cheer him up.

"Some of us will make it," he said. "Some of us will make it."

It didn't help. The GI got what he somehow knew was coming.

The Chocklett twins, Harold and Harry, were both present. How they managed to be in the same company is still a mystery, since it was against Army policy. But they weren't together long, for Harry was captured at Mortain.

AT FIRST REUNION — Capt. Pulver, right, is shown with the author at Company B's first reunion. The gathering was at Kansas City in June of 1988. Reunions have been held each year since at various locations around the country.

For the first time I was able to learn how they got separated. His brother Harold escaped the German sneak infiltration in darkness and fog the first night of the battle. He crawled to the rear to warn the headquarters and mortar platoons in time to thwart the German advance.

Harry, who had remained in his foxhole, was captured the next morning, Aug. 6, two days after his 19th birthday. He was ordered to tend German wounded in a nearby barn. When British Spitfires appeared, however, he left the barn and dived into a shell hole, but not soon enough to avoid getting a piece of shrapnel in his chest.

When he surfaced to examine his situation, he found that the barn had disappeared. He was recaptured and walked down the hill into Mortain, where a medic injected antibiotics directly beneath the wound. Harry complained about the method, but was told that the Germans had found that the closer the medication to the wound, the quicker the healing.

"My wound healed up fine," he said.

Harry was moved with the other prisoners by truck through Paris and the Argonne forest to a camp near Munich. "We could tell that our side was winning and that we would be liberated when the guards started to treat us better," he said. On April 29, Gen. Patton's troops arrived to end his incarceration.

I also learned more about the final days of my good friend Walter Paige, who was killed Aug. 1 at Tessy-sur-Vire.

I had noticed during the latter part of July that Walt was unconcerned about his safety and was making comments about the ridiculousness of war. I had had to order him once to share my hole during an artillery barrage.

Harry confirmed this attitude. "He didn't seem to care any more," he said. "I saw him walking around in the open when the rest of us were down taking cover."

I now think that Walt was trying to get it over with — a form of battle fatigue. I once had that feeling myself during the Normandy action.

A visitor to the reunion was Marc Kennedy, son of another good friend Warren Kennedy, who was first a mortarman and then a medic. Kennedy volunteered as a "doc" after many medics were knocked out of action by our own planes bombing us at Malmedy.

Marc said his father had written shortly after the change in assignment that he had "fouled up." I knew what he meant because the medic's duties were far more dangerous than that of an ammo-bearing mortarman. The proof was the two Silver Stars earned by Kennedy after the transfer.

On one of the bus tours we learned that the driver had been a member of the Ninth Air Force and had participated in the 1,000-plane bombing run that hit us as well as the enemy. Since this same air force hit us several times later during the war, we changed its name to the Ninth Luftwaffe.

At the end of the bus trip, the driver made a little speech and very gracefully apologized for the mistakes. Even though these words came 45 years after the event, they were the first and only words of regret we had heard from any member of that Air Force unit, so they were greeted with cheers.

After four days the war talk ended and we all went home — maybe to read some poetry about the moon.

Capt. Murray Pulver, who had been on a farm in civilian life, was a natural leader who was courageous and inspiring. He had an uncanny instinct for correct battle tactics. In addition he was lucky. Although slightly wounded three times, he escaped death so narrowly on so many occasions as to make one wonder if divinity was involved.

One of his officers, Lt. Hunn — a good man as well — wrote his wife that "every man in this company has the firm conviction that Capt. Pulver is blessed with divine guidance. Things I have seen make me believe the same. He has led us on several missions that looked absolutely hopeless and we came out with flying colors and the casualties were so slight that they could be discounted. There must be some reason for it."

I believe that Capt. Pulver, whether lucky or blessed from on high, single-handedly turned the tide of battle of Hill 285 at Mortain. I was aware that something had happened at Mortain to stop the Germans after our unit had let them through. Telling about falling back on a hinge, I wrote: "In the meantime, the Jerries were free to move toward the area occupied by the headquarters platoon and our mortar section. These troops put up a spirited defense and slowed the enemy advance, a factor which I believe was extremely important to us when the fog lifted."

The detailed answer to what happened has been provided in Capt. Pulver's memoirs, published in a book called "The Longest Year." The fog is lifting, a tank is creeping forward out of the gloom, and in Capt. Pulver's words: "The sergeant handed me the bazooka. I aimed it over the stone wall. That monster came out of the fog not more than 10 yards away. I fired hitting it right under the turret. The tank came to a stop. I swear that I could have reached up and touched the muzzle of the cannon if I had been tall enough. The concussion of the bazooka blast killed all of the occupants of the tank, but the tank's motor continued to run and did so for most of the day. Sgt. Maybee, Sgt. Goertz and the jeep driver crawled over and shook my hand. My face was a bloody mess. The backlash of the bazooka shell had sprayed little pieces into my face, but no serious harm was done. It just broke the skin."

This was followed immediately by a fire fight against German infantry. "We got them all without any of the five of us getting a scratch. It was like an old Western with the Indians attacking a circled wagon train."

He now felt so "gung ho" that he tried to knock out the company jeep, which had been captured and was housed in a barn. He would have succeeded if his rifle grenade hadn't misfired. He barely escaped with his life as he crawled away under intense small arms fire.

He then rallied two platoons of Company A (not his company), whose officer had been wounded, and got them to repulse an attack by troops of the First SS Panzer Division. He later was wounded a second time when a mortar shell damaged his teeth and gave him a "fat lip." Through all this, he stayed on duty and his company held Hill 285 and blunted the Nazi effort to cut off Patton's armored columns.

It was a day worthy of a Congressional, but the witnesses are deceased now and there's no way to prove it. But you'd better believe it happened the way Capt. Pulver remembers it. The good men don't have to make things up. They go out and do it.

Never underestimate the public relations value of a free cup of coffee.

Veterans of World War II have been beating the American Red Cross over the head for charging for a slug of caffein.

Letters to the Ann Landers column revive this hoary complaint, along with some other alleged misdeeds. "Don't tell me about the American Red Cross," one writer growls. "It happened long ago, but I remember it like it was yesterday."

"Gouging," another writer charges, while another closes his witnessing of Red Cross callousness with, "From that day on I had nothing good to say about the Red Cross."

It's a funny thing, though, that my experience with the Red Cross was exactly the opposite.

After we had captured Tessy-sur-Vire, France, and a day after the last enemy shell had dropped on us, a Red Cross canteen was set up about 100 yards behind our quarters. Many combat soldiers and I enjoyed coffee and doughnuts, and, some may not believe this, we were charged nothing.

Maybe this service was free because we were technically "on base." Landers has explained that Red Cross officials told her they "had to charge for off-base food and lodging because the British charged, and the British High Command pressured the U.S. Army to insist that the Red Cross charge also." The key word here seems to be "off-base."

Another charge against the Red Cross was that it was a skinflint about loaning money to GIs for worthy reasons. My personal experience was that the Red Cross was prudent in husbanding the money given it by the American people.

On a delay-en-route leave from Camp Blanding to my home in the

Detroit area, I had to transfer at the Washington D.C.. train station. One of the men who had gone through basic training with me asked if I would loan him $11. He said he had lost his dough in a crap game on the train and the Red Cross wouldn't loan him funds to continue his journey.

"I'll pay you back just as soon as I get home," he promised. The Red Cross read this guy correctly. But I didn't. I never saw the $11 again.

Curious about how often the Red Cross (which is you and I giving money to this organization) gets stung, I checked with the Traverse City office. The average loss is $500 a year.

Incidentally, when my leave ended and I was due to return to service, I was felled by a sudden illness. Would the U.S. Army believe my failure to report? We called the Red Cross, which investigated my case and made me legitimately late. All the same, the Army looked on my tardiness with great suspicion and I was shunted from one officer to another to re-explain my dereliction. The Red Cross report, however, got me safely through.

Another Landers correspondent reported that the Navy charged $25 a pint for blood given the wounded, the money being taken from the serviceman's pay. Could this have been Navy policy rather than Red Cross procedure?

Again my experience was entirely different. Countless times I saw blood being given by Army medics on the battlefield. That any wounded man had to pay for these life-giving transfusions is beyond belief.

Furthermore, the very fact that the medics wore Red Cross emblems on their helmets indicated the origins of compassionate and immediate tending of the wounded on both sides. The Red Cross movement was born from the previous lack of concern for the wounded on Europe's battlefields.

The international scope of the Red Cross was demonstrated to me at Mortain when I saw our medics greeting a German medic bearing a huge Red Cross flag into our lines. They greeted each other as brothers.

Perhaps part of the press problem for the Red Cross is that American GIs most of the time were given VIP treatment when off base. If they walked into a bar, someone would usually pop for a drink. In Paris, I rode the Metropole without paying. The uniform was our pass. While recovering from an illness in a military hospital near New York City, I was included in a group of recovering combat veterans who were treated by a New York club to dinner and theatre in the Big Apple. In general, the GI was well treat-

GERMAN WOODEN BULLET — The red wooden bullet in this show case is just to the right of the pewter spoon. All of the bullets pictured and the spoon were carried by the author in his pants pocket throughout most of the war.

ed by civilians. "Except when the lousy Red Cross charged him for a lousy cup of coffee."

What should be remembered, I believe, is that the Red Cross function primarily is to provide disaster relief and to serve as a go-between for the military and civilians. It does many other worthwhile things as well, but those are the two main jobs, and it has done them well.

It is possible to hold a pea in front of an eye and blot out the sun.

But that doesn't mean that the sun is no larger than a pea.

After about five decades, I finally have the definitive answer to the purpose of the German wooden bullet.

The solution came in the mail from Marty Black of Crystal Lake, Ill. It supports the theory provided initially by Larry Rice of Traverse City.

But before delving further into the answer, the question needs to be explained.

On July 16, 1944, during a hedgerow battle near St. Lo, France, I was in one of my frequent prone positions communing with the verdant Normandy pasture while bullets and shells were flying about.

Near me I noticed two German bullets. One was the normal kind, but the other was a red wooden pellet set in the usual metal casing. I pocketed the cartridges for later examination and discussion, provided there would be a later time. As it turned out, I carried them in my left pocket during the remainder of the war and I still have them. They are now in a special case hanging on my office wall.

I showed the wooden bullet to other GIs and we guessed as to its purpose. The first guess was that it was for short-range firing, perhaps when the soldier has circled his victim and doesn't want to risk firing back into his own lines with a normal bullet. But we thought it was improbable to expect such sophisticated tactics in the midst of the confusion of combat.

Our other theory was that the red pellet was a tracer bullet. I tended to favor that guess. Later I came to believe that both German bullets contributed to my good luck — a hex on the enemy with his own ammo. I still view them with affection.

The wooden bullet question surfaced at a reunion of Company B, 120th Infantry in 1988 — the first gathering of these men since the end of the war. Eilene Hunn, widow of Lt. Edward Hunn, had a personal reason for raising the question, since her husband had been wounded by a piece of wood at Thirimont, Belgium, during the Battle of the Bulge. Was he a casualty caused by the wooden bullet? No one in Company B had the answer, Just theories.

I mentioned this unanswered question in a newspaper column written after the reunion. Larry Rice read the column, called me and said the wooden bullet was the German version of a blank cartridge. This sounded like the truth so I published his version. He said he had some of the bullets, had fired them, and found that they disintegrated.

At the next reunion I told my fellow veterans of this discovery, but they were not convinced, and Mrs. Hunn had lingering doubts, too. So when I returned home I got in touch with Rice again. He gave me a box of the cartridges to show at the next reunion. The German word "blabpatronen" appears on the box. According to my German dictionary that word translates as "pale cartridge," or what we could call a "blank." Rice also said that the blanks were used by the Germans on maneuvers to give a more realistic experience to their training.

The proof of Rice's explanation came in a letter from Black, an airline pilot who gets around the United States and Europe and who is a World War II buff, having visited many battle sites.

While attending a gun collectors' show in Cleveland, Black learned about a book that explains the purpose of the wooden bullet. Through the magic of a copying machine, he sent me a portion of an article by Capt. C. Shore, who has collected several kinds of German wooden bullets for various weapons.

"When fired the wooden bullet disintegrates almost immediately," he states, "and sometimes it is possible to see the fluffy, harmless residue falling like snow a few inches from the muzzle. But there are times when slivers of the wood can be picked up a few yards from the muzzle." This caused the German military to specify that the wooden bullets would not be fired at an "exercise enemy" within a range of 25 meters, Shore says.

In his own experience, he fired "scores of these cartridges at a target at ten yards range without once finding any impression upon it, and in the majority of cases no sliver of wood touched a target at five yards."

Shore gives high praise to the Germans for use of the wooden bullets in training. "It produced noise and afforded real handling training, particularly to machine gunners, since on firing enough gas was provided to drive the recoiling portions (of the weapon) to the rear," he points out.

"Later (in France and Germany)," he writes, "a good many Spandau belts and saddle type magazines were found with the 7.9mm wooden bullets interspersed with normal types of ammunition. The most likely explanation of this was that with the very high rate of fire of these guns...such an introduction conserved live ammunition without detracting from...the killing power of the weapon."

Shore provides much more technical evidence to clinch the matter. The wooden bullet was for practice and for conservation of ammo for the automatic weapons. Both sides were getting plenty of "practice" at St. Lo. My wooden bullet was probably meant for an enemy "burp gun," as we called it. The wooden bullet I found was harmless. It's doubly harmless now in my office under glass.

A word one doesn't see often outside philosophy books is "empiricism." Empiricists are those who subscribe to the theory that all knowledge is derived from experience.

Accordingly, if you can't see it, feel it, smell it, hear it or whatever, it doesn't exist, or adds nothing to what we know about the universe.

Those who snore and don't believe they do because they've never heard themselves snoring are good examples of empiricists. I confess some sympathy for this point of view, since I have been mightily accused of being a "disturber of the night" while feeling innocent about it all.

I was first introduced to snoring as an infant while sleeping in the same room with my parents. At first I thought some angry animals had invaded our bedroom, but, in time, after repeated exposures to this mysterious noise, I grew accustomed to the sound and accepted it as a natural accompaniment of sleep.

But many people have never been able to adjust to snoring by someone else. They claim that this noise keeps them awake, not realizing that if they relaxed and tuned in to the rythmic sonorities of their rasping neighbor they would soon be lulled into a complementary slumber, and perhaps help orchestrate the evening sounds into something awesome to hear. I believe adequate research might show that happily married couples give such tandem resonance to their unions.

At one time in my life I came close to sharing the popular antipathy to snoring. This happened while I was a very young man on a date with a young girl who had worked hard all day as a waitress. After a late-night movie and while journeying home in a car, she fell asleep, which, in a way, was understandable in view of her long work hours. But I felt that she had really abandoned me when she began to snore, softly at first as though apologetic, and then at full roar as she obviously dismissed me from her life — forever, I should add.

I was first accused of being a snorer of gargantuan proportions while in the U.S. Army in England waiting in a camp for shipment to France. I had caught a bad cold and was hardly able to breathe during the day. So when I went to sleep that night in a Quonset hut filled with tired men needing their rest, I must have been in perfect condition for a night of mouth-breathing vibrations of the soft palate. But I knew nothing of this until met by loud complaints from my hut-mates the next morning. Some went so far as to examine the rivets and bolts in our Quonset to see if any had been displaced by my rattlings. I thought they went a bit far and showed little understanding for the effects of a cold. And since I had heard none of it, I tended to doubt their sincerity.

In France, after a particularly long, frightening and exhausting day of combat in July, I had occasion to wonder if there might, after all, be something to these charges. After digging a hole and flopping in it, I passed out completely. In the morning, I was told by those nearby that they had feared our defense line was being telegraphed to the enemy by the sounds roaring from my slit trench. As it was, an enemy plane droned overhead during the night and dropped a bomb a hedgerow or two ahead, they said. This bit of

SOME CO. B VETERANS — These men of Co. B are shown at the 50th anniversary of D-Day during a reunion in 1994 at the Park Place Hotel, Traverse City, Michigan.

knowledge had escaped me.(If a tree falls in the forest and no one is near to hear it, has the tree really fallen?) In this case, I acknowledged that a bomb had been dropped by visually checking out the crater it caused.

I suggested to those still complaining that I would be happy to be discharged from service as a menace to our troops if they would testify in my behalf, but none was willing to turn my snoring into a rewarding disability. They had troubles enough of their own without signing forms to get me out of the war. Furthermore, no one felt sorry for anyone else during that time.

Later, while living in a "keller" in Germany, I was bedded down nightly with about 20 other GIs. I noticed that I received no accusing reports in the morning about "sounds in the night," as the crossword puzzles put it. Either the level of tolerance was higher with this group, or I was being out-done by a Texan who had recently joined us. He didn't snore, however. His specialty was grinding his teeth. But here again I had to accept hearsay that he was wearing out his molars eveery night, for I never heard a thing.

Now that I am in the twilight golden years, with unlimited oppor-tunities for afternoon naps, I have started receiving word once again that I'm snoring. Sometimes I am awakened and told to stop it. "Stop? Stop what?" I ask in bewilderment. How can an innocent believe such calumny without convincing evidence? When will these unproven accusations cease? When will the empiricists rise again?

While watching a TV program depicting the pros and cons of life in Castro's Cuba, I was intrigued by the testimony of a Cuban who had oper-ated his own one-man metal-working shop during Batista's reign.

The Cuban said the Castro government took his shop away and paid him wages for the same work. His income dropped to one-fifth of its previous level.

But he listed all the governmental benefits that had come to his fam-ily as a result: free education, free health care and other programs. He felt that in the end he was better off.

In fairness to the viewer, it was explained that the TV documentary was planned by Castro himself. The other side of the coin was screened in an earlier hour of television.

I was reminded of my own experience with socialism — in the U.S. Army during World War II. Soldiers owned nothing, not even themselves. That was the reason for the GI identification. Each of us, in effect, was Government Issue, completely under the control of our officers, fed, clothed, transported and bedded down somewhere each night, totally at government expense.

Since we owned nothing, not even ourselves, there was little incentive to do more than was absolutely necessary. Prototypes of Beetle (of the comic strip) were spawned in great numbers. Many under communism feel the same way: little pay, little work.

I tended to resist this attitude, but even I succumbed when it came to washing socks. Why bother? I just buried them after they had become so rigid as to fit only the correct foot. I then asked for and was issued a brand new pair. No one questioned the needs of a combatant.

Financially I could have reasoned that I was about as well off as I was while working for a utility company in Detroit. As I recall, my salary at the utility was around $200 per month. When I finally rose through the Army ranks to a T/4, the equivalent of a buck sergeant, I was able to increase the monthly support of my wife and child from $80 to $125, while paying $7 monthly for $10,000 worth of life insurance and keeping $27.20 for myself.

Since I had little opportunity in combat to spend money, I supplemented the home income with accumulated wads of strange francs or marks. The best medium of exchange among GIs was candy, cigarettes or some prized ration item, such as a can of eggs and bacon.

My wife was able to get along fairly well on her reduced income, because at home most things were rationed or unavailable. Furthermore, property taxes were canceled, life insurance premiums were waived and I believe we even were able to stop paying on a land contract.

The sour note in socialism of course is the lack of freedom. The

WALTER PAIGE'S GRAVE — The author looked up Walter Paige's grave (the first time in 1962) in the military cemetery near Omaha Beach, France. This visit was made in 1999.

Cuban on TV couldn't mention that for fear of dire reprisals. The hour-long rebuttal that preceded Castro's version of life in Cuba documented case after case of denial of human rights, even to those who had fought for the revolution in the beginning.

During a lull in the fighting in Europe, after 60 days of combat, I indulged in the GIs favorite release mechanism when things have improved a bit —bitching. Thus on Sept. 15, '44 I wrote:

"Two months of combat service today. I take no credit for it. A mule could have done the same thing better. (I carried two boxes of machine gun ammunition for the machine gun squad.) For me, the Army has been something like a jail. I have no pride of service. I'm too degraded for that. The only thing I'll take pride in is survival. That will indicate endurance, a fair share of luck and some courage."

"I still hate the Army more than I do the enemy," I wrote. "Of course my reason tells me that I should subvert this feeling, but nonetheless it's there. I hate it because it debases every sense of justice, culture or ideals that I formerly lived by. It trained me inadequately for a job I had little aptitude for. (The machine gun was too complicated a weapon for me to master.) It forces me to remain quiet while others direct my every activity as though I were a 4-year-old."

I then got around to a real problem. Others had been issued the Combat Infantryman's Badge, worth $10 more a month, while in my case, I was told they would "look into it." I also was still a private, even though promised a recommendation to private first class.

As I read that letter today, I am shocked that I was so bitter. The officer who censored my letter didn't delete a word, nor did he turn me in. As a matter of fact, it might have helped me later to a promotion to awards and decorations non-com and the T/4 rating. With the job came freedom of many kinds and respect, even from officers.

My basic problem was the one that makes socialism suffocating, a lack of freedom to be oneself. The Army today is far different, a volunteer organization with enormous incentives to develop oneself and make much more money as well. When I checked in 2002, an infantryman starts at a monthly rate of $1022, plus generous benefits. The volunteer GI does get more respect.

The "mourning wall" in Washington, D.C., or the carved list of Americans who died in Vietnam, seems to me to be a poor memorial to the unfortunates of that disastrous war.

Its effect is to stun the soul with remorse, sadness and defeat —

hardly a spiritually uplifting tribute to the outstanding courage of the Vietnam soldier who, although he did not bring home a victory laurel, performed at a level of heroism unequalled by Americans since the Civil War.

War memorials in France, for example, located at the well-filled cemeteries of American dead, are beautiful tributes to the sacrifices of U.S. soldiers. The soaring statuaries at these sites are not depressing. They stand proud in recognition of the courage of the fighting men who served their country.

In contrast French memorials at World War I sites emphasize sadness and death. Perhaps there is no glory in war, but there is shining courage to be recognized. The sorrow of it all needs to be relieved by the grandeur of courage, no matter the outcome. No one gets a big thrill out of having people feel sorry for him. There's no respect in it.

In *A Bright Shining Lie*, Neil Sheehan's book about John Paul Vann and America's role in Vietnam, the author says this war is "without heroes." If he means this conflict ran longer than any other American war, that it ended without victory, that political and military leadership was inept, that its veterans were made to feel outcasts upon their return, that morale was low at home and in some places in the field, that drugs were rife among the troops, and that many principled young men abandoned their citizenship rather than fight in it — then he has a case for claiming the entire effort was not heroic, but a tragic flop.

However, to equate heroism with victory for a worthy cause is a mistake. Heroism comes in various degrees, but in each there is the strong element of bravery — win or lose, mistaken or not.

Medals have been given to soldiers who failed. They may have charged a machine gun nest, fallen on a grenade, or died trying to help someone else. Courage is heroism.

So what of the American GI in Vietnam?

Brig. Gen. Ellis W. Williamson commanded the first American combat troops in Vietnam in 1965. I wrote to him because he had been my boss while commanding the 1st Battalion, 120th Infantry, 30th Division in Europe in World War II.

He replied that "The American young man never ceases to amaze me. As you well recall he did so well against the highly mechanized and effective German forces. In Korea he held up against a strong enemy and continued to do well in spite of terrifically unpleasant weather conditions. In this war our young men are once again showing their worth under strained conditions and doing so remarkably well."

The general spoke of the difficulties: "We can easily beat him (the enemy) into the ground and destroy him every time we can catch him and make him stay still. It is so hard, however, to return to an area where the civilians have made honest efforts to cooperate with us and find that their leaders were beheaded the night before. Things of this sort go on around us all the time."

The last line of his letter sums it up: "The American people back home would be extremely proud of our young men if they could observe them at any time." The fact, however, was that in the end many American people were not proud.

Two years later (November 1967) this unit with the 4th Division was to lose 287 men killed and more than 1,000 wounded in a fight for Base Area 609.

So these men didn't win. But they fought in the worst conditions possible for a soldier. They fought in jungles, on mountains, in the midst of hostile civilians, with no purpose other than to fight and stay alive for a year and rotate home. Ground was not taken and held. Battles were fought, body counts taken, objectives achieved and handed back to the enemy.

Meanwhile, at home, for the first time in recent American history, there was no solid support from the people. On the contrary, demonstrations persisted against the war, draft cards were burned, college students stayed in college to avoid serving, and some went to Canada.

In view of the conditions under which the Vietnam soldier fought, how can it be denied that they were far greater heroes than those who took part in other wars, with the exception of the Civil War in which no one claims there were no heroes on the losing side.

Vietnam in my opinion was the ultimate testing ground for courage. Veterans of that war doubly merit the words of acclaim that appear on a Traverse City Veterans' Memorial: "Yesterday's hero, today's glory, tomorrow's exemplar."

ADDENDUM

What finally happened to...

Gibson — He carried a small Bible in his left breast pocket. Sometime after the Cesspool experience, he thought he had been wounded by a shell fragment. The buddy who was tending him couldn't find any blood to indicate where the wound was. Finally, he discovered a shell fragment embedded in the Bible. Gibson was unharmed. He was the only member of the machine gun section since St. Lo to survive the war while still in the front line.

Sgt. Horne — He suffered a serious leg wound in the Bulge battle. I am told that he recovered, stayed in the army and served in Korea.

Warren Kennedy — I visited him three times after the war. He chuckled about being greeted as a war hero when he returned to his office job. He is now deceased. However, I correspond each Christmas with his son Marc who lives with his family in Texas.

Wally Miller — He stayed in the army and saw service in Korea where he was wounded in the cheek by a Chinese soldier who was immediately dispatched by a fellow GI. I met him again at a Company B reunion in Kansas City. He is now deceased.

Sgt. O'Brien — He suffered a serious leg wound from a shelling while our unit was still bogged down at the Cesspool.

Walter Paige — His remains lie in the Omaha Beach cemetery in France. His parents, upon my recommendation, decided to leave his body in France as part of the remembrance of the American presence there.

Lt. Hunn — This truly outstanding combat soldier, stayed in the service and, tragically, was killed in the early "surprise" fighting in Korea.

Capt. Pulver — He is still leading Co. B, which at this writing continues to have annual reunions around the country. Capt. Pulver made a special project out of looking up former Co. B members and urging them to form ranks again once a year.